WEST COS ECCCESIAL
1

THE PRAISES OF ISRAEL

PSALMS 73–106

THE PRAISES OF ISRAEL

Volume Two

Psalms 73-106

Dudley Fifield

First Published 2009

ISBN 978-0-85189-178-1

© 2009 The Christadelphian Magazine and Publishing Association Limited

Printed and bound in England by:

THE CROMWELL PRESS GROUP
TROWBRIDGE
WILTSHIRE   BA14 0XB

CONTENTS

One further volume is in preparation:
VOLUME 3 – BOOK V – PSALMS 107–150

PREFACE

THIS work on the Book of Psalms was written over a period of some twenty-five years; Psalms 107 – 150 (see Volume 3) being the product of recent study. Consequently it is possible that readers will detect a development in style between earlier and later studies. The writer is, after all, twenty-five years older!

Originally they appeared in the pages of *The Bible Student* and we are grateful to the Editors of that magazine for agreeing so readily to their reproduction.

Inevitably, given the period of time involved, our thinking on some of the Psalms has changed. It would, however, have been a monumental task to have made substantial changes in those that were written in earlier years. We have therefore, apart from some minor editing, left them in their original form.

Because they were written in this way there is also some repetition of thought and ideas. However, as readers are most likely to read the Psalms on an individual basis, 'dipping in' as it were, this might prove to be more of a benefit than a disadvantage.

When this venture began it was not anticipated that the study of all 150 psalms would be completed, or that they would be published in book form. I am grateful to the Christadelphian Magazine and Publishing Association, the Editor and his staff for making this possible.

This is the second volume of a proposed three-volume work. This volume contains Psalms 73–106.

PSALMS OF ASAPH

THERE are twelve psalms which bear the ascription "A Psalm of Asaph". One of these we have already considered (Psalm 50) and the other eleven (Psalms 73 to 83) form the opening section of what is commonly referred to as the Third Book of Psalms.

Asaph was a Levite, the son of Berechiah and could trace his lineage back to Gershom, the second of Levi's sons (1 Chronicles 6:39-43). He was, together with Heman and Ethan (also known as Jeduthun), one of the three singers chosen to lead the music when the ark of God was brought up from the house of Obed-Edom to the tabernacle David had prepared at Jerusalem (15:16-19). In the tabernacle he was appointed to minister before the ark continually (16:37), whereas Heman and Jeduthun ministered in the tabernacle of Moses at Gibeon (verses 16:39-42).

Asaph was referred to as "the chief" among the singers, and clearly he was a musician also for he "made a sound with cymbals" (verse 5). Like Samuel, Gad and Heman he was also a seer, a prophet (2 Chronicles 29:30). This raises the interesting question as to what extent we can detect a prophetic element in the psalms attributed to him, although it has to be said that some of these psalms appear to belong to a much later time than Asaph and his contemporary, King David. Why is this? The answer appears to lie in the fact that, like Heman and Jeduthun, Asaph was the founder of what has been termed "a guild of singers and musicians" who continued to use his name. In the days of Jehoshaphat, Jahaziel, "a Levite of the sons of Asaph", prophesied the deliverance of Judah from the hand of Ammon and Moab (20:14-17).

In the first year of Hezekiah, when the house of God was cleansed, "the sons of Asaph; Zechariah, and

Mattaniah" were prominent in the work and afterwards joined with the other Levites "to sing praise unto the LORD with the words of David, and of Asaph the seer" (29:13,30). Again, when Josiah held the Passover at Jerusalem in the eighteenth year of his reign (2 Kings 23:21-23), "the singers the sons of Asaph" took their place in that solemn assembly (2 Chronicles 35:15).

After the captivity the sons of Asaph are recorded as returning to the land with Zerubbabel (Ezra 2:41) and when the foundation of the Lord's house was laid, "the Levites the sons of Asaph" were there "with cymbals to praise the LORD, after the ordinance of David king of Israel" (Ezra 3:10). Later they were singers "over the business of the house of God" (Nehemiah 11:22) and were involved in the solemnities connected with the dedication of the walls of the city (Nehemiah 12:35).

Clearly the house of Asaph played an illustrious part in the history of Israel. To these singers and musicians psalms were committed for their safe keeping and performance and these became "Psalms of Asaph", although only some of the songs were written by their forbear. At the time of the bringing up of the ark it is actually recorded that David committed a psalm into the hands of Asaph and his brethren. The psalm is a combination of Psalm 105 and 96 (1 Chronicles 16:7). Interestingly, the name Asaph means 'to receive' or 'to gather' (*Strong*).

Which psalms were written by Asaph himself must remain a matter of some conjecture, but that all of those that bear his name were intended to be sung in the House of God by this Levitical choir there can be no doubt.

Characteristics of Psalms

It has been noted that the Psalms of Asaph have certain predominant features. This is not to say that these characteristics and themes are not present in other psalms also, but they appear to be recurring themes in those songs associated with the sons of Asaph. The main features might be summarised as follows:

Firstly, there is the prophetic element to which we made passing reference above. In that particular comment our thought was principally of fore-telling events but we need to remember that other function of the prophet of forth-telling, that is teaching, and in this respect it is a characteristic of the songs of Asaph to interpret the past history of Israel as a means of warning and encouragement to subsequent generations. It may be remembered that Psalm 50 (the Psalm of Asaph that stands in isolation) was concerned with the giving of the Law at Sinai, but the feature noted above can be seen, for example, in Psalm 74:12-15; 77:10-20; 78:4-72; 80:8-11; 81:5-7; 83:9-12.

Secondly, there is the emphasis upon God as the Shepherd of Israel who led them from the captivity of Egypt to their promised inheritance and who continues to care for them and tend them as a shepherd does his flock. See Psalm 74:1; 77:20; 78:52,70-72; 79:13; 80:1, and perhaps Psalm 82, having regard to its use by the Lord Jesus in John 10 in the context of the good shepherd.

Thirdly, as we might expect with a prophet, in much of the language of the psalms God Himself is the speaker and this, of course, is something that these psalms have in common with all the prophetic writings.

Fourthly, it is possible to detect an emphasis running through all of the psalms upon God as the Judge and, even where this is not stated explicitly, the thought of God's judgement seems to be the underlying theme, as for instance in Psalm 73, the first of the Psalms of Asaph in this group.

The characteristics identified will be noted in the context of the psalms as we deal with them in turn, with others perhaps not so readily apparent from a straightforward reading of the songs.

PSALM 73

THIS is the most personal of all the psalms of Asaph. Most of the others approach God from a national rather than an individual perspective. It addresses a problem that troubled many in ancient Israel and has continued to cause distress to men and women of faith through the ages. We can still be perplexed by the prosperity of the wicked and the sufferings of the righteous; although perhaps with less justification than those of ancient times, for the sacrifice of the Lord Jesus Christ and all that it involves should enable us, from the time of our baptism, to appreciate the reality of our situation.

We suggest that, in part, the problem in ancient Israel arose from a misconception of the Law. We know that the Law was regarded as a law of works that promised blessing for righteousness and cursing for wickedness. It has to be remembered, however, that this applied to Israel on a national basis and was never intended to apply universally either to the righteous or the wicked. It was the nation that prospered or suffered, and consequently there could always be individuals in both categories who did not share in the common good or evil and who consequently might be judged by their fellows to be sinners or righteous merely by their personal circumstances. There was always a danger of judging men by the quantity of their possessions rather than by the quality of their life.

However, this was not the precise problem that Asaph wrestled with (we feel that this psalm was actually penned by the Levitical singer). The psalm falls broadly into two sections. In the first Asaph describes the temptation into which he had fallen and the manner in which he wrestled with his doubts and perplexities (verses

2-16). In the second he tells how he resolved his doubt and uncertainty and found the answer to the question that troubled him. It will be noted that our division of the psalm begins at verse 2. This is because the psalm emphasises first not his doubt but his conviction. He tells of the conclusion of the matter; the truth to which he had been led as a result of the trial of his faith:

"Truly God is good to Israel, even to such as are of a clean heart." (verse 1)

Of the word rendered "truly" *Strong's Concordance* says, "a particle of affirmation, *surely*". 'Yes, it is so and surely (RV) after all my anxious questionings I know that God is good'. Good to Israel; not all Israel, but those who are "Israel indeed" for they are pure of heart, the quality without which no man can see God (Matthew 5:8) or enter into His presence (Psalm 24:4).

"As for Me" (verses 2,3)

"But as for me, my feet were almost gone; my steps had well nigh slipped." (verse 2)

The pronoun "me" is emphatic in the original text, as if to indicate that in his shame and sorrow he felt unworthy to be numbered amongst the Israel of God. It is as if he said, 'I should have known better'; for his feet were almost gone, literally, 'inclined, turned aside in the wrong direction' and instead of the sure-footedness in perilous situations that David had spoken of (Psalm 18:33), his steps had almost slipped in life's journey. The reason is explained in the next verse:

"For I was envious at the foolish, when I saw the prosperity of the wicked." (Psalm 73:3)

As he beheld them he wished his lot in life was like theirs, prosperous, like the foolish (RV, the arrogant) who in their pride and infatuation with themselves boasted of their comfort and security.

At this point perhaps we all stand in danger. The Lord's "yoke is easy" and his "burden is light" (Matthew 11:30), but nevertheless it is a burden and it is a yoke, although taken up willingly and joyfully. It is possible for us, shouldering the responsibilities of life in the Truth, sometimes finding it difficult to cope with the ordinary affairs of life because of ecclesial duties and our duty of care for our brethren and sisters, to look at those who prosper in the world and to envy their apparent ease and comfort – their lack of responsibilities, beyond those that are the common lot of all men, and to long to share their way of life.

The Apparent Prosperity of the Wicked (verses 4-9)

It is important to recognise that in his description of the happiness of the wicked, the Psalmist is describing not the reality of the matter but rather circumstances as they appeared to him in the midst of his time of trial. Thus he cries:

"For there are no bands in their death: but their strength is firm. They are not in trouble as other men; neither are they plagued like other men."   (verses 4,5)

The reference to their death might seem premature at this early stage of the argument, but the picture that Asaph presents is one that can be readily understood: a life of unrestrained wickedness characterised by ease and comfort, everything their heart desired, culminating in a peaceful death in which there were no pangs (RV margin). They did not die in pain and anguish but they slipped quietly away, for their strength was firm (AV margin, "fat"). They enjoyed a life of unbroken health undisturbed by disease and suffering. Why, he cries, "they are not in trouble as other men; neither are they plagued like other men". Two different Hebrew words are used for "men": firstly *enosh*, describing the frailty and weakness of men; secondly *adam,* the more dignified title given to man first before the Fall.

They do not appear subject to the natural weakness that flesh is heir to, neither in time of calamity, when perhaps famine plagues men, are they affected. Others might suffer but they appear to be immune, secure in their prosperity – for this reason:

"Pride compasseth them about as a chain; violence covereth them as a garment."   (verse 6)

The word "chain" signifies a necklace. Chains of this kind, probably of gold or some other precious metal, would be worn by both men and women as an insignia of rank, of wealth and status. Theirs is a chain of pride, as if it encased the neck making it stiff and unyielding. The stiff-neck is so often the symbol of human stubbornness and pride (Psalm 75:5).

Similarly they would be clothed in sumptuous, bright coloured garments, again a symbol of position and rank, but obtained by violence. They had grown rich by their oppression of the poor whom they had spoiled and plundered:

"Their eyes stand out with fatness: they have more than heart could wish. They are corrupt, and speak wickedly concerning oppression: they speak loftily. They set their mouth against the heavens, and their tongue walketh through the earth." (verses 7-9)

The verses speak of unrestrained and shameless pride; hearts revelling in inward satisfaction, believing that they have everything of which imagination could conceive.

The word "fatness" does not necessarily convey the ideas we might normally associate with it. Indeed it is said that the word can indicate a sleek, self-satisfied look; the countenance of the man of this world who imagines he has everything that heart could desire. The self-satisfaction and smug assurance shines from his eyes which protrude, completing the picture of the fullness of his prosperity.

They sneer and scoff, delighting in the success of their way of life. They speak loftily (literally, 'from on high'), that is, haughtily, for they see no reason to disguise their wickedness. There is no shame or fear but they delight in their riches, seeing in them a proof of their strength and superiority over other men.

The RV says not "*against* the heavens", but "*in* the heavens". Thus they exalt themselves and speak as though they were God Himself. They imagine that their words give them authority over all the earth to do as they deem fit.

Men Follow their Example (verses 10-12)

It has been pointed out that the "Therefore" which commences verse 10 is co-ordinated or connected with the "Therefore" of verse 6. That is, arising from their prosperity and untroubled life, there were two consequences: firstly they were filled with pride and arrogance (verses 6-9); secondly, others were influenced by their example:

"Therefore his (or, my) people turn hither, and full waters are swallowed by them."

(verse 10, *Speaker's Commentary*)

The meaning of the Hebrew text is, admittedly, obscure. The rendering above, we believe, gives the best sense. Corrupted and won over by their example, those of a like disposition follow them and drink fully of their wickedness, enjoying the pleasures of sin (Job 15:16).

Obsessed with the way of life that they pursued, they even doubted the reality of God Himself. Theirs was not an intellectual but a moral atheism, for they determined in their hearts to shut God out of their lives in the false confidence that the providential hand of God was not at work in their lives. They question His omniscience and doubt His power for they are blinded by their material wealth:

"And they say, How doth God know? and is there knowledge in the most High? Behold, these are the ungodly, who prosper in the world; they increase in riches." (verses 11,12)

His Trial of Faith (verses 13-16)

Faced with the apparent unbroken prosperity and success of the wicked, the Psalmist is moved to contemplate his own experiences and to cry, "Surely in vain have I cleansed my heart" (verse 13, RV). For if the wicked were rewarded in this way what value was there in seeking God, what reward was there in righteousness?

Like the priests under the Law (Exodus 30:17-21) he had washed his hands – they literally, he symbolically – for he had a spirit of innocency, a clearness of conscience (verse 13), but unlike the wicked (verse 5) he had been plagued all the day long and chastened every morning (verse 14). It had been a continuing experience and there is a lesson we need to learn about living the Truth. Chastening is a mark of God's love. It is an indication that He accepts us as His sons and daughters. Inevitably, in seeking day by day to be influenced by the word of God we will experience a striving of heart and mind that is totally foreign to the godless man. It is a consequence of endeavouring to live in the light of God's word, and the conflict that we know within ourselves day by day is an essential part of God's chastening hand, instructing us in the way of righteousness.

The Psalmist, however, felt a sense of responsibility to the children of God in general. He says, "If I had said (i.e., to himself) I will speak thus; behold I had dealt treacherously with the generation of thy children" (verse 15, RV). If he had paraded his doubts before his brethren and sisters, spoken openly of his perplexity at the prosperity of the wicked, then he could have undermined the faith of some. Again we need to learn that lesson today. We must express our convictions not our uncertainties. If we have doubts we must resolve them in meditation and prayer, in seeking the counsel perhaps of one wiser in the ways of God than ourselves. This is so in all aspects of life in the Truth, but perhaps particularly true if we are assailed by doubts that affect a first principle of our faith. Such an experience, that can sometimes overtake the strongest, is not the time to write or speak publicly of our doubt. Like the Psalmist of old we must have a sense of responsibility and settle within ourselves the questions that trouble us, knowing that to broadcast them will only cause anxiety and produce uncertainty in the minds of our brethren and sisters.

As Asaph pondered the problem that caused him such anxiety, it was a great weariness to him. A burden had been laid upon him that it seemed human thought alone could not resolve (verse 16).

The Place of Understanding (verses 17-20)

But there was an answer, for when he went into the sanctuary of God then he understood their end (verse 17). Asaph, of course, was a priest and as such he ministered in the tabernacle of David and presumably, at a later date, in the temple itself. The language of verses 18 and 19 is suggestive of a particular Old Testament event:

"Surely thou didst set them in slippery places: thou castedst them down into destruction. How are they

561

brought into desolation, as in a moment! they are utterly consumed with terrors."

The language recalls the fate of Korah, Dathan and Abiram (Numbers 16:31,35), and the subsequent use of the censers that these wicked men had used in their rebellion against Moses and Aaron is significant. Plates were made of them for a covering of the altar that they might be for a memorial unto the children of Israel (Numbers 16:36-40). Might it not be that as he entered the sanctuary and witnessed this memorial, Asaph was reminded of the fate of these wicked men and his instruction began as to the truth of the matter. Whether this conjecture be true or not, the fact remains that it is only in God's light that we shall see light (Psalm 36:9). It is by divine revelation, by meditation upon the word of God, that we shall see things in their true perspective, understanding that the wicked have an "end" but the righteous have a continuing place in the purpose of God. The wicked have peace and prosperity for a little while, then inevitably, the judgement of God and the coldness and stillness of the grave. The righteous may suffer the chastening of God as they pass through this vale of tears, but beyond there awaits them glory and immortality in the kingdom of God for which this present life is but a time of preparation:

"For our light affliction, which is but for a moment, worketh for us a far more exceeding and eternal weight of glory; while we look not at the things which are seen, but at the things which are not seen: for the things which are seen are temporal; but the things which are not seen are eternal."   (2 Corinthians 4:17,18)

Not for ever does God appear to sleep, but in the language of the psalm a time always comes when He arouses Himself; a time when because there is no remedy the wicked must pass away:

"As a dream when one awaketh; so, O Lord, when thou awakest, thou shalt despise their image."
(Psalm 73:20)

The use of the word "image" in this passage is particularly appropriate. Although often used of idols it means literally, 'a representation', from a root meaning 'to shade, a phantom, i.e., an illusion' (*Strong*). Hence all their pomp and pride in their achievement is counterfeit. It is an illusion with no real substance or value.

Confession of Error

"Thus my heart was grieved, and I was pricked in my reins. So foolish was I, and ignorant: I was as a beast before thee."   (verses 21,22)

The word rendered "grieved" is very emphatic. It is an indication of the agony of mind experienced as he brooded over the prosperity and untroubled way of life of the wicked. The result was bitterness and envy burning within as he wrestled with the problem that presented itself to him. He was "pricked in the reins" (i.e., kidneys), regarded as the seat of emotions.

The reason for his dilemma is acknowledged. It was because he had been foolish (*Strong*, stupid, brutish). He had begun to think like those whom he envied (see Psalm 49:10,12,13). He had lowered himself to the level of the beasts of the field who have no communication with God and consequently no knowledge or understanding of His ways.

Faith Triumphant

"Nevertheless I am continually with thee: thou hast holden me by my right hand. Thou shalt guide me with thy counsel, and afterward receive me to glory. Whom have I in heaven but thee? and there is none upon earth that I desire beside thee. My flesh and my heart faileth: but God is the strength of my heart, and my portion for ever."   (verses 23-26)

The beauty of thought and expression contained in this triumphant declaration of the Psalmist's faith is, we believe, best appreciated by reading and quiet meditation. Words of explanation are in danger of detracting from, and not adding to, their significance. It is with some trepidation therefore that we express some thoughts on the passage itself, and comment more generally on the approach to the words shown by many commentators that indicates how far they have departed from simple Bible truth.

Literally, the word rendered "nevertheless" means 'but as for me'. It is a contrast with the delusions and insecurities of the wicked. His fellowship with God was a continuing experience for He had taken hold of his right hand, and because now he was led by God's counsel there lay before him a glorious future which he would enjoy in resurrection splendour. Consequently he could say that in God alone were all his longings and desires fulfilled for, though bodily powers might fail, God was the rock (Hebrew) of his heart and his portion or inheritance for ever. He longed for the day when he would share in all its fullness the life of God (see Psalm 16:2 [RV, "I have no good beyond thee"] 5,6,11).

It is strange how so many orthodox writers find difficulty in this passage in Psalm 73. Saddled first with a restricted view of divine revelation, they cannot comprehend how such as Asaph should be able to express thoughts which they recognise must surely refer to the eternal glory which God has promised – a hope which they associate almost entirely with the New Testament. They add confusion to confusion by describing it as "heavenly glory", for they turn their gaze from the earth to heaven above. They seem to be completely oblivious of the fact that this man who had sung his songs before the ark of God would have known and rejoiced in the promises that God had made to Abraham and to David. He knew that these revolved around God's purpose with the earth and that the blessings associated with them could be gained only by resurrection from the dead. It was these great truths, expressed so powerfully and persistently in the scriptures he knew, that enabled Asaph to see the truth of the matter regarding the end of the wicked and the reward of the righteous.

Conclusion

"For, lo, they that are far from thee shall perish: thou hast destroyed all them that go a whoring from thee. But it is good for me to draw near to God: I have put my trust in the Lord GOD, that I may declare all thy works."

(verses 27,28)

Literally the Hebrew says, "They that go far from thee shall perish". To depart from God, the "fountain of life"

(Psalm 36:9) can mean only everlasting darkness and death.

Those who behaved in such a way, who for a time the Psalmist had envied, committed whoredom, that is, spiritual harlotry. By their apostasy they broke the covenant that God had likened to the marriage bond (Hosea 1-3; Isaiah 54:5,6, etc.).

In contrast, however, Asaph now says of himself, "It is good for me to draw nigh to God". As one writer renders the words, "And as for me nearness to God is my good" (William Kay, *Psalms with Notes*). He who had once asked what profit there was in serving God now declares his trust in God's works, His sovereign care and providential love. It is all his desire that he might declare the things that God has done for him.

PSALMS 74 & 79

PSALM 74 bears the superscription, "Maschil of Asaph". On the word "maschil" we have commented previously. There are thirteen psalms with which the word is associated and eight of these have been dealt with in earlier chapters (Psalms 32, 42, 44, 45, 52-55).

The word is derived from a verb meaning to be prudent and intelligent, hence to instruct. It is a psalm designed for instruction – not as the "michtam" psalms, which were primarily for private meditation and instruction, but rather for public use, for the instruction of the people generally.

The psalm also has a subscription which appears (in error) at the head of the next psalm (see Thirtle, *The Titles of the Psalms*). This is, "To the chief Musician, Al-taschith". The word "Al-taschith" means literally 'destroy not' and it indicates that God's special blessing was desired at a time of intense national distress and anxiety, when it seemed that the very existence of the nation was in danger.

It seems appropriate at this juncture to point out that Psalm 74 is closely connected in thought and language with Psalm 79. Both appear to have been written at the same time and against the same background of events. It seems beyond reasonable doubt that they are from the pen of the same author. We have found all writers on the Psalms that we have consulted unanimous in this view and we see no reason to question this conclusion.

The following comparison of the two psalms, extracted from the *Cambridge Bible* (A. F. Kirkpatrick, page 439), might be of interest.

Psalm 74		Psalm 79
verses 1,9,10	How long? forever?	verse 5
verses 3,7	The desecration of sanctuary	verse 1
verse 1	God's wrath	verse 5
verse 1	Sheep of thy pasture	verse 13
verse 2	Thine inheritance	verse 1
verses 10,18,22,23	The reproaches of the enemy	verses 4,12
verses 7,10,18,21	God's name	verses 6,9

The unanimity of thought, however, disappears completely when the various writers seek to identify the period in Israel's history to which the psalms belong. The following are amongst the suggestions made:

1. The time of the Maccabees.
2. The invasion of Shishak, King of Egypt in the reign of Rehoboam.
3. The fall of Jerusalem before Nebuchadnezzar and the ensuing captivity in the days of Zedekiah.
4. The invasion of Sennacherib in the reign of Hezekiah (a view favoured by the Christadelphian authors we have read).

As to the actual author of the psalms, we have not encountered a single writer prepared even to make a guess.

The emphasis of the language in both psalms gives some credence to the times of Hezekiah: particularly the references to "the reproach of the enemy" would have a counterpart in the scorn and derision of Rabshakeh and Sennacherib. Personally, however, we find difficulty in this view because of the references to the temple and the city of Jerusalem. These were not sacked by the enemy in the days of Hezekiah (See Psalm 74:7; 79:1,2) and consequently we believe that we must look elsewhere to establish the circumstances in which the psalms were written.

For different reasons we are not convinced that the psalms were written during or immediately after the time when Nebuchadnezzar destroyed both the city and the temple. The reference in Psalm 74:9, "there is no more any prophet" presents a difficulty because of the ministry of Jeremiah; and the plaintive, "How long?" of both psalms would not seem appropriate in view of Jeremiah's prophecies of the length of the captivity. Perhaps these difficulties are not insurmountable and some explanation could be offered, but reading the two psalms we feel that it is impossible to escape the conclusion that although the city had fallen before an invader and the house of God defiled and in part destroyed, both were still standing and, at the time of writing, remained under Jewish occupation.

We venture to offer another suggestion as to the time these psalms were written. We know that in the latter part of his reign Hezekiah formed a friendship with Merodach Baladan, King of Babylon. When his son Manasseh succeeded him he continued that alliance and, possibly to cement it – perhaps on the advice of his counsellors for he was only eleven years old when he began to reign – he allowed the worship of the gods of Babylon to find a place in the life of Judah. It was not only the religious practices of Babylon but also the abominations of all the surrounding nations that became part of everyday life in Judah. It is difficult to find a more dreadful description of human wickedness than that which existed in the reign of Manasseh (see 2 Kings 21:1-18; 2 Chronicles 33:1-10).

Manasseh reigned for fifty-five years, longer than any other king of Judah, but apart from the description of his wickedness we know virtually nothing about him or of historical events that occurred during his reign. Kings devotes just eighteen verses and Chronicles twenty verses to this period. However, the latter part of the Chronicles record of his reign tells us briefly of something regarding which we have no detailed knowledge (2 Chronicles 33:11-19). The Lord brought upon him the king of Assyria who carried Manasseh away to Babylon in chains. There, after an unspecified time, he was released and returned to his throne as a consequence of humbling himself and turning again to the Lord his God. Josephus says this captivity happened in the twenty-second year of his reign, and

secular history helps us for approximately at that time
Merodach Baladan was defeated in battle by Esarhaddon
of Assyria who established his throne in Babylon. What
was more natural than that Esarhaddon should seek to
put down and bring into submission those who had allied
themselves with Merodach Baladan? – consequently his
action against Manasseh, king of Judah. We have no
detail in scripture, but it follows surely that an invasion of
the land would not be directed simply at its king.
Undoubtedly the land of Judah was ravaged, the city of
Jerusalem spoiled and the temple defiled, if not destroyed.
We can imagine that although there was no general
captivity in this period, an Assyrian force would have
remained to preserve order and a governor appointed who
would have been either an Assyrian or an individual
trusted by the Assyrians. We suggest that it is against this
background that both Psalms 74 and 79 were written.
From contemporary records and the writings of Josephus
it appears that the captivity of Manasseh lasted for about
eight years. We can well imagine then the feeling of
despair that would overtake the righteous with no
prophetic word to indicate when this time of trouble might
end. Looking ahead to the uncertainty of the years to
come, well might the thought have arisen in the heart of
godly men – "Al-taschith", destroy not, as they looked to
the Lord for deliverance.

Like other writers we cannot hazard a guess as to the
authorship of the two psalms. It would be nice to think
that it was the young Jeremiah, but the chronology falls
short by our reckoning by about thirty years. Nevertheless
it seems likely that the psalms were known to him (see
Jeremiah 10:25; 23:1).

Psalm 74 can be divided into three parts:

1. A vivid description of the havoc caused in the city and
   sanctuary because God has cast away His people
   (verses 1-9).
2. A plea to God to act. For His sovereignty in both
   nature and history is recognised and it is His honour
   that is at stake (verses 10-17).

569

3. A further entreaty that God might not abandon His people to their enemies but have respect to the covenant He had made (verses 18-23).

Verses 1-9

As he considers the ruin and havoc created by the invader and the absence of any sign of deliverance, the Psalmist is moved to ask whether this situation will prevail perpetually:

"O God, why hast thou cast us off for ever? Why doth thine anger smoke against the sheep of thy pasture?"
(verse 1)

Smoke is a metaphor used to describe the fire of God's anger that had burned against them although they were the sheep of His pasture. It was this fact that Israel were His sheep, the objects of His love and compassion that causes the Psalmist to cry:

"Remember thy congregation, which thou hast purchased of old; the rod of thine inheritance, which thou hast redeemed; this mount Zion, wherein thou hast dwelt." (verse 2)

There are three factors in the work of God emphasised. Firstly, He had redeemed Israel out of Egypt (see Exodus 15:13). Then He had chosen "the rod" (AV margin, the "tribe") of Judah (Genesis 49:8-10). And finally, He had made Mount Zion His dwelling place. The word rendered "dwelt" means 'to reside' (*Strong*) and is the Hebrew verb from which the word *Shechinah* is derived, the term which was later used to describe the dwelling of God in the midst of His people.

The Psalmist pleads with God to lift up His feet, that is figuratively to stand and behold all that the enemy has done in the sanctuary (verse 3). He describes the work of the enemy as the "desolations". Literally the word means 'ruins', and it has been pointed out (*Speaker's Commentary*) that it is not a strong word implying total destruction. In this context we remember how some thirty or so years later Josiah undertook the repair of the temple – a fact which lends support to our suggestion that places the two psalms in the reign of Manasseh. The enemy roared even in the place where God met with His people ("congregation" – i.e., meeting place) and there they had set up their standards as signs or symbols of their own false worship (verse 4).

The two following verses are difficult in translation but not in general meaning. We follow the RV which presents the writer as though he was still beholding the desolators at work:

"They seemed as men that lifted up axes upon a thicket of trees. And now all the carved work thereof together they break down with hatchet and hammers."
(verses 5,6)

The enemy is compared to men frantically chopping down a wood or forest in their desperation to break down the woodwork of the temple, perhaps to carry away the golden decorations. The AV of verse 7 might imply that the temple had been put to the torch. But interestingly the word rendered "sanctuary" is plural (literally, "they have set thy sanctuaries on fire", see Leviticus 26:31). These would have been places of special importance to Israel because of their spiritual associations with events in the nation's history – places such as Gibeon (see 1 Kings 3:5). These places, with which the God of Israel had been pleased to associate His name, they had cast down to the ground:

"They said in their hearts, Let us destroy them together: they have burned up all the synagogues (literally, 'appointed places', from a root 'to meet') of God in the land." (verse 8)

So the Psalmist cries:

"We see not our signs: there is no more any prophet: neither is there among us any that knoweth how long."
(verse 9)

Instead of their own standards they saw only the emblems of false worship and foreign domination, and there was no prophetic voice to shed light in the darkness that enveloped them.

Verses 10-17

The cry once again, characteristic of both psalms is, "How long?". Would God suffer the reproach of the adversary and the blasphemy of the wicked to continue? (verse 10). The arrogant Assyrian boasted in his gods and ridiculed the God of Israel both in his taunts and in his deeds. Why, asks the Psalmist, do you draw back your hand even your right hand? His plea is, "Pluck it out of thy bosom" (verse 11). It is a prayer for God to rise up as in days of old when He had smitten the Egyptians (see Exodus 15:12) and destroy these arrogant oppressors.

The Psalmist's prayer is made in the assurance that God had shown Himself to be sovereign in establishing the nation of Israel, in delivering them from the darkness of Egypt, and he had every confidence that God could do the same again:

"For God is my King of old, working salvation in the midst of the earth. Thou didst divide the sea by thy strength: thou brakest the heads of the dragons (sea monsters) in the waters. Thou brakest the heads of leviathan (crocodiles) in pieces, and gavest him to be meat to the people inhabiting the wilderness. Thou didst cleave the fountain and the flood: thou driedst up mighty rivers." (verses 12-15)

The sea creatures and crocodiles are symbols of Egyptian power, and the reference is clearly to the destruction in the Red Sea. This wonder had been performed in the sight of all nations (Joshua 2:10; Psalm 77:14) and the Egyptians washed up on the seashore had become meat to the beasts of the wilderness. As God's might was shown in the destruction of the Egyptians, He had also asserted His sovereignty when He smote the rock so that the waters poured forth for their sustenance, and dried up the river Jordan that they might cross over into their inheritance. Truly God was their King from days of old.

As God had asserted His sovereignty in history, so also it was manifest in nature for He had appointed the heavenly bodies to rule over the earth. Its fixed laws demonstrated not only His power but His faithfulness: they were established and maintained by Him. Thus:

"The day is thine, the night also is thine: thou hast prepared the light (i.e., the moon) and the sun. Thou hast set all the borders of the earth: thou has made summer and winter." (verses 16,17, RV)

Verses 18-23

Encouraged by his recollections of God's power manifest in history and nature the Psalmist returns to prayer:

"Remember this, that the enemy hath reproached, O LORD, and that the foolish people have blasphemed thy name. O deliver not the soul of thy turtledove unto the multitude of the wicked: forget not the congregation of thy poor for ever." (verses 18,19)

The reproaches of the enemy, the blasphemies of the foolish, weighed heavily on the Psalmist's heart. Like Rabshakeh, at a later date the enemy would see in their victory a cause to malign the God of Israel. The word "foolish" carries the meaning of moral perversity, and its use in the Psalms and Proverbs leads us to conclude that these were the blasphemies of the foolish in Israel who presumed that their God had forsaken them.

But let them be confounded pleads the Psalmist – "deliver ... thy turtledove", save "thy poor". The dove was a favourite symbol amongst the people of Israel. They delighted in it we are told (Edersheim) above all others, for they regarded it as the most appropriate epithet to describe their covenant relationship with God. This arose out of the way they thought about the Song of Solomon as a representation of the love of God, their Bridegroom, for them, His bride. The word 'dove', of course, is particularly associated with the language of the Song of Solomon (see 1:15; 2:14; 4:1; 5:2; 5:12; 6:9). Hence the plea that follows:

"Have respect unto the covenant: for the dark places of the earth are full of the habitations of cruelty."
(verse 20)

Most appropriately the cry is for God to remember His covenant, for the Psalmist knew that God remained faithful to the word He had spoken. The dark places of the earth were the lands to which God's people had been carried captive; they were truly "habitations of cruelty", places where violence had found a home for it was part of the fabric of their society. Kay (*Psalms with Notes*) translates this as "homesteads of violence".

The concluding verses of the psalm repeat the prayers previously expressed:

"O let not the oppressed return ashamed: let the poor and needy praise thy name. Arise, O God, plead thine own cause: remember how the foolish man reproacheth thee daily. Forget not the voice of thine enemies: the tumult of those that rise up against thee increaseth continually." (verses 21-23)

His concern is that having presented their cause before the Most High, the oppressed should not be turned away ashamed because they had trusted in vain. Rather, he cries, let the poor, those who are crushed and downtrodden, have reason to praise thee.

His final appeal is that God will plead His own cause, for Judah's cause is God's cause, and in delivering them the enemy and the foolish would no more have reason to reproach and blaspheme His name. Although the tumult of the oppressor was rising up before God continually, the Psalmist knew that the Lord would not suffer their taunts and arrogance indefinitely, for –

"Why do the heathen rage, and the people imagine a vain thing? The kings of the earth set themselves, and the rulers take counsel together, against the LORD, and against his anointed ... He that sitteth in the heavens shall laugh: the Lord shall have them in derision ... Yet have I set my king upon my holy hill of Zion."

(Psalm 2:1-6)

PSALM 79

It seems appropriate, given the connection between the two psalms established earlier in this chapter, to consider Psalm 79 with Psalm 74. As indicated, it has the same background and, almost certainly, the same author. It is a lamentation over the same national disaster discussed in Psalm 74, although there is a different emphasis. Whereas Psalm 74 dwelt particularly upon the temple, this song is more concerned with the city and people of Jerusalem. Again in Psalm 74 there is an underlying hope of deliverance, whereas in Psalm 79 there is a sombre tone of almost unrelenting sadness, relieved only by the expression of faith in the final verse. So much so that one writer described it as "the funeral anthem of the nation" –

574

mistakenly we believe, for it was not yet the end of the Kingdom of Judah. Nevertheless he has captured, in a sense, the spirit of the psalm.

It would be true to say that Psalm 79 is not one of the better known psalms amongst us, but clearly it was known and remembered by faithful men of God, for it is quoted by both Jeremiah and Daniel:

Psalm 79:6,7	**Jeremiah 10:25**
"Pour out thy wrath upon the heathen that have not known thee, and upon the kingdoms that have not called upon thy name. For they have devoured Jacob, and laid waste his dwelling place."	"Pour out thy fury upon the heathen that know thee not, and upon the families that call not on thy name: for they have eaten up Jacob, and devoured him, and consumed him, and have made his habitation desolate."

Psalm 79:1,8,9	**Daniel 9:18**
"Thy holy temple have they defiled." "O remember not against us former iniquities: let thy tender mercies speedily prevent us: for we are brought very low. Help us, O God of our salvation, for the glory of thy name: and deliver us, and purge away our sins, for thy name's sake."	"O my God, incline thine ear, and hear; open thine eyes, and behold our desolations, and the city which is called by thy name: for we do not present our supplications before thee for our righteousnesses, but for thy great mercies."

Neither is verbatim, but free quotations – Daniel particularly so. Nevertheless, it is clear that Jeremiah, prophesying of the destruction of the city before Nebuchadnezzar, recalls these words of Psalm 79 when the city had suffered before the might of Assyria and many had gone into captivity. Remembering the fact that Asaph was a seer, perhaps we can appreciate that this plaintive cry was, against the background of the Psalmist's time, itself a prophecy of that yet more dreadful destruction to come because of their apostasy.

Similarly, Daniel looking back to the overthrow of the kingdom would see that event clearly foreshadowed in this psalm and would appropriate its words in his wonderful prayer on behalf of his people. There is, apparently, no

575

metric structure to the psalm and consequently no obvious structural division. Writers tend to divide it in different ways according to their understanding of its content and for convenience we do likewise:

1. The Psalmist's grief because of the ruin of the city (verses 1-4).
2. His prayer that God will turn His anger away and punish the enemy (verses 5-8).
3. Prayer for God to remember because of the honour of His name (verses 9-12).
4. A final expression of the thanks with which God's mercy would be acknowledged (verse 13).

Verses 1-4

These first four verses contain the Psalmist's terrible lament over the way the land had been overrun, the temple desecrated, the city left in ruins and the people slaughtered. The language is so explicit that it needs little comment to explain its meaning:

"O God, the heathen are come into thine inheritance; thy holy temple have they defiled; they have laid Jerusalem on heaps. The dead bodies of thy servants have they given to be meat unto the fowls of the heaven, the flesh of thy saints unto the beasts of the earth. Their blood have they shed like water round about Jerusalem; and there was none to bury them. We are become a reproach to our neighbours, a scorn and a derision to them that are round about us."

(verses 1-4)

As in Psalm 74 (verse 2) both land and people are described as God's inheritance. They belonged to Him and they were both His portion as He should have been theirs. The word "defiled" indicates not the destruction of the temple but the presence of the enemy in its precincts (Psalm 74:4). The words "servants" and "saints" almost certainly refer to Israel's status as the people of God rather than to any particular righteousness pertaining to them, and these words of verse 2 seem also to have been alluded to by Jeremiah (7:33).

The words of verse 4 appear to be a quotation from Psalm 44:13 which was written against the background of

Sennacherib's invasion in the days of Hezekiah. It would be appropriate to recall them now for whenever Jerusalem was threatened, the nations round about (Edom, Moab, Ammon, etc.) rejoiced and sought to take advantage of the situation.

Verses 5-8

"How long, LORD? wilt thou be angry for ever? shall thy jealousy burn like fire?"   (verse 5)

"How long?" This plaintive cry of both Psalm 74 (verse 10) and Psalm 79 surely reflects the aching heart and longing soul whose cry is echoed in the Book of Revelation (6:10). The appropriateness of this connection will become more apparent as we come to the end of this study. How long would God's jealousy burn like fire? The Psalmist would know that He had declared, "For the LORD thy God is a consuming fire, even a jealous God" (Deuteronomy 4:24), and would recognise that these things had come upon the nation because they had forgotten the covenant and in His jealousy the Lord would not share their allegiance with any other. Nevertheless he beseeches the Almighty: "Pour out thy wrath upon the heathen that have not known thee, and upon the kingdoms that have not called upon thy name" (verse 6). Surely there is a play here upon the words of verse 3, "Their blood have they shed (literally, poured out) like water". Now in retribution God was called upon to pour out His wrath.

They had devoured Jacob and laid waste his dwelling place (verse 7). This is not the temple, God's dwelling place, but literally it conveys the idea of 'pasture'. This is, perhaps, more correctly translated, "laid waste his pasture" (see RV and margin); that is the land itself which God had given to His flock. The section closes with a plea that God would "remember not against us the iniquities of our forefathers" (verse 8, RV). It might appear that the Psalmist was pleading with God not to hold them responsible for the sins of their fathers which, of course, God had explicitly stated should not happen (Deuteronomy 24:16; see also Ezekiel 18). However, verse 9 makes it clear that the thought is rather of a continuing apostasy, a walking in the sins of their fathers. What they suffered was the result of their own iniquity, because they

577

had not turned away from the sins of previous generations. Reflecting upon the name of God (Exodus 34:6), the writer pleads that God would "prevent" (literally, 'come to meet') them with His tender mercies that their necessity might be met and answered by the goodness of God (verse 8).

Verses 9-12

If verse 8 has introduced us to the meaning of the name of God, verse 9 continues the emphasis:

> "Help us, O God of our salvation, for the glory of thy name: and deliver us, and purge away our sins, for thy name's sake."

In forgiving and delivering, God would show Himself to be true to the name He had revealed when He caused all His glory to pass before Moses in the Mount. The word translated "purge" is that normally rendered "to make an atonement"; hence, to cover or forgive their sins.

By manifesting Himself on behalf of His people God would give an effective answer to all those round about who rejoiced in Judah's calamity. No longer would the nations be able to cry, "Where is their God?". Instead He would be known amongst the nations in the sight of His people by revenging their blood which had been shed (verse 10). The words are based upon the song of Moses recorded in Deuteronomy 32 (verse 43).

The verse that follows beseeches the Lord to show pity to those who had been carried away to Babylon by Esarhaddon. The reference to the prisoner, whose sighing the Psalmist asks might come before the Lord, is assumed by every writer we have read to be used in a plural sense to encompass all who had been taken to Babylon. However, given the background described, could not the allusion be to a particular prisoner, to Manasseh, whose repentance had been reported in Jerusalem? The mercy that the Psalmist desired to be shown to him he asks to be extended to all those who had been carried away with him, for, "According to the greatness of thy power (literally, arm, see Exodus 15:16) preserve thou those that are appointed to die" (Psalm 79:11). As the Hebrew idiom has it, preserve thou 'the sons of death'. It has been pointed

out that the idiom does not necessarily mean that they
were under sentence of death, but that their confinement
in Babylon was as a living death (compare Isaiah 42:7).

In contrast to the mercy shown to the captives the
Psalmist pleads:

"And render unto our neighbours sevenfold into their
bosom their reproach, wherewith they have reproached
thee, O Lord."   (verse 12)

Many link the idea of sevenfold recompense with the
vengeance of Lamech (Genesis 4:24) and the words of the
Lord Jesus (Matthew 18:21,22). However, these references
are to the vengeful spirit of man and the forgiving spirit
enjoined upon Peter by the Lord Jesus. The plea of the
psalm is for God to render a full recompense to the
neighbouring nations (i.e., Edom, Moab and Ammon)
because they had reproached the God of Israel in rejoicing
over the trouble He had brought upon His people, and
doubting His power and sovereignty over the nations.

Verse 13

The psalm concludes with an expression of the thanks
that the sheep of His pasture would render to their
shepherd if He heard their cry and responded accordingly:

"So we thy people and sheep of thy pasture will give
thee thanks for ever: we will shew forth thy praise to all
generations."

The Apocalypse

We have already intimated a connection between the cry
of the Psalmist, "How long LORD" (verse 5) and the spirit
of God's persecuted people in the Book of Revelation
(6:10). But further connections are apparent. We have
considered the significance of the sevenfold recompense
that must surely remind us of "the seven trumpets", "the
seven thunders" and "the seven vials". There are also
some remarkable links with Revelation chapter 11. We list
them for comparison overleaf:

Psalm 79	**Revelation 11**
"O God, the heathen are come into thine inheritance; thy holy temple have they defiled" (verse 1).	"Rise, and measure the temple of God ... But the court which is without the temple leave out ... for it is given unto the Gentiles" (verses 1,2).
"The dead bodies of thy servants have they given to be meat ... and there was none to bury them" (verses 2,3).	"And their dead bodies shall lie in the streets" (verse 8).
"We are become a reproach to our neighbours, a scorn and derision to them that are round about us" (verse 4).	"And they that dwell upon the earth shall rejoice over them, and make merry, and shall send gifts one to another" (verse 10).
"Pour out thy wrath upon the heathen that have not known thee" (verse 6).	"And the nations were angry, and thy wrath is come ..." (verse 18).

A comparison might also be made between verse 13 of the psalm and verse 17 of Revelation 11. Would we be seeing too much if we suggested that there is a point of contact between Esarhaddon and the "beast that ascendeth out of the bottomless pit" (Revelation 11:7)? After Sennacherib's hasty departure and the rise of Merodach Baladin they might well have imagined that the Assyrian had disappeared from the political map for ever. How wrong they were!

Upon Shoshannim Eduth

Psalm 79 is one of two psalms, the other being Psalm 59, that have this subscription; the only difference being that the first word is singular in Psalm 59 but plural in this psalm. It means 'lilies', 'testimonies' and we have already written (Psalm 59) on its association with the spring (Passover to Pentecost) and the giving of the Law at Sinai. Thirtle points out that in both psalms it is used by way of contrast with the safety and security that firstly David, and secondly Israel, should have known in the land.

In both psalms the emphasis is upon "the city" (see Psalm 59:6,14 and 79:1-3). This also provides a point of contact with Revelation 11, discussed above. Note the references to "the holy city" (verse 2), "the great city" (verse 8), and "the tenth part of the city" (verse 13). We cannot now enter into a consideration of the 11th chapter of Revelation but there is a principle that should be noted. Quotations from the Old Testament in the Apocalypse do not necessarily relate directly to the same event or to the same time period as the Old Testament scripture. Rather it is often a similarity of circumstance that holds the key to interpreting the words of the Apocalypse, with the actual events and their time of occurrence having no direct relevance to the Old Testament scriptures from which they are drawn. This we feel confident is the way that Psalm 79 is used in Revelation 11.

PSALM 75

PSALM 75 bears the superscription, "A Psalm or Song". We have commented before on these epithets, suggesting that possibly by the addition of the word *shir* (a song) the Psalmist is indicating that not only was the psalm sung in set worship in the sanctuary, but it was also sung in a more general way by the people at large to celebrate God's deliverance.

There is also a subscription, "To the chief Musician on Neginoth", indicating that the psalm when sung was accompanied by stringed instruments.

Background

This psalm answers so effectively the questions posed in Psalm 74 that it is difficult to escape the conclusion that it is connected with that psalm historically. Whether it has the same author one cannot say with any certainty, but it would be appropriate if it did. Here we find the answers to the questions posed, "How long?" and "Shall the enemy blaspheme thy name for ever?" (Psalm 74:10). We suggest therefore that the psalm would have been written shortly after the Babylonians defeated Esarhaddon and before the repentant Manasseh with the captive Israelites were returned to their land.

Structure

It is a short psalm (ten verses) and opens with an expression of thanksgiving to God by the people of Judah for the manifestation of power on their behalf. To this ascription of praise the Lord responds (verses 2-6), assuring them that at the appropriate time He will always respond to the cry of His people. The Lord's words are then echoed upon earth by His people (verses 4-8), before the psalm closes with a repetition of the ascription of praise with which it opened (verse 9), followed by a response again from God Himself (verse 10).

Verse 1

The theme of the psalm is an expression of thanksgiving for the manifestation of God's power on behalf of His people, and a meditation upon the way in which He responds to the cry of His servants when the enemy oppresses them. The Psalm opens:

"We give thanks unto thee, O God; we give thanks for thy name is near; men tell of thy wondrous works."

(verse 1, RV)

The repetition of the words, "we give thanks" is not a poetic device to give emphasis. In the first phrase the Hebrew is in the perfect tense, hence, "We have given thanks," whereas the second phrase is in the present tense. It is as if the Psalmist has fused together the past and present. Just as they, as a people, had given thanks in previous generations for the mighty works wrought on their behalf, so now there is a continuation of that praise for the deliverance recently effected. They gave thanks for His name was near. By His name, God was made known in their midst and by it He had performed wondrous works to destroy the enemy. It was near in the sense that God's presence had drawn near to His people to succour them and comfort them in their humiliation. There was a sense in which when there was no answer of God and they cried, "How long?", the name of God came from far (see Isaiah 30:27). However, in the assurances of the Law He was always near. Never was there a time when He was not totally in control and always aware of the predicament of His people:

"For what nation is there so great, who hath God so nigh unto them, as the LORD our God is in all things that we call upon him for?"   (Deuteronomy 4:7)

Verses 2,3

Abruptly God responds. There is an answer from heaven for all those who, in their hearts, still felt anxiety and perplexity because of the recent calamities, for:

> "When I shall take a set time (see AV margin) I will
> judge uprightly." (verse 2)

God is the righteous judge who at the set time will act. He
will execute His judgements, not according to man's
expectations, but at the time appropriate to the carrying
out of His will and purpose. The difference in translation
between the text of the AV, which uses the term
"congregation", and other translations, arises from the
fact that the Hebrew word *mo'ed* has both the significance
of an assembly and of a set time. This is because it carries
the root idea of 'something fixed', whether it be a place
(i.e., of assembly) or a time (see Habakkuk 2:3).

The second "I" carries great emphasis. It is as though
God said, "I, whatever men may do: I, whatever men may
think" (*Cambridge Bible*). The emphasis is carried
forward into the next verse, for though –

> "the earth and all the inhabitants thereof are
> dissolved: I (literally, 'I, myself, I') bear up the pillars of
> it. Selah." (verse 3)

Thus, in the critical circumstances in which they had
found themselves when the world itself (their world)
seemed to have broken down and dissolved in terror and
confusion, God gives them the assurance that he has "set
up" (RV) the pillars of the earth. He has laid the
foundations, established order and ordained the
fundamental laws which rule the earth, both physically
and morally (see 1 Samuel 2:8). In short, God is in control
and, consequently, if in faith and patience we wait, God
will eventually manifest Himself on our behalf.

Verses 4-8

The "Selah" indicating a pause for meditation, marks an
appropriate break between the words of God Himself and
the words of the Psalmist which follow. On the basis of
what God has spoken the writer issues a warning to all
who behave presumptuously in speaking not only against
His people but against God Himself:

> "I said unto the fools (literally, 'shiners' or 'boasters',
> *Strong*), Deal not foolishly: and to the wicked, Lift not
> up the horn: lift not up your horn on high: speak not
> with a stiff neck." (verses 4,5)

The Hebrew word translated "lift up" is used four times in the psalm: once in verses 4,5 in the negative sense of "lift not up" and three times in a positive way in verse 6 (translated "promotion"); verse 7 (translated "setteth up") and verse 10 (translated "be exalted"). In the AV the phrase occurs twice in verses 4 and 5, but only once in the Hebrew text where the idiom requires the double negative in the translation. The meaning of the Hebrew word *ruwm*, translated thus on these occasions, is of the lifting up of the head in deliverance, victory and triumph. Underlying it is the idea of strength, hence the graphic figure of "lifting up the horn" (verses 5,10), a metaphor taken from the habit of animals of lifting up their horns in token of strength in victory over their adversaries. Thus the usage in verse 5 is in direct contrast with the other occurrences: 'In your arrogance, "lift not up the horn" as though your strength will prevail, for ultimately it is only those whom God "lifts up" who will be truly exalted in the earth.' So also the further word of warning, "Speak not with a stiff neck", or as the RV margin renders it, "Speak not insolently with a haughty neck". The words recall the song of Hannah:

"Talk no more so exceedingly proudly; let not arrogancy come out of your mouth." (1 Samuel 2:3)

We have already noted that "the pillars" (Psalm 75:3) is an allusion to verse 8 of Hannah's song and further connections are apparent. "He putteth down one and raiseth up another" (Psalm 75:7) is an echo of 1 Samuel 2:6,7, and the words of the final verse, "the horns of the righteous shall be exalted" are surely based upon, "and he shall give strength unto his king, and exalt the horn of his anointed" (1 Samuel 2:10).

This most interesting connection with the song of Hannah gives to the psalm a truly Messianic spirit that we might not otherwise have detected. The song of Hannah is the background to the song of Mary (Luke 1:46-55) and these connections make it clear that the true fulfilment of Psalm 75, whatever its more immediate implications, is to be found in the day when the Lord Jesus shall come in glory. The message for us of the verses already considered is obvious. Although men might say,

"Where is the promise of his coming?", we wait in faith and patience, knowing not the day or the hour, but confident that God is in control and that at the appointed time He will send the Lord Jesus again, for nothing can frustrate those things which He has ordained.

The Psalmist continues:

> "For promotion (i.e., lifting up, exaltation) cometh neither from the east, nor from the west, nor from the south. But God is the judge: he putteth down one, and setteth up another." (verse 6)

Everything we have read about verse 6 expresses the difficulty that expositors, both Christadelphian and others, have found in this verse.

If "lifting up" does not come from east, west or south, it must come from the north, and yet the contrast between verses 6 and 7 clearly teaches that it comes from the Lord. We feel that the answer is actually very simple once the background to the psalm is understood. Judah would not look to the north for their deliverance, for that was where the Assyrian reigned and where Manasseh was held prisoner and his fellow captives languished. But the truth was that God was in control and Esarhaddon's brief supremacy was to come to an end before the might of Babylon.

> "The most High ruleth in the kingdom of men, and giveth it to whomsoever he will." (Daniel 4:17)

Thus the hand of God was at work amongst the nations, for "God is the judge: he putteth down one, and setteth up another" and with Esarhaddon gone the Lord, through the hand of the Babylonians, caused Manasseh and the captives to return to their land.

> "For in the hand of the LORD there is a cup, and the wine is red; it is full of mixture; and he poureth out of the same: but the dregs thereof, all the wicked ... shall wring them out, and drink them." (verse 8)

God's judgements upon the Assyrian oppressor are likened to a cup of wine which He gives to the wicked to drink. The wine is red (RV, foameth) and mixed with herbs and spices, and the initial idea is of the attractiveness of the path they pursue. They are intoxicated by it; they can see no further than the initial joy and sense of fulfilment they feel. But there is a lesson which all who set themselves against the God of Israel must learn, for they must drink that cup of His wrath to the full, to the dregs. They will be wrung out until they are all consumed to their confusion and shame. Note that it is God who pours out the wine for, following the theme of verses 6 and 7, He is in total control and He gives to the wicked that which shows them for what they really are, and ends in His righteous judgement. The figure of the cup of God's wrath is common in scripture (see for example, Isaiah 51:17-23; Jeremiah 25:27; 49:12; Ezekiel 23:32; Obadiah 16, etc.).

Verses 9,10

In the assurance that God would deliver them out of all their troubles, the Psalmist cries on behalf of all the people of Judah:

"But I will declare for ever; I will sing praises to the God of Jacob." (verse 9)

His declaration of what God has accomplished will be continuous, but surely he is carrying us forward to the kingdom age when with immortal voices the faithful of all ages shall truly declare God's glory for ever. Surely it is significant that the praise is offered to the God of Jacob who brought him back to the land from his servitude to Laban in Padan-aram, as Manasseh and his fellow captives would now be brought back from their captivity in Assyria.

To this promise of continuous praise God responds in the final verse which, as we have intimated earlier, carries us forward to the establishment of God's kingdom on the earth:

"All the horns of the wicked also will I cut off; but the horns of the righteous shall be exalted." (verse 10)

In that victory we hope to share, for –

"He that overcometh, and keepeth my works unto the end, to him will I give power over the nations."

(Revelation 2:26)

587

PSALM 76

JUST as Psalm 75, this also bears the superscription, "A Psalm or Song of Asaph". It also has a subscription, "To the Chief Musician, to Jeduthun" – perhaps more accurately, "belonging to Jeduthun". It will be recalled that David appointed three, Asaph, Heman and Ethan, to lead the singing in the tabernacle (1 Chronicles 15:17-19). In later references, Ethan is referred to as Jeduthun, and it would appear that this second name was given to him because of the special character of the singers he led (1 Chronicles 25:1-6). The name Jeduthun is derived from a word which means, 'to hold up the hands in praise or confession' and it seems that these were the specific duties of the choir he led. Their duty lay in this direction and the three psalms which carry this subscription (38, 61 and 76) are certainly marked by this characteristic (Thirtle, *The Titles of the Psalms*, page 228).

Background

The internal evidence of the psalm, which will be noted in our general consideration, points, we believe beyond question, to the destruction of Sennacherib's army in the days of Hezekiah. Historically therefore it is earlier than the two preceding psalms which we have related to Manasseh. There is nevertheless an appropriateness about its place in the Psalter which must surely have led the compilers of the Psalms to place it after Psalms 74 and 75. They too were concerned with Assyrian aggression, and if in Hezekiah's day they had seen the visible hand of God destroy the invader, so now in their day they had seen, through the ways of providence, God achieve a like victory over the Assyrian oppressor. It was therefore most appropriate that this psalm which praises God for His victory over Gentile power should be included in this particular place by the compilers of the Psalms. The

588

Septuagint Version actually adds the words, "A Song for the Assyrians".

Structure

The metre of the song clearly indicates that it falls into four stanzas, each consisting of three verses. Two stanzas, the first and the third, are concluded with "Selah" indicating the need to pause and reflect before moving on to the next section.

The four stanzas, would appear to break down into the following headings:

1. Jerusalem the abode of God (verses 1-3).
2. The destruction of the invading army (verses 4-6).
3. God the Judge of men and the Saviour of His people (verses 7-9).
4. Consequently let Israel and all nations pay homage to Him (verses 10-12).

Verses 1-3

"In Judah is God known: his name is great in Israel."
(verse 1)

Literally, 'In Judah God has made himself known', that is by the wonderful manifestation of His power whereby He had destroyed the Assyrian host. Grammatically the participle of the verb expresses present action. But as a result of this action His name is great also in Israel. The conjunction of Judah and Israel is significant for at this time the Northern Kingdom had been overthrown; it had ceased to exist. Nevertheless it was Hezekiah of all the kings of Judah who made a determined effort to win the people of the Northern Kingdom back to the worship of their God.

In 2 Chronicles 30 we have the record of Hezekiah sending letters to Ephraim and Manasseh inviting them to come to the house of the Lord to keep the Passover (verses 1-9). However, the general reaction was that they "laughed them to scorn, and mocked them" (verse 10). There were some, nevertheless, who responded, for "divers of Asher and Manasseh and of Zebulun humbled themselves, and came to Jerusalem" (verse 11). Later in the chapter (verse 18) there is reference also to Ephraim

589

and Issachar so it would appear that a considerable number of Israel had joined themselves to Judah.

Israel, of course, was the covenant name of the nation and its use in parallel with Judah was an indication that Hezekiah and those over whom he ruled were now recognised as the Israel of God, and consequently it was an assurance to them that all God's promises remained inviolate although the Northern Kingdom had disappeared.

> "In Salem also is his tabernacle, and his dwelling place in Zion." (Psalm 76:2)

It is unusual to find the ancient name of Jerusalem used in the later books of scripture. Our minds are directed almost instinctively to the very first occasion that it was used in Genesis 14 when Melchizedek met Abraham after his pursuit and defeat of the four kings. It is interesting to remember that this was a northern confederacy that came down from the same general area as the Assyrians. On that occasion also the godly seed had triumphed over the seed of the serpent. The association of Melchizedek, a king-priest, with these events must be of some significance in pointing our attention to the future glory, for he was the first king-priest to reign in Salem. How appropriate then that this psalm should direct our thoughts to the last (see Hebrews 7:1-17). The meaning of Salem (i.e., peace) would also be significant, for God had brought peace to His people as a result of this victory.

The word "tabernacle" translates a Hebrew original that is not usually associated with the tabernacle or the temple where God dwelt in the midst of His people. It means literally a 'hut', in the sense of boughs entwined together to make a shelter, hence the booths associated with the Feast of Tabernacles. The word translated "dwelling" means literally a 'habitation', and of itself carries no direct association with the "dwelling place of God". However, both words (*Strong*) have a secondary meaning that has strong scriptural evidence to support it. The first word can mean 'lair' and the second a 'den'. The RV margin renders them as 'covert' and 'lair'. The first word occurs in this sense in Psalm 10, "As a lion in his den" (verse 9); the second in Psalm 104: "The young lions

... lay them down in their dens" (verses 21,22), and again in Amos 3, "Will a young lion cry out of his den ...?" (verse 4).

The figure then is of God as a lion going forth from His mountain lair to destroy. He is presented as the lion of the tribe of Judah and the words are surely resonant of the day when God's power and glory shall be manifest in the Lord Jesus Christ, who of course bears this title himself (Revelation 5:5). The words of the psalm and the destruction of the Assyrian host prefigure the victory of the Lord Jesus Christ, when "the LORD also shall roar (like a lion) out of Zion, and utter his voice from Jerusalem" (Joel 3:16; see also Hosea 11:10). It was at Jerusalem that the Lord wrought this terrible destruction.

> "*There* brake he the arrows of the bow, the shield, and the sword, and the battle. Selah."   (Psalm 76:3)

Emphatically the word "there" tells us the very place where the destruction took place. Ancient historians have various 'flights of fancy' as to the fate of Sennacherib's army, but the scriptures are clear. It was at Jerusalem, for:

> "It came to pass that night, that the angel of the LORD went out, and smote in the camp of the Assyrians an hundred fourscore and five thousand: and when they arose early in the morning, behold, they were all dead corpses."   (2 Kings 19:35)

Who arose early in the morning? – the inhabitants of Jerusalem (see also Isaiah 31:8,9).

So God destroyed all their instruments of war. They were of no avail to resist "the sword of the LORD" wielded by the angel (figuratively, of course) who went out (from Zion) and smote the Assyrian camp. Psalm 46, which was also written at this time, emphasises the message of Psalm 76:

> "God is in the midst of her (Jerusalem); she shall not be moved: God shall help her, and that right early (margin, 'when the morning appeareth') ... Come, behold the works of the LORD, what desolations he hath made in the earth. He maketh wars to cease unto the end of the earth; he breaketh the bow, and cutteth the spear in

sunder; he burneth the chariot in the fire. Be still, and know that I am God: I will be exalted among the heathen, I will be exalted in the earth."

(Psalm 46:5,8-10)

Verses 4-6

Following the theme already developed, these verses describe the destruction of the invading army:

"Thou art more glorious and excellent than the mountains of prey. The stouthearted are spoiled, they have slept their sleep: and none of the men of might have found their hands. At thy rebuke, O God of Jacob, both the chariot and horse are cast into a dead sleep."

(Psalm 76:4-6)

Apparently there is no contrast in the Hebrew text. A consensus of opinions suggest that the RV is to be followed in this instance: "Glorious art thou and excellent, from the mountains of prey". "The mountains of prey" is a metaphor for the Assyrian invaders as God now returns, glorious in His majesty, having gone forth as a lion from Jerusalem and devoured the prey. There is an appropriateness about the figure of the lion and his prey, for it is written of the Assyrian that as a lion he "filled his holes with prey, and his dens with ravin" (Nahum 2:12; see also 3:1).

The fierce lion of Assyria was no match for the Lion of Judah, for "I will break the Assyrian in my land, and upon my mountains tread him under foot" (Isaiah 14:25). The mighty men of Assyria ("the stouthearted") were spoiled, for they slept the sleep of death. Again there is an appropriateness about the language for they laid themselves down to sleep and, in the morning, they were all dead: "They shall sleep a perpetual sleep, and not wake" (Jeremiah 51:57). Their hands did not respond; it was as though they were paralysed. The *Speaker's Commentary* has a most interesting comment:

"This phrase is remarkable; it seems to represent a death which comes suddenly, yet with a momentary interval of consciousness; the sleeper, awakened by a sudden pang, endeavours in vain to put out his hands and grasp his weapons, but falls back overwhelmed by the deep sleep, which in the next verse is said to fall on chariot and horse, i.e., the whole army of the invaders."

(Speaker's Commentary, Psalms, page 344)

Verses 7-9

It might be expected that, having witnessed such a notable victory over their enemy, the people of Judah would have rejoiced and exulted in the defeat of such a dreadful foe. It is surely an indication of the fact that the scriptures are the words of God and not the words of man that, in his contemplation of God's righteous judgement and deliverance, the Psalmist shows none of these emotions. Rather, he is filled with a sense of awe and wonder and describes the judgement poured out in solemn and measured tones. It is almost as if he were moved to ask himself how he could stand before such a glorious and righteous God. What would be his fate if he were to provoke Him to anger?

"Thou, even thou, art to be feared: and who may stand in thy sight when once thou art angry? Thou didst cause judgment (sentence, RV) to be heard from heaven; the earth feared, and was still, when God arose to judgment, to save all the meek of the earth. Selah."

(verses 7-9)

David had written that "the meek shall inherit the earth; and shall delight themselves in the abundance of peace" (Psalm 37:11) – words quoted by the Lord Jesus when he said, "Blessed are the meek: for they shall inherit the earth" (Matthew 5:5). So it was that, far from a lifting up of the heart, because God had pronounced judgement from heaven upon the proud Assyrian who was powerless before His irresistible might, the Psalmist expresses the people's consciousness of their own weakness and their dependence upon God, for it is the meek of the earth that He saves.

Verses 10-12

There is only one conclusion to which his meditations on this fearful judgement and act of deliverance could lead him: Israel and all nations must recognise His sovereignty and pay homage unto Him.

"Surely the wrath of man shall praise thee: the remainder of wrath shalt thou restrain."   (verse 10)

This is evidently a difficult verse to translate and to understand. It is as if God says that ultimately all the wrath of men must be silenced and all rebellion quelled that their voices might turn to praise. In keeping with this thought, in parallel with it, the next phrase extends the picture: "the residue of wrath shalt thou gird upon thee" (RV). It is as if God gathers up all that remains of the wrath of man and adorns Himself with it like a garland of victory, for:

> "Vow, and pay unto the LORD your God: let all that be round about him bring presents unto him that ought to be feared." (verse 11)

Those vows that Israel had made in their hour of peril must now be paid in solemn tribute to God. Moreover the nations round about must also recognise and acknowledge His sovereignty and bring their gifts and offerings to lay before Him. The words of course have an historical background, for the Second Book of Chronicles declares that:

> "Many brought gifts unto the LORD to Jerusalem, and presents to Hezekiah king of Judah: so that he was magnified in the sight of all nations from thenceforth." (32:23)

The words, "that ought to be feared" are represented in the Hebrew text by a single word, and this is translated by the *Speaker's Commentary* as "the terrible". Others render it, "unto the fear", and the same expression occurs in Isaiah's prophecy, "Let him be your fear" (8:13). We rejoice in the love of God, but let us never take our Heavenly Father for granted; let us never presume upon His goodness. In reverence and fear let us remember that He is also "the terrible" as manifest in judgement against Senacherib's host for:

> "He shall cut off the spirit of princes: he is terrible to the kings of the earth." (verse 12)

Behind the first phrase is the figure of the vintage, as princes are cut off as grapes from the vine – a common method of describing God's judgements (see Isaiah 18:5; Revelation 14:18). Well might the nations fear if only they understood the lessons of history and the dreadful judgement that God will yet pour out upon those who despise Him and do not fear His name.

PSALM 77

OTHER than the fact that it is a psalm "of" or "for Asaph" there is no indication as to the authorship or historical background. It has to be admitted that the internal evidence of the psalm is not sufficiently strong to point unerringly to any one particular individual or time period. We feel nevertheless that it is always good to have some historical circumstance to which the psalm could apply because this gives us a framework on which to develop our thoughts and meditations. This is one of a number of scripturally unidentified psalms that, on a personal basis, we feel a kind of intuition about. The more we read it, the more convinced we become that it was written by Hezekiah at the time of his sickness and the threatened assault on Jerusalem by the Assyrian invader.

The psalm is personal, exploring the innermost feelings of the writer's heart. He penned his words at a time of great anxiety concerning his own welfare, but even this sense of personal tragedy was almost overwhelmed by his concern about an imminent catastrophe that seemed likely to fall upon the nation as a whole. Thus after telling of his determination to express his prayer unto God (verse 1) the writer explains what had brought him to this conviction. First of all he expresses the disquiet and personal distress which he had experienced (verses 2-4). He tells how his endeavour to consider his past experience, that therein he might find relief in the present troubles, had brought him no assurance (verses 5-9). However, he turns again to reconsider the work of God on behalf of His people and finds in the marvels worked of old, particularly the way in which God had manifested Himself at the time of the Exodus, the consolation he seeks (verses 10-20). It is in that confidence, gained from these meditations, that he can declare his trust in both the visible and providential hand of God (verse 20).

We know that Hezekiah's sickness and the Assyrian invasion coincided because he reigned for twenty-nine years (2 Chronicles 29:1) and it was in the fourteenth year of his reign that Sennacherib took all the fenced cities of Judah (2 Kings 18:13). As a result of his prayer God added fifteen years to his life (2 Kings 20:6) and this simple calculation makes it clear that at the time of the invasion Hezekiah was a sick man. Others had assumed temporary authority in Jerusalem, amongst whom was Shebna the scribe, an unscrupulous and unreliable man (see Isaiah 22:15-19). It is at this time surely that Hezekiah, lacking his characteristic vigour and steadfastness, tried to buy off the Assyrians with treasures both from his own house and the house of the Lord (2 Kings 18:13-16), but all to no avail (2 Kings 18:17). No doubt they had heard that the king was sick.

Verses 1-4

In his distress the Psalmist determines to make his prayer unto God:

> "I will cry unto God with my voice; even unto God with my voice, and he will give ear unto me."
>
> (verse 1, RV)

As is often the case, the Psalmist emphasises the conviction to which the events related in the remainder of the psalm have led him. Perhaps we can see how, in this sense, both the first and last verses of the psalm stand alone. The first as a declaration of intent; the last as a recognition of God as the Shepherd of Israel (verse 20).

Verses 2-4

> "In the day of my trouble I sought the Lord: my sore ran in the night, and ceased not: my soul refused to be comforted."
>
> (verse 2)

Almost all commentators follow the RV in altering the sense of "my sore ran in the night", to "my hand is stretched out in the night" – that is, in the attitude of prayer. However, the difficulty they feel with the Hebrew is obvious and most write without conviction. The Jewish authorities have used the translation, "my wound", the association with "hand" arising from the idea of being struck as with the hand of God. We therefore retain the rendering of the AV and understand the "sore" which ran in the night to refer to Hezekiah's boil (Isaiah 38:21), although there is no direct linguistic link. The prayer is no hastily contrived petition, but like Jacob he wrestles with God through the night. In his case, however, there is no blessing in the morning to comfort, for –

"I remembered God: and was troubled. I complained (meditated, *Strong*), and my spirit was overwhelmed. Selah" (verse 3)

Through the long watches of the night God had held his eyes from closing. Sleepless, his pleadings finally reduce him to such a state of lassitude that he can no longer utter the words that stir in his heart.

Verses 5-9

In his attempt to find solace he had "considered the days of old, the years of ancient times". He had remembered his own experiences when in contemplation of past mercies to the people of Israel he had played upon the harp and sung his songs in the night season. It is as if the peace and solitude of the night had been occasions when he had been able to turn to God in meditation and prayer. He recalled how he had "communed with his own heart and made search". In this way God had given him comfort and solace in the past (verses 5,6).

But the recollection of past spiritual refreshing served now only to aggravate his anxiety and sense of bewilderment, for he was sick unto death, and the Assyrian was pillaging the land. So his plaintive cry rises up:

"Will the Lord cast off for ever? And will he be favourable no more? Is his mercy clean gone for ever? Doth his promise fail for evermore? Hath God forgotten to be gracious? Hath he in anger shut up his tender mercies? Selah." (verses 7-9)

The emphasis is upon the ages to come, for had God forsaken His people? Had He abandoned the promises that He made? These things, God's lovingkindness and His promises, were the foundation of his faith and it is only when we remember the desperateness of Judah's plight at that time that we can appreciate how it was possible for a man like Hezekiah to ask such questions in his heart. In the sixth year of his reign Shalmanezer had carried away captive the Northern Kingdom. It was no more. Now with the Assyrian rampaging through the land all the strong cities had fallen and the host of Sennacherib had surrounded the city of Jerusalem. In the words of Isaiah, the Assyrian waters (the Euphrates) had overflowed their banks, they had engulfed the land "even to the neck" (8:7,8). Only the head, Jerusalem, remained to be subdued and Hezekiah the man on whom the people rested was sick unto death.

If we would measure the faith of the man we must do so by realising the blackness of the day that could cause such doubts to be expressed in his heart, and marvel that he was able to triumph in the face of such dreadful adversity.

Verses 10-19

The way in which he did so stands as an example to us of how we, in prayer and meditation, can find comfort and consolation in the midst of life's perplexities. He recognised that these thoughts, the distress that he felt as he sought an answer from God, arose not from any change in God's will and purpose but in his own weakness. He remembered "the years of the right hand of the most High" – the times when God had blessed him abundantly and he had rejoiced in the tokens of God's favour (verse 10). It is a lesson that we need to learn. We speak of God's goodness, of His providential hand. If we believe that God has blessed us in all the good we have known in our pilgrimage, then let us be sustained by these memories when days of trouble and adversity come, knowing that He has said: "I will never leave thee, nor forsake thee" (Hebrews 13:5). For:

> "All things work together for good to them that love God, to them who are the called according to his purpose." (Romans 8:28)

To this point in the psalm the writer had looked merely to his own experience. He has searched his own heart in looking for an answer of God, but now he turns to the recorded history of God's dealing with His people in the past:

"I will remember the works of the LORD: surely I will remember thy wonders of old. I will meditate also of all thy work, and talk of thy doings."   (verses 11,12)

It is in celebrating past deliverance and meditating upon these wonders that he will find solace in the present distress. But it is one act of deliverance above all others, that his mind focuses upon – the Exodus. Not only is it God's greatest work on behalf of His people but it is the foundation of all others, for by it the nation was first established and recognised as His special people.

The Psalmist's thoughts seem to revolve around the language of Exodus 15 in particular.

Psalm 77	Exodus 15
"I will remember the works of the LORD" (verse 11).	"The LORD is my strength and song" (verse 2).
"Thy way, O God, is in holiness" (verse 13, RV mg).	"Who is like thee, glorious in holiness?" (verse 11).
"Who is so great a God as our God?" (verse 13).	"Who is like unto thee, O LORD, among the gods?" (verse 11).
"Thy wonders of old" (verse 11).	"Doing wonders" (verse 11).
"Thou hast declared thy strength among the people" (verse 14).	"Thou hast guided them in thy strength" (verse 13).
"Thou hast with thine arm redeemed thy people" (verse 15).	"Thy right hand, O LORD, hath dashed in pieces the enemy" (verse 6).
'The waters saw thee, O God, the waters saw thee; they were afraid: the depths also trembled" (verse 16, RV).	"The depths were congealed in the heart of the sea" (verse 8). "Thou didst blow with thy wind, the sea covered them: they sank as lead in the mighty waters" (verse 10).
"Thou leddest thy people like a flock by the hand of Moses and Aaron" (verse 20).	"Thou in thy mercy hast led forth thy people which thou hast redeemed: thou hast guided them by thy strength unto thy holy habitation" (verse 13).

When the comparison is made and the source of the Psalmist's meditations becomes more apparent, little

599

further comment seems necessary. The very grandeur of the language used, the manner in which the sea is personified as fearing and trembling before its Creator should fill us with a sense of wonder and awe.

We notice that the people redeemed at the time of the Exodus are described as "the sons of Jacob and Joseph" (verse 15). This clearly was meant to cover all Israel and the fact that many of the Northern Kingdom who had joined themselves to Judah (2 Chronicles 30:18) were now within the besieged city, gives added point to the description in this context.

Notice also that, moved by the Spirit, the writer gives us additional information – detail that is not found in the Exodus record. The passage describes what might be called 'a night crossing' (Exodus 14:20), accompanied by a hurricane-type wind, torrential rain, thunders and lightnings that burst through the darkness (literally, 'the lightnings gave shine') and also apparently an earthquake, for "the earth trembled and shook" (verse 18).

The phrase rendered "in the heaven" is translated by the RV as "in the whirlwind" and this rendering certainly maintains the symmetry of the picture. It should be noted, however, that the word means literally 'a wheel' and is connected with the chariots of God (Habakkuk 3:8). It is linked with the living creatures of Ezekiel 1 (verses 15-21 etc.) and these allusions give an added dimension to the language of the Psalmist, as if to emphasise that the glory of God was manifested for the deliverance of His people and the destruction of the oppressor. It was as if the chariots of God overwhelmed the chariots of Pharaoh.

Many have thought, needlessly, that this psalm is incomplete. They regard the last verse as too abrupt an ending. But surely there is an appropriateness about it that teaches a great spiritual lesson:

> "Thy way was in the sea, and thy paths in the great waters, and thy footsteps were not known."
>
> (verse 19, RV)

How God had accomplished this must remain in a sense beyond human comprehension. God's way through the sea had opened up – the path by which He led them through the midst of the waters. His footsteps were not known for there was no physical manifestation of His person. He was seen only in the storm and turbulence of that dreadful night. In the morning the Egyptians were gone; they had perished in the sea. There must have been a great calm, a naturalness about the scene after the convulsions of the night that could almost be described as unnatural.

How better could the Psalmist describe that moment than to say of the Shepherd of Israel:

"Thou leddest thy people like a flock by the hand of Moses and Aaron." (verse 20)

The phrase "by the hand of" should not be overlooked. It might so easily be read as no more than an expression of the part Moses and Aaron played in the event as leaders of the people. But the words "by the hand of" are imbued with deeper meaning. It was the rod of God in the hand of Moses that became a serpent (Exodus 4:20). The Lord spoke to Aaron by the hand of Moses (Numbers 16:40) and gave command unto the children of Israel by the hand of Moses (Numbers 15:23). Further examples can be quoted which indicate clearly that Moses stood in God's stead. He was the mediator of the covenant (Galatians 3:19). His voice was God's voice. It is the language of God-manifestation, for Moses was God's representative in the midst of His people.

The abruptness with which the psalm ends speaks of the answer to all the Psalmist's perplexity and anxiety.

"Be still, and know that I am God." (Psalm 46:10)

In this confidence Hezekiah could say in expressing the conclusion reached:

"I will cry unto God with my voice; even unto God with my voice, and he will give ear unto me."

(Psalm 77:1, RV)

601

PSALM 78

PSALM 78 is described as a "Maschil of Asaph"; that is, it was intended for instruction. The didactic nature of the psalm is immediately apparent for in recounting events from Israel's past history, it does so, not to elevate the nation or to praise prominent individuals from the past, but to emphasise the manner in which the nation had continually turned away from their God. Like a refrain there is a similar form of words repeated on three occasions in the psalm:

"And they sinned yet more against him by provoking the most High in the wilderness. And they tempted God in their heart by asking meat for their lust."

(verses 17,18; see also verses 40,41; and 56,57)

The passages do not appear to mark any divisions of thought in the song but rather to emphasise the nature and character of Israel's apostasy throughout this period of her history.

It is the longest of the psalms, apart from Psalm 119. However, because it recapitulates historical events it does not need the detailed consideration of many shorter psalms. The past history is related as a warning to the present generation and those yet to come that they might not fall into the same condemnation.

As to the author of the psalm it is impossible to say. As far as the time of writing is concerned, it appears that there are two possibilities. It should be noted that the history related deals with the time from the Exodus to the Lord's choice of Zion as the place of His habitation and the establishment of David on the throne. There is also a distinctive emphasis upon the name Ephraim (see verses 9 and 67), the latter reference contrasting the fact that God had rejected Ephraim and chosen the tribe of Judah.

The two alternatives as to the time of writing are:

1. Shortly after the division of the kingdom when the wickedness of Jeroboam the son of Nebat, a man of Ephraim, had become apparent. There would no doubt have been some perplexity and anxiety in Judah as to what the future might hold for their royal house. The words of this psalm, recapitulating the apostasy of Israel through successive generations with its subtle emphasis upon Ephraim, would have served as a warning to them and also as a source of encouragement, that if they learned the lessons of the past, their house would stand. For God had chosen Zion and rejected the tabernacle of Joseph and the tribe of Ephraim.

2. For very similar reasons the psalm might also have been written in the days of Hezekiah when God finally overthrew the Northern Kingdom. In this respect one might have expected the history of Israel's apostasy to have continued beyond the establishment of David upon the throne and on balance, primarily for this reason, we are inclined to favour the first suggestion.

The first section of the psalm (verses 1-8) indicates the primary reason for Israel's apostasy. God had laid upon them the responsibility to teach their children that each subsequent generation might instruct the generation following. By this means God's Truth would be kept alive in the earth. Their failure to do so had resulted in the apostasy of successive generations, and was now perpetuated in the way of Jeroboam the son of Nebat which established the pattern followed by every king of the Northern Kingdom, except the last.

Verses 1-8

The writer as a prophet who speaks forth the word of the Lord addresses Israel:

"Give ear, O my people, to my law: incline your ears to the words of my mouth. I will open my mouth in a parable: I will utter dark sayings of old." (verses 1,2)

It was the duty of a prophet not only to foretell but also to forthtell. He had a responsibility to interpret the past that the lessons might be applied in the present and the future.

Thus he "(opened his) mouth". Often simple phrases in scripture have a profound significance. This is one such expression, for the mouth is opened that divine wisdom might be poured in. It was written of the Lord Jesus, prophetically, that "grace is poured into thy lips" (Psalm 45:2). As a consequence men "wondered at the gracious words that proceeded out of his mouth" (Luke 4:22). In similar fashion Paul exhorted the saints at Ephesus to pray for him "that utterance may be given unto me, that I may open my mouth boldly, to make known the mystery of the gospel" (Ephesians 6:19). So also it is written of the Lord Jesus that "he opened his mouth and taught them ..." (Matthew 5:2; see also Acts 8:35; 10:34; 2 Corinthians 6:11).

The Psalmist opened his mouth in a parable in "dark sayings of old". The word rendered "parable" has a range of meanings, amongst which is the simple idea of a teaching or a comparison. In this sense it is not difficult to understand the use of the word in connection with Israel's past history. The "dark sayings" are more difficult to understand, for the phrase carries the idea of an enigma, something that is hard to perceive. Perhaps it is best understood in the sense of Israel's continual apostasy which in the face of all that God had done for them must appear as an enigma, something hard to be understood in rational terms. Why did they fail? How were they able to forget God and His goodness so easily? It was in the contemplation of such questions as these that the lessons would be learned for present and future generations. This particular verse was, of course, quoted by Matthew in connection with the Lord's teaching in parables:

"All these things spake Jesus unto the multitude in parables; and without a parable spake he not unto them: that it might be fulfilled which was spoken by the prophet, saying, I will open my mouth in parables; I will utter things which have been kept secret since the foundation of the world." (Matthew 13:34,35)

Note that in keeping with our earlier observation the Psalmist is called a prophet. Matthew follows neither the received Hebrew text nor the Septuagint. If his words are an interpretive comment, then given the context of the psalm, "the foundation of the world" must refer to the establishment of the nation of Israel; in effect the deliverance from Egypt was the foundation of their world.

The context of the first eight verses of the psalm give us the secret of the Lord's teaching in parables. The parables and dark sayings had been received from their fathers. They were not to be hidden from their children (verse 4), for God had established a testimony in Jacob and appointed a law in Israel "that they should make them known to their children" (verse 5). Moreover, this was done "that the generation to come might know them, even the children which should be born; who should arise and declare them to their children" (verse 6).

The emphasis upon "the children" demonstrates that the parables were intended to appeal to those who were of a childlike disposition, who had open hearts and ready minds to receive them. It also indicates one of the primary reasons for Israel's continued apostasy. They had failed to teach their children and there had been an absence among them of that childlike spirit that was ready to receive God's word and put their trust in Him.

The words regarding "a testimony in Jacob and ... a law in Israel" are not general references to the law but specific precepts relating to the responsibility of every Israelite to instruct his children in the law of God and in the history of His people, that they might be handed down from generation to generation (see Exodus 10:2; 12:26,27; 13:8; Deuteronomy 4:9; 6:20-25).

This is a continuing responsibility. It remains with us to this day, for we must teach our children that they in turn might teach their children. This is the way in which God keeps His truth alive in the earth. If we might extend it beyond the immediate context of family, it is by "the foolishness of preaching" (1 Corinthians 1:21). Paul says to Timothy:

"I am appointed a preacher, and an apostle, and a teacher of the Gentiles." (2 Timothy 1:11)

"Hold fast the form of sound words, which thou hast heard of me." (verse 13)

"The things that thou hast heard of me among many witnesses, the same commit thou to faithful men, who shall be able to teach others also."   (2 Timothy 2:2)

The purpose of teaching the children in this way was –

"that they might set their hope in God, and not forget the works of God, but keep his commandments: and might not be as their fathers, a stubborn and rebellious generation; a generation that set not their heart aright, and whose spirit was not stedfast with God."
(Psalm 78:7,8)

The words "and not forget" are an echo of the Book of Deuteronomy. The recurring words of warning there are "lest thou forget" (see Deuteronomy 4:9,23; 6:12; 8:11,14,19;9:7). The reference to "a stubborn and rebellious generation" recalls the condemnation of the son who would not hearken to his parents, whom no chastisement could reform, for whom there remained only the penalty of death (Deuteronomy 21:18-21).

Verses 9-11

Just as the psalm closes with the rejection of Ephraim in whose lot the tabernacle resided (verse 67), so the historical section begins with a reference to Ephraim:

"The children of Ephraim, being armed, and carrying bows, turned back in the day of battle."   (verse 9)

Clearly the historical record in the psalm is intended to describe the nation in total, but reading forward from verse 9 one could almost imagine that it is spoken, in the main, of Ephraim alone. However, reading carefully we note that in verse 12 the record turns from Ephraim to their fathers, and continues to speak of their fathers throughout the psalm until the next reference in verse 67.

Why then is Ephraim singled out in this way? We know that because of the prominence of that tribe the name of Ephraim came to stand for the Northern Kingdom as a whole and the idolatory of Jeroboam, in which he was undoubtedly encouraged by the tribe to which he belonged, may well have been in the Psalmist's mind. The actual historical circumstance to which verse 9 refers is a matter of some conjecture. There is a suggestion of indecision and cowardice in the day of battle. Perhaps this was intended as an assurance to Judah that if they remained faithful to their God they had nothing to fear from their northern brethren. *Smith's Bible Dictionary* in the entry on 'Ephraim' suggests that the reference is to the event recorded in 1 Chronicles 7:20-27 when the sons of Ephraim, while they still sojourned in Egypt, made an unwise incursion into the land of promise to take away the cattle of the inhabitants of Gath. It is an interesting conjecture but not totally convincing. The emphasis upon Ephraim, as those who did not keep the covenant of God and refused to walk in His law, is perhaps because of the tribe's pretensions to leadership and predilection to unfaithfulness. They were leaders in apostasy. Again, without concrete evidence as to the reason, we note that when first numbered, the tribe of Ephraim were forty thousand and five hundred (Numbers 1:33). At the end of the wilderness journey, unlike most of the tribes, they had a substantial decrease in numbers, being only thirty-two thousand and five hundred (Numbers 26:37).

Is there a suggestion here that because of their rebellious spirit they had suffered more from the plagues and judgements of God than most of their brethren because they were at the heart of the rebellion in the wilderness? In the establishment of the Northern Kingdom, it is important to remember that it was of the Lord: "This thing is from me", God told Rehoboam (1 Kings 12:24).

Although the kingdom was divided the Lord still expected the allegiance of the northern tribes to His covenant and to His law. Jeroboam, however, because he feared the defection of the people to the house of David, established a different and false system of worship (1 Kings 12:25-33). Thus the Psalmist declared:

"They kept not the covenant of God, and refused to walk in his law; and forgat his works, and his wonders that he had shewed them." (Psalm 78:10,11)

Verses 12-16

They forgot the lessons that they should have learned from their fathers, for "marvellous things did he in the sight of their fathers, in the land of Egypt, in the field of

Zoan". There is a curious reference to Zoan in the Book of Numbers which tells us that "Hebron was built seven years before Zoan in the land of Egypt" (Numbers 13:22). Zoan was the principal city of the Hyksos dynasty, known as the Shepherd Kings, who invaded Egypt and usurped the throne. Perhaps they were also responsible for building Hebron. However, after their passing, Zoan became the chief city of a number of Pharaohs and there can be no doubt that it was the city of the Pharaoh of the Exodus. "The field of Zoan", where God showed His wonders, is referred to in the Egyptian inscriptions and is a large fertile plain stretching to the east of the city. (*Smith's Bible Dictionary*).

After this brief reference to the plagues, to which he returns later (verses 43-53), the Psalmist speaks of the dividing of the sea and the pillar of cloud and of fire that led them by day and by night (verses 13,14). "He made the waters to stand as an heap". The language is taken from Exodus 15: "The floods stood upright as an heap, and the depths were congealed in the heart of the sea" (verse 8). Regarding the word rendered "congealed", *Strong* says "to thicken as unracked wine, curdled milk, frozen water". Could it be then that God, having divided the sea, caused it to freeze so that the children of Israel passed over between two walls of ice which melted to overwhelm the Egyptians?

> "He clave the rocks in the wilderness, and gave them drink as out of the great depths. He brought streams also out of the rock, and caused waters to run down like rivers." (verses 15,16)

Two different Hebrew words are used for "rock". The one relates to the occasion at Rephidim when Moses was commanded to strike the rock, and the other to the occasion at the end of their journey when he was told to speak to the rock in Kadesh. The "great depths" of the rock or cliff implies a mighty reservoir of water, and the picture is of rivers of water running out to provide an abundance of water that followed and sustained them throughout their time in the wilderness (see 1 Corinthians 10:4).

Verses 17-31

But even while they were receiving these blessings their hearts turned aside from God:

"And they sinned yet more against him by provoking the most High in the wilderness." (verse 17)

The two occasions when God sent quails among them seem to be joined together because on both occasions they murmured against Moses and against God and tempted God in their hearts. "Can God furnish a table in the wilderness? Can he give bread also?" In this way they tried God. They said, 'If we are your people then prove it. If you are able, give us flesh to eat'. They doubted His love; they questioned His ability to provide for them. The two records in Exodus 16 and Numbers 11 are alluded to, for it is in the second of these that a fire was kindled at Taberah when the anger of the Lord burned against them (verses 18-21).

The reason for their provocation was that "they believed not in God and trusted not in his salvation" (verse 22). They had experienced the deliverance from Egypt yet they still did not believe that God could fulfil all that He had promised. In every expression the Psalmist demonstrates that there was nothing natural about the manna:

"He ... opened the doors of heaven, and ... rained down manna upon them ... (he gave) them of the corn of heaven. Man did eat angels' food." (verses 23-25)

Angels' food – not because the angels (AV margin, 'the mighty') needed it for nourishment but because they were instrumental in providing it. As He rained manna upon them so He caused the winds to blow that brought the quails. They are also said to have rained upon them (verse 27). So they ate and were filled for He gave them their desire and before their hunger was assuaged, while the flesh was yet in their mouths, the wrath of God came upon them (verses 26-31; see Numbers 11). Many perished in the plague and the place was called Kibroth-Hattaavah (the graves of lust).

The lesson for us is that if we really desire something with all our hearts, though we call God's love into question by our yearning, then He may grant our request. The end of the matter, however, might be a spiritual disaster. The words of another psalm penned regarding the same incident are most instructive:

> "He gave them their request; but sent leanness into their soul." (Psalm 106:15)

God fulfilled their desires but the result was spiritual malnutrition.

Verses 32-39

All these things which they had suffered still failed to produce any real reform and this section of the psalm appears to dwell on the murmuring and unbelief that was manifest on the return of the spies:

> "For all this they sinned still, and believed not for his wondrous works." (verse 32)

On that occasion God said:

> "'How long will this people provoke me? and how long will it be ere they believe me, for all the signs which I have shewed among them?'" (Numbers 14:11)

It was at this time that Moses pleaded on behalf of the people recalling in his prayer the wonderful words by which God had declared His name when He caused His glory to pass by (Numbers 14:17-20; see also Exodus 34:6,7).

Although God hearkened unto Moses and did not destroy the people, He sentenced the rebellious generation to perish in the wilderness:

> "Therefore their days did he consume in vanity, and their years in trouble." (verse 33)

They were as a breath, fleeting and transitory, carried away by God's wrath. These words should be compared with a similar description in Psalm 90 (verses 7-9), a psalm of the wilderness written by Moses about this very generation that perished.

Although there were temporary reformations there was no lasting change of heart. Their repentance was superficial and soon they reverted to their old ways, always falling into the same old rut (verses 34-37). However, their unfaithfulness served to demonstrate the grace and forbearance of God:

"But he, being full of compassion, forgave their iniquity, and destroyed them not: yea, many a time turned he his anger away, and did not stir up all his wrath. For he remembered that they were but flesh; a wind that passeth away, and cometh not again."

(verses 38,39)

In the face of all their murmuring and provocation God maintained His lovingkindness, for He remembered the weakness and transitory nature of human life.

Verses 40-55

Having thus contrasted Israel's continual rebellion with the unchanging goodness of God, the Psalmist begins the sad story anew. He passes now from the events of the wilderness back to the deliverance from Egypt which he had left at verse 12.

Having reiterated his refrain about the manner in which they provoked God and rebelled against Him (verses 40,41), he recalls their perversity in forgetting the wonders performed in the field of Zoan (verses 42,43). He recounts the manner in which God had brought the plagues upon Egypt; not in the order of the Exodus record, apart from the first and the last, and omitting three, for what reasons we have been unable to discover. In the execution of these judgements upon Egypt the angels were His agents: "He cast upon them the fierceness of his anger ... by sending evil angels among them" (verse 49). Not wicked angels of course, but angels whose mission was to bring evil circumstances upon those who merited God's anger. Perhaps the reference to the work of the angels is a fitting introduction to the record of the death of the first-born (verses 50,51). The reference to "the tabernacle of Ham" (verse 51) arises because Ham was the father of Mizraim which was the ancient name for Egypt (see Genesis 10:6).

Having described the waywardness of the people in the wilderness, the Psalmist tells now of the manner in which God had been the Shepherd of His people, guiding them like a flock through the wilderness until He brought them to this mountain, the border of His sanctuary (verse 52-

611

54). Here surely is a reference to the fulfilment of the words of Exodus 15:

> "Thou shalt bring them in, and plant them in the mountain of thy inheritance, in the place, O LORD, which thou hast made for thee to dwell in, in the Sanctuary, O Lord, which thy hands have established. The LORD shall reign for ever and ever." (verses 17,18)

Some think that the reference is to the land of promise in its entirety, but the emphasis upon "the place" is one that runs through scripture. It was known from the beginning and men of faith looked to the day when God would be manifest there (see Genesis 22:2,3 i.e., Moriah). Bringing them into the land, God cast out the Canaanites before them and divided the land among them by lot (Psalm 78:55; see Joshua 23:1-5).

Verses 56-58

Briefly these verses reiterate Israel's continued unfaithfulness in the time of the Judges. No lessons had been learned from the past, but again they tempted and provoked the Most High. They dealt treacherously (RV) with Him as their fathers had done. They were like a deceitful bow that continually failed to hit the mark. Moreover they provoked the Lord who would, in His jealousy, share their allegiance with no other (Exodus 20:5), by embracing the idols of the Canaanites and worshipping in their high places.

Verses 59-64

Because of their wickedness God once more punished them. He "greatly abhorred Israel (literally, 'rejected them', *Strong*)" (verse 59) and "forsook the tabernacle of Shiloh, the tent which he placed among men" (verse 60).

During the entire period of the Judges the tabernacle was at Shiloh (see Joshua 18:10; Judges 18:31; 1 Samuel 4:3). Later, without the ark, it was moved to Nob (1 Samuel 21) and again to Gibeon (1 Kings 3:4). God forsook the tabernacle at Shiloh when the ark of the covenant was taken by the Philistines. He "delivered his strength into captivity, and his glory into the enemy's hand" (Psalm 78:61). The ark never returned to Shiloh or to that tabernacle where God had been pleased to dwell in the midst of His people. Generations later the prophet Jeremiah was to say to a people that trusted, in their complacency, that the temple in their midst was a guarantee of their security:

"But go ye now unto my place which was in Shiloh, where I set my name at the first, and see what I did to it for the wickedness of my people Israel."

(Jeremiah 7:12)

The implication is that it was allowed to fall into disrepair and ruin.

His people were delivered into the hand of the Philistines (Psalm 78:62) so that their young men were consumed by fire and the maidens were consequently unable to marry. Their priests fell by the sword, but because of the extremity of the times their widows were unable to mourn for them in the customary way (verses 63,64).

Verses 65,66

The God of Israel, however, remained true to His purpose and, as always, there was a remnant who trusted in Him and looked for His deliverance. Thus the Lord did not leave His "glory" in alien hands indefinitely, but suddenly, like a man of war awaking out of sleep and shouting in expectancy of the battle, He smote the enemy causing them to turn back and become a perpetual reproach. This work was, of course, accomplished, through the hands of Samuel, Saul and David to whom God gave the victory.

Verses 67-69

It was at this time that it became manifest that God had rejected the tabernacle of Joseph at Shiloh, for it was not Ephraim that He had chosen (verse 67) but Judah. It was Mount Zion that He loved (see Psalm 87:2) and it was to the tabernacle of David that the ark was eventually restored. There God allowed Solomon to build Him a house like the heavens in its grandeur and like the foundations of the earth in its stability (verses 67-69).

Verses 70-72

The psalm concludes with the selection of David as king. The royal line is established through which the Lord's anointed would eventually come: "He chose David also his servant" (verse 70). All men might regard themselves in some sense as servants of God, but few indeed are acknowledged by Him as "my servant" – a mark of special distinction. It was used also of Abraham (Genesis 26:24), Moses (Numbers 12:7), Joshua (Judges 2:8), Job (Job 1:8), and the Lord Jesus Christ (Isaiah 42:1). It emphasises the special relationship that David enjoyed with the Lord, and the qualities he possessed that commended him to God in a way that was true of few others. He was taken from watching over his father's flock to be the shepherd of God's people, a task for which he was ideally suited and to which he faithfully applied himself throughout his long reign:

"So he fed them according to the integrity of his heart; and guided them by the skilfulness of his hands."

(Psalm 78:72)

For Psalm 79 comments see pp 566–574–581

PSALM 80

WE continue our consideration of the Psalms of Asaph. Again we have no clear evidence as to the authorship of the song, and as far as the circumstances that led to its being written are concerned we are dependent on the internal evidence. A careful reading suggests the following factors that need to be taken into account:

1. It is a time when Israel once more faces remorseless enemies who threaten her existence as a nation (see verses 2-7,12,13).

2. Israel's neighbours rejoice in the calamities that have overtaken her (verse 6).

3. There is some emphasis upon the northern tribes (verses 1,2) suggesting that all Israel is involved in the Psalmist's prayer for deliverance.

4. There is an outstanding individual whom the Psalmist describes as "the man of thy right hand ... the son of man whom thou madest strong for thyself" (verse 17). In this man the nation's hope for deliverance rested.

These facts lead us once again to consider Hezekiah, for in the historical record there is no other man whose circumstances and character meet the criteria outlined above.

Although the Northern Kingdom fell in the sixth year of Hezekiah's reign, Samaria having first been besieged for three years by Shalmaneser of Assyria, the evidence points to a determined effort by Hezekiah in the first year of his reign to reform not only his kingdom, Judah, but also to turn the hearts of the Northern Kingdom back to the God of their fathers. His efforts met with only very limited success but, nevertheless, it seems appropriate that the psalm should have been written at that particular time. In our studies in the psalms we have referred on a number of occasions to Hezekiah's invitation to the northern tribes to join with Judah in celebrating the Passover (2 Chronicles 30). There are some points of contact between the language of the psalm and the historical record in Chronicles.

We note first that the references to God's anger and the parlous plight of both kingdoms is consistent with the accession of Hezekiah to the throne (see 2 Chronicles 29:1-15). In particular we note the following words:

> "Wherefore the wrath of the LORD was upon Judah and Jerusalem, and he hath delivered them to trouble, to astonishment, and to hissing, as ye see with your eyes. For, lo, our fathers have fallen by the sword, and our sons and daughters and our wives are in captivity for this. Now it is in mine heart to make a covenant with the LORD God of Israel, that his fierce wrath may turn away from us."   (2 Chronicles 29:8-10)

In his representation to the Northern Kingdom Hezekiah twice uses the words, "turn again unto the LORD" (30:6,9). A like phrase runs as a refrain through the psalm, "Turn us again" (verses 3,7,19).

The reference to Ephraim, Benjamin and Manasseh (verse 2), although being a scriptural allusion which we will develop later, has an echo in the historical record for "all Israel ... threw down the high places and the altars out of all Judah and Benjamin, in Ephraim also and Manasseh, until they had utterly destroyed them all" (2 Chronicles 31:1).

The introduction of the Psalm, "Thou that dwellest between the cherubims" (verse 1) and the plea "to cause thy face to shine" (verse 3), surely a reference to the priestly benediction (Numbers 6:25), also have a possible echo in 2 Chronicles, for –

> "the priests the Levites arose and blessed the people: and their voice was heard, and their prayer came up to his holy dwelling place, even unto heaven."   (30:27)

The dependance of the people upon good King Hezekiah is emphasised a little later when Sennacherib came up against Jerusalem:

"And he ... spake comfortably to them, saying, Be strong and courageous, be not afraid or dismayed for the king of Assyria, nor for all the multitude that is with him: for there be more with us than with him: with him is an arm of flesh; but with us is the LORD our God to help us, and to fight our battles. And the people rested themselves upon the words of Hezekiah king of Judah."

(2 Chronicles 32:6-8)

This surely was one who could be described as the man of God's right hand whom He had made strong for Himself.

As far as the structure of the psalm is concerned it can be divided as follows:

1. A prayer for God to show favour to His people (verses 1-3).
2. How long will they continue to be the subject of God's anger? (verses 4-7).
3. God brought a vine out of Egypt (verses 8-11).
4. The vine wasted (verses 12-16).
5. The man of God's right hand (verses 17-19).

Verses 1-3

The opening verse of the psalm joins together all Israel, both northern and southern kingdoms.

"Give ear, O Shepherd of Israel, thou that leadest Joseph like a flock; thou that dwellest between the cherubims, shine forth." (verse 1)

Israel is the covenant name of the nation as a whole but Joseph is indicative of the Northern Kingdom only. The plea is that the Shepherd of Israel who led Joseph like a flock should shine forth from between the cherubim, that is from God's dwelling place in the temple at Jerusalem (Exodus 25:22; 2 Samuel 6:2).

The reference to God leading Joseph like a flock is a reference to His providential hand working in the midst of His people, and recalls both Jacob's words when blessing the sons of Joseph and his blessing upon him in Genesis:

"And he blessed Joseph, and said, God, before whom my fathers Abraham and Isaac did walk, the God which fed me (Hebrew, 'shepherded me') all my life long unto

617

this day, the Angel which redeemed me from all evil, bless the lads." (Genesis 48:15,16)
Similarly:

"But his bow abode in strength and the arms of his hands were made strong by the hands of the mighty God of Jacob; (from thence is the shepherd, the stone of Israel:) even by the God of thy father, who shall help thee." (Genesis 49:24,25)

The prayer is that God would manifest Himself as in days of old for the reference to Ephraim, Benjamin and Manasseh is not simply a mark of identification for the northern tribes, but it is also a reference to the camp of Israel in the wilderness. These three tribes camped to the west of the tabernacle, and not only so but when the children of Israel broke camp and followed the pillar of cloud and the pillar of fire, their position in the procession was immediately behind the ark of the covenant (see Numbers 2:18-24; 10:21-24).

When "the LORD came from Sinai, and rose up from Seir unto them; he shined forth from Mount Paran" (Deuteronomy 33:2). Now Hezekiah's prayer was that God would shine forth from between the cherubim, stir up His strength, and come to save His people (Psalm 80:2) at this time when both kingdoms were in distress and he had made a determined effort to rekindle the faith and zeal of his northern brethren.

"Turn us again, O God, and cause thy face to shine; and we shall be saved." (verse 3)

It could be that the prayer is simply that God will restore the kingdoms to their former state of blessing, but perhaps there is rather more to the words. The prophet Jeremiah at a later date was to write:

"I have surely heard Ephraim bemoaning himself thus; Thou hast chastised me, and I was chastised, as a bullock unaccustomed to the yoke: turn thou me, and I shall be turned; for thou art the LORD my God. Surely after that I was turned, I repented." (Jeremiah 31:18,19)

Thus the prayer would not simply be for restoration of former blessings but also a recognition that first must come national repentance. Only God could produce it, create the circumstances in which it would spring forth. As God had chastised Ephraim and he had learned the lesson, turned again to God and repented, so Hezekiah desires God to manifest Himself in a similar way – if need be to chastise so that the hearts of the people might be turned to Him and then in the instruction received, to find in their hearts the repentance that was so needful:

"Before I was afflicted I went astray: but now have I kept thy word." (Psalm 119:67)

Verses 4-7

"O LORD God of hosts, how long wilt thou be angry against the prayer of thy people?" It is said that the name and title of God used here is rare in the psalms. It would be more correct to say that it is rare outside the psalms that have an undoubted link with Hezekiah (see for example Psalms 46,48). It is a characteristic of Isaiah's prophecy and its use in the psalms associated with Hezekiah is linked to this usage. Its emphasis in this psalm is another indication that it falls into the category of psalms connected with that righteous man.

Here is a recognition of God's universal sovereignty: Lord of all the angelic hosts; Lord of the armies of Israel. Will He now exercise His power on their behalf? Will He lead them once more as in days of old? How long would He be angry (*Strong*, "smoke against") at the prayers of His people? When we think of the prayers of God's people we describe them in terms of the incense burned for a sweet smelling savour to the Lord. It is as if the fire of God's wrath had produced a cloud of thick smoke (see Exodus 19:18 – same word) that the prayers offered could not penetrate. Their sins had separated them from God; their prayers were not heard.

He had fed them with the bread of tears and given them tears to drink in good measure (verse 5). It was as if tears were their daily portion and so acute was their grief that the tears were poured out unto a "great measure". The word "measure" means literally 'a third', clearly of some larger measure. It is suggested that the measure could have been the bath which would have contained nearly

619

three gallons. Figuratively the Psalmist expresses the depth of their suffering and sorrow. In another psalm written in Hezekiah's days the writer had cried:

"My tears have been my meat day and night, while they continually say unto me, Where is thy God?"
(Psalm 42:3)

So now:

"Thou makest us a strife unto our neighbours: and our enemies laugh among themselves." (Psalm 80:6)

It was not the great powers like Assyria and Egypt that rejoiced over their calamity but those who were round about them, Edom, Ammon and Moab, always, like scavengers, ready to quarrel among themselves over Israel's land, rejoicing in every misfortune that befell God's people. So it ever was and ever will be until the Lord shall come. Thus the Psalmist repeats the prayer and sentiments already expressed:

"Turn us again, O God of hosts, and cause thy face to shine; and we shall be saved." (verse 7)

Verses 8-11

We traced the reference to God as the Shepherd of Israel to the blessing of Jacob upon Joseph and his sons. The inference in verse 1 appears to be a prayer that God would fulfil that ancient promise now in respect of Ephraim and Manasseh as the representatives of the Northern Kingdom. In like fashion it seems possible that the use of the vine as a figure of Israel is prompted by that same blessing of Jacob upon Joseph:

"Joseph is a fruitful bough (Hebrew, 'ben' – son / branch), even a fruitful branch by a well; whose branches run over the wall." (Genesis 49:22)

Joseph was likened to a vine and the figure came to stand for all Israel and everything that she should have been.

"Thou broughtest a vine out of Egypt (RV). Thou hast cast out the heathen, and planted it. Thou preparedst room before it, and didst cause it to take deep root, and it filled the land. The hills were covered with the shadow of it, and the boughs thereof were like the goodly cedars. She sent out her boughs unto the sea, and her branches unto the river." (verses 8-11)

As the vine-dresser prepares the ground, clears away the stones, the thorns and the thistles, all that would hamper growth, so God had done for His vine. He brought it out of Egypt and transplanted it in the land of Caanan (Exodus 15:17). He cast out the nations before them and provided everything that was necessary for their spiritual development. As the prophet Isaiah expressed it in his song of the vineyard (Isaiah 5:1-7):

> "What could have been done more to my vineyard, that I have not done in it?"   (verse 4)

Israel had taken root, they had established themselves in the land, filling their inheritance. They had covered with the shadow of their branches the mountains of the south; they had extended that influence to the cedars of Lebanon in the north. Moreover, the vine had "sent out her branches unto the sea, and her shoots unto the River" (RV) – in other words from the Mediterranean Sea in the west to the River Euphrates in the east. These of course, are the boundaries of the land that God promised to Abraham and the words of Deuteronomy 11 seem to provide a background for the words of the psalm:

> "Every place whereon the soles of your feet shall tread shall be yours: from the wilderness (i.e., the hills) and Lebanon, from the river, the river Euphrates, even unto the uttermost sea shall your coast be."
>
> (verse 24; see also Genesis 15:18-21)

These were the approximate boundaries in the days of David and Solomon (2 Samuel 8:1-14; 1 Chronicles 18:1-13; 1 Kings 4:21) and they remain the borders of the land yet to be occupied by the people of Israel when the Lord shall come.

Verses 12-16

> "Why hast thou then broken down her hedges, so that all they which pass by the way do pluck her? The boar out of the wood doth waste it, and the wild beast of the field doth devour it."   (verses 12,13)

It was customary to protect vineyards by building fences round them (Isaiah 5), but because they had brought forth wild grapes (verse 4) the defences had been broken down and not only had those who passed by spoiled it but it had

621

been ravaged by the wild beasts of the nations. So the Psalmist pleads with a play upon the words, "to turn us again" (verses 3,7,19) that God Himself, the Lord of hosts, would "turn again" (RV) and "look down from heaven, and behold, and visit this vine to protect that which (RV margin) thy right hand hath planted, and the branch that thou madest strong for thyself" (verses 14,15). There are differing meanings, each standing on their own from one point of view, but growing out of each other from another perspective; all of them true of those to whom the words are applied.

The word "branch" (*ben*) means literally 'son'. So the Psalmist can speak first of Israel, for the vine was God's son in the national sense, which He had established (made strong) for Himself. "Out of Egypt have I called my son" (Matthew 2:15; see Hosea 11:1); "Israel is my son, even my firstborn" (Exodus 4:22). But in a different sense he who sat on Zion's throne also became God's son when he was anointed king. He was a branch of the vine, "made strong" as the representative of God's people, who embodied in his royal office all that Israel nationally should have been before the Lord. In the immediate sense the reference is to Hezekiah. However, the words have a deep Messianic significance and refer ultimately to the Lord Jesus Christ. The Targum renders it: "And upon Messiah the king, whom thou hast made strong for thyself" (see *Cambridge Bible*).

Nevertheless, the vine was burned with fire and cut down. If it bears no fruit it is worthless. So they (the people of Israel – the figure of the vine being dropped) "perish at the rebuke of thy countenance". Not merely has God hidden His countenance, but in anger His face had been turned against them.

Verses 17-19

The thought of the psalm turns to the one who alone could bring deliverance to this people under the hand of their God. Initially, as we have indicated, it was Hezekiah "the man of thy right hand ... the son of man whom thou madest strong for thyself" (verse 17).

There is here a play upon the events concerned with the birth of Benjamin (Genesis 35). When he was born his mother called him, as she died, Benoni, the 'son of my sorrow', but his father called him Benjamin, the 'son of my right hand'. The meanings are reflected in the experience of Hezekiah, for when he was sick unto death the people undoubtedly thought that, as the representative of the nation, he had been smitten because of their sin (Isaiah 53). He was a 'son of sorrow' yet lifted up to become 'the son of God's right hand'. He is one of the most remarkable types of the Lord Jesus Christ in the Old Testament scriptures. The Lord also, because of his human nature, was 'a son of sorrow' yet made strong by his Father for the conquest of sin. He was the Son of His right hand, the son of man whom He made strong for Himself. The title "Son of Man", indicating that all man was intended to be was fulfilled in him, speaks of the dominion that God will ultimately give him over all the earth (Genesis 1:26-28; Psalm 8; Hebrews 2:5-10). He, the only begotten Son of God, the Israel of God, is also the true vine; and the lessons of Israel are ours to learn, lest we too be cast forth as a branch that is withered that men gather up and cast into the fire (John 15:6).

So the psalm concludes with the Psalmist's assertion that if God blesses, then "will not we go back from thee". In the new bond of allegiance he asks God to quicken them that they may call upon His name (verse 18). In this hope the Psalmist repeats the prayer of verses 3 and 7:

> "Turn us again, O LORD God of hosts, cause thy face to shine; and we shall be saved."   (verse 19)

"Upon Gittith"

The psalm bears this subscription. The three psalms that bear this title (7,80,83) are shown by Thirtle to be connected with the Feast of Tabernacles (*The Titles of the Psalms*, pages 55-58) and in particular with the winepress connected, of course, with the harvest (Deuteronomy 16:13). The appropriateness of this title to the psalm we have considered, with its emphasis upon the vine that should have brought forth its fruit to God, is evident. The background of the Feast of Tabernacles was a reminder to them not only of the joy of harvest but also of the fact that

God was their keeper. The writer of Psalm 80 lived in this consciousness and looked for the fulfilment of all his desires to the "Shepherd of Israel ... that leadest Joseph like a flock" (verse 1).

PSALM 81

MOST writers seem to agree that this psalm is connected with the New Year and the Feast of Tabernacles. They reach this conclusion mainly because of the words of verse 3:

"Blow the trumpet at the time of the New Moon. At the full moon, on our solemn feast day."   (NKJV)

On the basis of this verse alone it could be argued, legitimately, that the reference is to the beginning of the seventh month of the religious year, Tizri, which was also the first month of the civil year. It was marked by a day of trumpet blowing (Leviticus 23:23-25; Numbers 29:1-6) and followed on the fifteenth day of the month by the celebration of the Feast of Tabernacles (Leviticus 23:39). There was no specific command to sound trumpets at the beginning of Tabernacles, but there was a general instruction to sound the silver trumpets "in the day of your gladness, and in your set feasts" (Numbers 10:10, RV).

What carries a great deal of weight with writers is the fact that the Jews have regarded this song as their New Year Psalm and by an ancient tradition it has also been associated with the Feast of Tabernacles. This brief résumé of the argument might be regarded as a prima facie case for the view presented. There are, however, difficulties involved. The context, as will be seen when we examine the content of the psalm, speaks not of Tabernacles but of Passover (see verses 4-7). The assumption that the reference is to the beginning of the seventh month fails to recognise that the words are equally true of every month. For each new moon the beginning of a new month was celebrated by the sounding of the silver trumpets (Numbers 10:10). Although the passage in Numbers 10 refers "to your set feasts", it must

625

be admitted that there is no evidence that the trumpets were sounded at Passover. However, the feast referred to in the psalm was described as a solemn occasion (verse 3) and there is a particular event in the reign of Hezekiah that meets the requirements both of verses 1 to 3 and of the context of the psalm. This is the Passover celebrated by Hezekiah in the first year of his reign. When he ascended the throne his first act was to cleanse the temple (2 Chronicles 29:3-19) and restore its worship (verses 20-36). When this was accomplished Hezekiah sent letters to all Israel inviting them to come to Jerusalem to keep the Passover. Because of the deficiency of the priests this was not kept in the month Abib, the appointed month, the first month of the religious year, but in the second month (30:1-3). Although some mocked the king's messengers (verse 10), a great multitude assembled in Jerusalem (verse 13) to keep the passover on the fourteenth day of the second month.

Among the northern tribes mentioned specifically as being represented on this occasion were Asher, Manasseh, Zebulun, Ephraim and Issachar (verses 11,18), and such was the spirit of the feast that it was kept with great rejoicing:

"So the children of Israel who were present at Jerusalem kept the Feast of Unleavened Bread seven days with great gladness; and the Levites and the priests praised the LORD day by day, singing to the LORD, accompanied by loud instruments."

(verse 21, NKJV)

Such was the elation felt by the people that they determined to keep the feast for another seven days (verse 23) and the emphasis is upon the fact that they kept it with gladness. The whole congregation of Judah, the priests, the Levites and those who had come down from Israel rejoiced (verse 25):

"So there was great joy in Jerusalem, for since the time of Solomon the son of David, king of Israel, there had been nothing like this in Jerusalem."

(verse 26, NKJV)

Thus, we believe, we have identified the event that occasioned the psalm. Like some of the psalms that were

626

written for Asaph, that is, for the choir of temple singers founded by him, the writer might have been Hezekiah himself; alternatively a contemporary, perhaps one of the sons of Asaph.

Structure of the Psalm

The difficulty of analysing the structure of any psalm will become apparent if a few psalms are selected at random and a variety of writers consulted. There will be similarities and also differences depending sometimes on how the writer interprets particular verses. Some writers refer to the metre of the psalm, seeing a poetic structure, although even here there will be disagreement which is confusing as, presumably, all writers of orthodox commentaries are students of Hebrew. In our experience, while consulting reference books to ensure that the obvious is not being missed through ignorance of the original Hebrew, it is best to read the psalm for ourselves and make our own breakdown of its various parts. We need to remember that, however we might divide or subdivide the verses, the different parts we discern are all related to each other and the psalm is in reality one. The main thrust of the psalm is not affected by the way we may divide it into sections and the divisions, if they serve no other purpose, help in presenting the meaning of the song in a convenient fashion.

We have approached Psalm 81 in this way and our own division of the psalm is given below.

Analysis

    1. The Passover and Exodus (verses 1-7).

    2. God speaks to His people (verses 8-10).

    3. Israel's failure to listen to their God (verses 11-14).

    4. The Psalmist's final reflections (verses 15,16).

Verses 1-7

The first three verses are a call to joyous celebration of the feast to be held as the new moon appeared at the beginning of the second month, and then on the fourteenth day of that month, and in the following two weeks as they rejoiced in keeping anew the Feast of Passover (verse 3).

All Israel were called to participate in this joyous event: the ordinary people (verse 1); the Levites who were in charge of the temple music (verse 2); and the priests whose duty it was to blow the trumpets (verse 3). Twice reference is made to the God of Jacob (verses 1,4), and this in conjunction with the fact that the feast is spoken of as "ordained in Joseph" (verse 5) is a clear indication that the feast referred to was celebrated by all Israel and not just by Judah.

The God of Jacob had manifested himself to that patriarch as a God of comfort and consolation. As he blessed the sons of Joseph he said:

"God, before whom my fathers Abraham and Isaac did walk, the God which fed me (literally, 'shepherded me') all my life long unto this day, the Angel which redeemed me from all evil, bless the lads."

(Genesis 48:15,16)

The recognition that God had been his shepherd throughout his life was an acknowledgement of a characteristic of God's care that we have previously noted as a specific feature of the Psalms of Asaph (77:20; 78:52,53,70,72; 79:13; 80:1).

Although there is no direct reference to God as the Shepherd of Israel, the use of the title, "The God of Jacob" in Psalm 81 must be seen as an implicit acknowledgement of that fact. The exhortation to "sing aloud unto God our strength" (verse 1) must also be appreciated as a means of describing the truth that all God had been to Jacob, He would be also to his children, Israel. So we too must learn the lesson that God is our strength. The strength derived from Him, however, is not the infusion of some overwhelming and irresistible power that enables us to overcome in adversity and trial. Rather, it is the confidence and assurance that come from the knowledge that God is our Shepherd who will never leave us or forsake us, for His angels encamp round about those who fear Him to deliver them.

They were to rejoice in this feast because –

"it is a statute for Israel, an ordinance of the God of Jacob. He appointed it in Joseph for a testimony."

(verses 4,5, RV)

It was a continual witness, a memorial to the care and love bestowed upon them by the God of their fathers.

When the "testimony" was appointed is stated specifically. It was "when He went throughout the land of Egypt" (verse 5, NKJV). The language recalls the words of Exodus:

"About midnight will I go out into the midst of Egypt: and all the firstborn ... of Egypt shall die."   (11:4,5)

There can be no doubt, we believe, that the reference is to the occasion when God passed over the homes of the Israelites. Thus the feast was appointed:

"Ye shall keep it a feast to the LORD throughout your generations; ye shall keep it a feast by an ordinance for ever."   (Exodus 12:14)

The concluding sentence of Psalm 81:5 is difficult: "Where I heard a language that I understood not." The Psalmist appears to become the spokesman for Israel at the time of the Exodus, as the first person singular is used, but the form of speech is continued through verse 7 where the speaker is clearly God Himself.

It is appropriate that the Psalmist should speak as the representative of Israel, particularly when we remember the continuity of their national life. The reference to a language that they understood not may suggest the tongue of the Egyptians which was foreign to them, and Psalm 114 would support such a view:

"When Israel went out of Egypt, the house of Jacob from a people of strange language."   (verse 1)

However, the context of the phrase suggests an alternative meaning. We note the connection that it was when God went through the land of Egypt that he heard the language he understood not. It is not the language of the Egyptian but the voice of God that they did not understand. Kay (*Psalms with Notes*) renders the phrase in verse 5: "The lip of one I had not known then heard I".

We do not always appreciate the extent to which Israel had forgotten God in the land of Egypt. He had become a stranger to them and they had embraced the idolatrous worship of the Egyptians among whom they lived:

"Put away the gods which your fathers served ... in Egypt." (Joshua 24:14)

It was necessary for God to make Himself known unto them in the land of Egypt that He might deliver them (see Ezekiel 20:5-8). Thus when God spoke it was in a language that they did not understand. Not that the words uttered were themselves unfamiliar to them but their meaning, the message they carried, was new to them because they had forgotten their God. Thus verses 6,7 express the words of God Himself spoken to them at that time as He enlightened and instructed them:

"I removed his shoulder from the burden; his hands were freed from the baskets. You called in trouble, and I delivered you; I answered you in the secret place of thunder; I proved you at the waters of Meribah." (NKJV)

God delivered them from the burdens placed on them by the Egyptians (Exodus 1:11; 2:11,23; 5:4,6,7; etc.). They were freed from the baskets, a reference to the containers depicted in ancient Egyptian paintings as used in the making of bricks – a task referred to particularly as being Israel's lot in Egypt (Exodus 1:14; 5:7-11).

In their trouble they called unto the God they had neglected. This is of course a generalisation and among the people there must always have been a faithful remnant who, no doubt, stirred up the hearts of their brethren in their distress:

"And the children of Israel sighed by reason of the bondage, and they cried, and their cry came up unto God by reason of the bondage. And God heard their groaning, and God remembered his covenant with Abraham, with Isaac, and with Jacob."

(Exodus 2:23,24)

God answered their cries in the secret place of thunder. This was when God revealed Himself to them at Sinai. The word translated "secret" means literally 'a hidden or covered place' (*Strong*). When God descended upon the mount –

"there were thunders and lightenings, and a thick cloud upon the mount, and the voice of the trumpet exceeding loud." (Exodus 19:16)

The Lord came down upon the mount but His presence was hidden from the people by the cloud. Into that secret place Moses went and spoke with God (Numbers 12:7,8). The "secret place of the most High" (Psalm 91:1) is ever the place of intimate and close association with God. It is a place of divine revelation and fellowship, a theme developed in the New Testament (Matthew 6:4-6,14-18) that we consider when we come to Psalm 91, which provides a more appropriate background.

Having delivered them from Egypt, God proved them at the waters of Meribah. Their faith was put to the test and the name Meribah, which means 'strife', was a continual reminder to them of their repeated ingratitude to their God, not just in the wilderness, but throughout their history (Exodus 17:7; Numbers 20:13; Psalm 78:20).

Verses 8-10

On the basis of the Exodus deliverance God speaks to His people. The words can be understood as if they were spoken at that time to the people in the wilderness. Nevertheless their character is such that they are appropriate to the nation at any time in their history:

"Hear, O my people, and I will testify unto thee: O Israel, if thou wilt hearken unto me; there shall be no strange god in thee; neither shalt thou worship any strange god. I am the LORD thy God, which brought thee out of the land of Egypt: open thy mouth wide, and I will fill it." (verses 8-10)

There is an intimacy about the language and a poignancy in the appeal that emphasises the closeness of the relationship with their God. "My People", "O Israel", God pleads with them, for "I am the LORD thy God". If they would but hearken to the word of God when He testified against them, the consequence would be that there was no strange god among them.

There are two different words translated "strange" in verse 9 and significantly the same two Hebrew words occur in Deuteronomy 32 in close connection with each other. The first word has associations with a strange woman with whom a man might commit adultery (verse

631

16). The second carries the idea of that which is foreign or alien. Thus Deuteronomy 32 testifies:

> "So the LORD alone did lead him, and there was no strange (i.e., alien) god with him."   (verse 12)

It was God who had delivered Israel; He alone had saved them. Thus their allegiance was to Him only. It could not be shared with any other and if they would but open their mouths, that is look to Him in faith to supply all their needs, then He would provide for them – whether water from the rock or manna in the desert (see Psalm 78:20-25). Such fidelity was demanded of them, for "I am the LORD thy God". The majestic words of the Decalogue are recalled (Exodus 20:2; see also Deuteronomy 5:6) for He was the Holy One of Israel. It was to the One that brought them out of the land of Egypt that they owed their national existence.

Verses 11-14

But Israel would not hearken. The pathos of the words reiterating the closeness of the relationship and the dreadful consequences of their actions is made clear:

> "But my people would not hearken to my voice; and Israel would none of me. So I gave them up unto their own hearts' lust: and they walked in their own counsels."   (verses 11,12)

It is surely the most dreadful thing that can happen to God's people. The RV in verse 12 says, "So I let them go after the stubbornness of their heart, that they might walk in their own counsels". God gave them over to their own desires and left them to their own devices.

It is a facet of human nature of which we need to be aware. If a man persists in evil and constantly refuses all attempts to persuade him to change his ways, then in time he will become so hardened in the way he has chosen that it will be virtually impossible for him to change. When a man reaches this state, then God confirms him in the way he has chosen. Romans 1 is a prime illustration of the principle. Because men –

> "changed the glory of the incorruptible God into an image made like to corruptible man, and to birds, and fourfooted beasts, and creeping things ... God also gave

them up to uncleanness through the lusts of their own
hearts." (verses 23,24)

"Who changed the truth of God into a lie, and
worshipped and served the creature more than the
Creator ... For this cause God gave them up unto vile
affections." (verses 25,26)

"And even as they did not like to retain God in their
knowledge, God gave them over to a reprobate mind."
(verse 28)

Similarly Paul writes in 2 Thessalonians 2 of one who
would work with –

"all deceivableness of unrighteousness in them that
perish; because they received not the love of the truth,
that they might be saved. And for this cause God shall
send them strong delusion, that they should believe a
lie: that they all might be damned who believed not the
truth, but had pleasure in unrighteousness."
(verses 10,12)

It was their choice; they received not the love of the truth,
and because they persisted in that way, they became
hardened in it and God sent them strong delusion that
they should believe a lie.

The plaintive cry over Israel is, "Oh that my people had
hearkened unto me, and Israel had walked in my ways!"
(Psalm 81:13). Then would the hand that chastened them
have been turned against their enemies, who would have
been subdued before them (verse 14).

Verses 15,16

The Psalmist's final reflections bring the song to a close:

"The haters of the LORD would pretend submission to
Him, but their fate would endure forever."
(verse 15, NKJV)

The changes in pronoun in the last two verses present a
difficulty in determining to whom the Psalmist refers. We
have followed the New King James Version which
presents us with the picture of a feigned loyalty. Those
who hated the Lord pretended that they would willingly
subject themselves to Him. Their hypocrisy, however,
would not profit them, for there was reserved for them the
coldness and blackness of the tomb forever.

Although many in Israel did not love God's ways and their apparent devotion was a charade, yet it remained true that if they had truly sought Him with all their hearts then "he would have fed them also with the finest of the wheat: and with honey out of the rock should I have satisfied thee" (verse 16).

All the blessings that God had promised Israel when He delivered them from Egypt were still available to a people who were prepared to turn in obedience to His word.

PSALM 82

ONE of the fundamental principles of the Law of Moses was that there should be "no unrighteousness in judgment". Those who exercised authority were not to "respect the person of the poor, nor honour the person of the mighty". Rich or poor, all were to be treated alike, for "in righteousness shalt thou judge thy neighbour" (Leviticus 19:15; see also Deuteronomy 1:16,17, etc.). It was however inevitable that, where human judges were concerned, there was a greater likelihood of the rich and powerful being treated with partiality than the poor and destitute. It has ever been and will be so until the Lord returns. It was for this reason that the law placed special emphasis upon the need to take care of the poor and needy:

"Ye shall not afflict any widow, or fatherless child."

(Exodus 22:22)

"Cursed be he that perverteth the judgment of the stranger, fatherless, and widow." (Deuteronomy 27:19)

Those who disregarded the divine edict would not go unpunished for, "A father of the fatherless, and a judge of the widows, is God in his holy habitation" (Psalm 68:5).

It is against this background that Psalm 82 was written, for it is an indictment of the judges in Israel who without compunction were accepting the persons of the wicked and failing to uphold the cause of the poor and fatherless, the afflicted and needy. Far from delivering them out of the hand of their oppressors they were allowing the rich and powerful to exploit them to their own advantage.

By its very nature the psalm is appropriate to many periods in both the history of Israel and Judah; in that sense its message is timeless. Nevertheless there are two alternatives that are worth noting. There is a striking parallel with the thought and language of the psalm in Isaiah's prophecy:

"The LORD standeth up to plead, and standeth to judge the people. The LORD will enter into judgment with the ancients of his people, and the princes thereof: for ye have eaten up the vineyard; the spoil of the poor is in your houses. What mean ye that ye beat my people to pieces, and grind the faces of the poor? saith the Lord GOD of hosts."   (Isaiah 3:13-15)

If this passage is referring to the same time then it would place the psalm in the latter part of Uzziah's reign, during the time that Jotham acted as regent, or even at the beginning of the reign of that wicked King Ahaz.

The other suggestion would relate it to the reformation begun by Asa (2 Chronicles 15) and accomplished by his son Jehoshaphat (2 Chronicles 19):

"And he (Jehoshaphat) set judges in the land throughout all the fenced cities of Judah, city by city, and said to the judges, Take heed what ye do: for ye judge not for man, but for the LORD, who is with you in the judgment. Wherefore now let the fear of the LORD be upon you; take heed and do it: for there is no iniquity with the LORD our God, nor respect of persons, nor taking of gifts."   (verses 5-7)

Presumably this had not been the case previously and the psalm could therefore apply to the end of Asa's reign or the beginning of Jehoshaphat's.

For the purpose of our consideration we divide the psalm as follows:

1. The assembly of the judges (verse 1).
2. A plea for righteous judgement (verses 2-4).
3. The consequences of their unscrupulous behaviour (verses 5-7).
4. The righteous judge (verse 8).

Verse 1

The psalm opens in a most dramatic way. The elders of Israel are gathered in formal counsel. In solemn assembly they meet to dispense judgement, but the seat of the presiding judge is vacant. Suddenly that place is filled, not by any human prince but by the great judge of all, the God of Israel, and the judges become the judged:

"God standeth in the congregation of the mighty: he judgeth among the gods." (verse 1)

From one perspective the psalm has a simple and powerful message about righteousness in judgement: from another it gives a wonderful insight into the principles of God-manifestation. To illustrate the point we reproduce again the first verse with the Hebrew titles in their original (anglicised) form: "Elohim standeth in the congregation of El: He judgeth among Elohim".

Many have been led to false conclusions because of their failure to understand the scriptural teaching about God-manifestation. Some commentators imagine that the picture is of God holding counsel in heaven and passing judgement upon the angels who, they fail to perceive, can do no unrighteousness in judgement.

"El" is, of course, singular in form and should properly be applied not to the princes but to God Himself. They, the judges of Israel, are the congregation of God, the Mighty One. They dispense justice on His behalf; they are His representatives in the midst of His people. They stand by His appointment and He, the Judge of all, presides over their assembly. This they had forgotten – hence the dramatic scene presented – for now the Lord "judgeth among the gods". This is a title applied to the judges of Israel:

"Then his master shall bring him unto the judges (Hebrew, *elohim,* literally, 'gods')." (Exodus 21:6)

"If the thief be not found, then the master of the house shall be brought unto the judges (Hebrew, *elohim*) ... the cause of both parties shall come before the judges (Hebrew, *elohim*)." (Exodus 22:8,9)

"Thou shalt not revile the gods (Hebrew, *elohim,* i.e., judges), nor curse the ruler of thy people." (verse 28)

They are called Elohim because they stand in God's stead before the people and speak forth His judgement.

In a similar sense Moses was to be to Aaron "instead of God" (Exodus 4:16) and as "god to Pharaoh" (Exodus 7:1). Thus the Psalmist says that the God who presides in the midst of them, judges amongst the gods (Elohim). They had been elevated to this station, one of the loftiest to which men could aspire. They had been invested with His royal dignity for they were His representatives in the midst of His people, and understanding this we appreciate more fully the words of the Lord Jesus (John 10:34) when he quoted the words of this psalm: "I said ye are gods" (verse 6) – a quotation to which we shall return.

Verses 2-4

So the judges of Israel are challenged:

> "How long will ye judge unjustly, and accept the persons of the wicked?" (verse 2)

Unscrupulously they had perverted judgement. They had honoured and curried favour with the wicked to their own advantage. Literally they had 'judged iniquity'. The judgement itself had been iniquity, the very opposite of judging righteously. The word rendered "accept" means literally "respect" (RV). They had shown partiality to the rich and powerful and apparently this situation had been allowed to continue for a long time. For "how long?" is the plaintive cry of the psalm. "How long?" – perhaps also in the sense: 'Will you *now* repent of your wickedness and turn from your evil ways?'

The abuse of their privilege was longstanding and without excuse, therefore they are reminded of their responsibilities:

> "Defend the poor and fatherless: do justice to the afflicted and needy. Deliver the poor and needy: rid them out of the hand of the wicked." (verses 3,4)

Their duty to the poor and afflicted, those in the direst of straits who were helpless and destitute (the meaning of the Hebrew words rendered "poor" and "needy"), so clearly emphasised in the law, was disregarded. There was no justice for the poor but the wicked were allowed to oppress them and, no doubt, judges and wicked grew rich together for they were virtually hand in glove with each other.

Verses 5-7

There is no response from the judges; they are blind to their moral perversion. They lack the knowledge and understanding to reform for they walk in darkness (verse 5). These men had become infatuated with their position and blinded by their pride in their office. Literally, "they walked to and fro in darkness". It was their conversation, their way of life, and they felt secure and confident, oblivious to the reality of their standing before God.

It is a strange thing about human nature that in the face of the obvious it can still continue to pursue wickedness, blindly convincing itself that whatever God's word says, it does not really matter. Not for nothing does the scripture describe it as "the deceitfulness of sin".

The consequences of those in authority, who should have been shepherds of the flock, behaving in this way were inevitable. The very foundations of their society, God's society, which should have been founded on righteousness and justice, were destroyed: "All the foundations of the earth (were) out of course" (verse 5).

So God remonstrates with them: "I have said, Ye are gods". In effect, 'I have appointed you to this privileged and exalted status'. "All of you (are) sons of the Most High" (verse 6, RV). The "I" is emphatic as if to leave them in no doubt of the One they represented and who regarded them in a special sense as His sons.

"Nevertheless" (RV), notwithstanding their exalted position, "ye shall die like men, and fall like one of the princes" (verse 7). Literally, 'ye shall die like Adam'. How appropriate that they should be reminded of the fate of one who like them was in a special sense a son of God (Luke 3:38); one who was made in the image and likeness of God and given dominion over the works of His hand (Genesis 1:26), for he too was God's representative, exercising authority on His behest in the midst of the earth. Like Adam they had denied their calling, degraded their exalted position. Like Adam they should die; they should fall as one of the princes. We suggest that the reference is to Korah, Dathan and Abiram, men who were not true to their princely calling (see Jude verse 6, RV).

Like Adam and those princes of old they should not die the common death of all men, but they would be judged and found guilty before God and sentenced accordingly to that which was their just desert.

John 10

It is appropriate at this juncture that we consider the use made of this psalm by the Lord Jesus when he was accused by the Jews of making himself God (John 10:33). The Lord Jesus responded by quoting the words of Psalm 82:6:

> "Is it not written in your law, I said, Ye are gods? If he called them gods, unto whom the word of God came, and the scripture cannot be broken; say ye of him, whom the Father hath sanctified, and sent into the world, Thou blasphemest; because I said, I am the son of God?"
>
> (John 10:34-36)

The principles of God-manifestation are at the heart of the argument. In effect the Lord said, 'If He called them Elohim, to whom the word of Elohim came; if they were designated "gods" because the word of God was spoken through them and they dispensed judgement on His behalf, then how much more appropriate that he who was that word made flesh could claim to be the Son of God'. They themselves had been called sons of God purely by reason of their office, how much more then was that title his by reason of the fact that he was the only begotten of the Father.

Of course the use of this scripture in this context has other implications. Those who accused him were the judges of his day. They had demonstrated that their motivation was no different from those assumed in the psalm. First, they had cast out of the synagogue the man born blind, whom the Lord had healed. (John 9:30-34). They excommunicated him for no reason other than he testified that it was the Lord Jesus who had given him sight. Secondly, they had sought to stone the Lord Jesus for no good cause (verse 32) except that they had murder in their hearts.

They knew their scriptures; they knew the context and they thought that they were 'the gods' in Israel. The Lord was warning them that they too would die like Adam and fall like one of the princes. There is more to be learned, however, for this incident in John 10 falls into the context of the Good Shepherd. They were the shepherds in Israel but they had shown their lack of concern for the flock by their treatment of the man born blind. The Good Shepherd had found him and cared for him. They, like the judges in Psalm 82, walked in darkness (9:38-41). But the Lord Jesus in contrast presented himself as the true representative of his Father, the Shepherd of Israel, for Psalm 82, a Psalm of Asaph, is as we have seen previously one of that series of songs that refers to the Shepherd of Israel (77:20; 78:52,53,70,72; 79:13: 80:1).

Verse 8
We come then to the concluding verse of the psalm. It stands in evident contrast to the unprincipled judges indicted by God:

"Arise, O God, judge the earth: for thou shalt inherit all nations."

Our first reaction might be to think of the Lord God Himself as the subject of the Psalmist's prayer, but we are in the realm of God-manifestation and if they could be called "gods" to whom the word of God came, how much more could the Psalmist, prophetically, look forward to the one who should reign for God in a day when He shall judge the world in righteousness (Acts 17:31). This is the one of whom another Psalmist had declared:

"Thy throne, O God, is for ever and ever: the sceptre of thy kingdom is a right sceptre."   (Psalm 45:6)

And again:

"Thou art my Son; this day have I begotten thee. Ask of me, and I shall give thee the heathen for thine inheritance, and the uttermost parts of the earth for thy possession."   (Psalm 2:7,8)

It is in the Lord Jesus that these words will be fulfilled.

All this is confirmed by the Lord's words in John 10, when he declared himself to be the Son of God and thereby made claim also to be David's seed and heir to his everlasting throne, for "I will be his father, and he shall be my son" (1 Chronicles 17:13). In that day when he sits on David's throne:

"He shall judge thy people with righteousness, and thy poor with judgment ... He shall judge the poor of the people, he shall save the children of the needy, and shall break in pieces the oppressor."   (Psalm 72:2,4)

PSALM 83

THIS is the last of the group of psalms (73 to 83) that bears the title "A Psalm of Asaph". We have noted previously that one of the recurring themes of these psalms is that of judgement. Psalm 82 spoke of God judging the judges of Israel for their injustice, whereas Psalm 83 speaks of God's judgement upon the nations that are round about Israel; not those in the distant parts of the earth, not the nations afar off, but those who are the more immediate neighbours of God's people. Ten nations are enumerated as being confederate together against them. They are (as AV): the Ishmaelites, Moab, the Hagarenes, Gebal, Ammon, Amalek, Tyre, the Philistines, Edom, Assur.

Some doubt might exist as to the exact location of Gebal but all those mentioned, with the exception of Assur, are nations with whom Israel 'rubbed shoulders' throughout her history in the land, and some of them had a particularly close relationship with God's people (i.e., the Ishmaelites, the Edomites and the children of Lot).

Background

The questions that naturally spring to mind are:

1. When was this psalm written?

2. Against what background was it penned?

As far as our reading is concerned we are aware of four suggestions. Two of these in our view can be dismissed immediately. These are the speculations of critical scholars that the psalm either relates to the times of the Maccabees or to the period after the exile (the Samaritan inhabitants of the land being the confederacy). There is no real evidence to support either of these views and the historical circumstances do not fit the facts of the psalm.

A third view is that the psalm relates to Sennacherib's invasion in the days of Hezekiah. Some interesting links can be established between the psalm and chapters in Isaiah's prophecy that undoubtedly refer to Hezekiah's time. However, the reference to Assyria appears to clinch the argument against this view. The psalm says:

"Assur (RV, Assyria) also is joined with them: they have holpen (RV margin, 'they have been an arm to') the children of Lot." (verse 8)

The Assyrians are not the leaders of the confederacy but they lend their support to it. The "children of Lot" are the principal protagonists and Assyria gives practical aid, perhaps by supplying mercenaries or by the provision of military advice and supplies. Although we do not believe that the psalm was written in the days of Hezekiah, we think that the connections with Isaiah's prophecy are relevant and we shall return to these later in this chapter.

The fourth suggestion, which receives support from most Christadelphian writers and many orthodox commentators, is that the psalm was written in the days of Jehoshaphat, against the background of the confederacy of nations who threatened Judah as described in 2 Chronicles 20. These events present a satisfactory historical perspective against which the theme of the psalm is enacted. Moab and Ammon (i.e., the children of Lot) and "with them other beside" (2 Chronicles 20:1), together with the Edomites (verse 10), present a great multitude and strike fear into the heart of Jehoshaphat, and all Judah. Jehoshaphat and the people present themselves before the Lord and make supplication unto Him. The words of the king's prayer strike a chord with the language of the psalm (2 Chronicles 20:5-12). Note particularly:

"O LORD God of our fathers, art not thou God in heaven? and rulest not thou over all the kingdom of the heathen? and in thine hand is there not power and might, so that none is able to withstand thee?"
(verse 6)

Consider this host says Jehoshaphat, for:

"Behold ... how they reward us, to come to cast us out of thy possession, which thou hast given us to inherit. O

> our God, wilt thou not judge them? for we have no might against this great company that cometh against us; neither know we what to do: but our eyes are upon thee."   (verses 11,12)

All Judah with their wives and their children stood before the Lord and the spirit of the Lord came upon Jahaziel the son of Zechariah, a Levite of the sons of Asaph, and he prophesied (verses 13,14). Is it possible that this particular son of Asaph was the actual author of the psalm? His message was clear: they were not to be dismayed by this great multitude for the battle was not theirs but the Lord's. "Ye shall not need to fight in this battle: set yourselves, stand ye still, and see the salvation of the LORD with you" (verse 17).

The following day, led by singers appointed by the king, Jehoshaphat led forth his army and when they began to sing and to praise, God took action against this great company that had come against them. He caused every man to turn his sword against his fellow so that they were swallowed up in the confusion that followed (see verses 22-24). So the conclusion of the matter was that –

> "they returned, every man of Judah and Jerusalem, and Jehoshaphat in the forefront of them, to go again to Jerusalem with joy; for the LORD had made them to rejoice over their enemies. And they came to Jerusalem with psalteries and harps and trumpets unto the house of the LORD. And the fear of God was on all ... those countries, when they heard that the LORD fought against the enemies of Israel. So the realm of Jehoshaphat was quiet: for his God gave him rest round about."   (verses 27-30; see Psalm 83:14-18)

Although the language of the psalm is different, the thoughts expressed are precisely the same. It could be that this psalm, which would be a very suitable prayer in the circumstances described in 2 Chronicles 20, was sung by Jahaziel amongst the singers who led Jehoshaphat and his army out.

Some Problems Considered

Although the psalm can be readily associated with these events of Jehoshaphat's reign, there are some difficulties.

First, there is the mention of Assyria in the psalm but no reference to this enemy of God's people in Chronicles. Secondly, the psalm names ten members of the confederacy, whereas Chronicles mentions only three with an implication (verse 1) that there were others involved.

With regard to Assyria, she had not yet emerged as the world power that she was shortly to become. The psalm tells us that she was not a primary antagonist but lent her support in some way to Moab and Ammon. If she was not represented significantly in the host gathered against Judah, then it is perhaps not surprising that there is no mention of Assyria in 2 Chronicles 20 which is dealing with the immediacy of the situation. We might ask, however, why should Assyria involve herself in such a conflict? What was her interest?

We know from non-Biblical history sources that Ahab of Israel was confederate with Benhadad of Syria in an inconclusive battle with the Assyrians from which they retreated to Nineveh with no advantage gained. Jehoshaphat, foolishly from the divine standpoint, subsequently allied himself with Ahab against the threat of Syria (2 Chronicles 18) and this would be sufficient reason for Assyria, in furthering her own territorial ambitions, to give assistance to this confederacy without becoming directly involved.

As far as the nations mentioned in the psalm are concerned, we suggest that we have encompassed in these surrounding nations all of Israel's immediate enemies, and pre-eminent among them were those whom we today would describe as Arab. These were bound together by a common hatred, not just of Israel but also of Israel's God and everything associated with Him. Note the language of the psalm:

"For, lo, thine enemies make a tumult: and they that hate thee have lifted up the head." (verse 2)

"They are confederate against thee." (verse 5)

The purpose of God's judgement is:

"That they may seek thy name, O LORD." (verse 16)

"That they might know that thou alone, whose name is JEHOVAH, art the Most High over all the earth."

(verse 18, RV)

We suggest therefore that although the psalm was probably penned in the days of Jehoshaphat, its message is timeless. It represents the attitude of Israel's neighbours, particularly the Arabs, throughout history. Thus, not all the nations mentioned needed to be involved in the confederacy that faced Jehoshaphat for the psalm represents the totality of the opposition, the attitude of them all towards Israel. This hatred, however, will be reflected at various times by different representatives of this group as the historical circumstances require. The reference to Assur can be seen as an indication that throughout history an added threat to Israel has come from the north, and these greater world powers have not been averse to using Israel's neighbours to further their own strategic and territorial ambitions.

The Principle Illustrated

Thus, references to Isaiah's prophecy, and the part played by Assyria in using these nations to her own advantage in Hezekiah's day (referred to above), are relevant for they are part of the recurring fulfilment of the psalm throughout history.

So also in the days of Nebuchadnezzar these nations were, like birds of prey, quick to offer assistance and feed on the carcase of Israel as the power from the north accomplished that which they could never achieve in their own strength.

Thus we read of Edom's "perpetual hatred" (Ezekiel 35:5) and other prophets testify to her cruelty and swiftness in taking advantage in the time of Israel's distress (see Obadiah verses 10,14; Amos 1:11; Joel 3:19; Psalm 137:7-9, etc.).

Particularly interesting in this connection is the section of Ezekiel's prophecy (chapters 25-35) that deals with God's judgements on the surrounding nations. In chapter 25 we have reference to Ammon (verses 2-6), Moab (verses 8-12), Edom (verses 12-14), and the Philistines (verse 15)

– all condemned because of their attitude towards Israel in the day of her distress.

Similarly in chapters 26-29 we have reference to God's judgements upon Tyre. The section opens with the words:

"And it came to pass in the eleventh year, in the first day of the month, that the word of the LORD came unto me saying, Son of man, because that Tyrus hath said against Jerusalem, Aha, she is broken that was the gates of the people: she is turned unto me: I shall be replenished, now she is laid waste."   (26:1,2)

The eleventh year was, of course, the last year of Zedekiah's reign. It was the year that the two-year siege of the city by Nebuchadnezzar came to an end and the city was broken up, the temple destroyed and the people carried away captive (see 2 Kings 25). In all this Tyre rejoiced.

Perhaps the most remarkable fulfilment of the psalm has been in our own days with the establishment of the State of Israel. For all the territory once occupied by these ancient nations is now, to a large extent, occupied by the Arab nations who are united together by one thing only – their hatred of Israel and their determination to "cut them off from being a nation" (verse 4).

The psalm had a remarkable fulfilment in the conflict of 1947/48 and in the Six-Day War of 1967. The part played by northern powers (i.e., Russia and others) in arming and supporting the Arab cause is a reflection of the truth that "Assur also is joined with them. They have holpen the children of Lot".

As we look with anticipation to the coming of the Lord Jesus, we do well to remember that we have the authority of scripture to assure us that the 'peace process' is a sham. The perpetual hatred remains. The ultimate aim of these nations is unchanged and the psalm has a continuing fulfilment.

We turn now to a more detailed consideration of the content of the psalm.

Verses 1-5

The psalm opens with a prayer that God would come to the rescue of His people who were threatened with annihilation by their enemies:

> "Keep not thou silence, O God: hold not thy peace, and be not still, O God." (verse 1)

In the face of overwhelming odds, when humanly speaking there seems no hope, the Psalmist recognises that in God only is there salvation. The enemies have no thought for God. They have totally disregarded Him. They imagine that His apparent inactivity and refusal to speak is an indication that He is powerless to intervene:

> "For, lo, thine enemies make a tumult: and they that hate thee have lifted up the head. They have taken crafty counsel against thy people, and consulted against thy hidden ones. They have said, Come, and let us cut them off from being a nation; that the name of Israel may be no more in remembrance. For they have consulted together with one consent: they are confederate against thee." (verses 2-5)

As previously noted, they are God's enemies and their hatred of His people is motivated by this fact: "For, lo, thine enemies ... they are confederate against thee".

Israel's right to dwell in the land is not political as the world perceives it, but religious. It is founded in the promises that God made to Abraham and David which were ratified through the blood of the Lord Jesus Christ. From the very beginning it is God who determined which territories Edom, Moab, Ammon etc. should occupy, and all these decisions were taken with Israel in mind. In our days the battle lines are drawn by the extreme Islamic groups who, irrespective of political aspirations, regard the land, and Jerusalem in particular, as theirs.

Although, in the Hebrew text, the actual words used are different, the thought pattern in these opening verses of the psalm recalls the language of Psalm 2:

> "Why do the heathen rage, and the people imagine a vain thing? The kings of the earth set themselves, and the rulers take counsel together, against the LORD, and against his anointed." (verses 1,2)

So these nations "make a tumult", "(take) crafty counsel", and "(consult) together with one consent". Their aim is to blot out the name of Israel for ever; to frustrate the purpose of God in them and thus bring to an end the worship of Israel's God.

All these words, particularly the emphasis upon their craftiness, give the idea of a secret agenda. Their true purpose and aim is concealed. This is particularly true in our day when world opinion seems to swing more and more towards the Arab cause. Only occasionally does the mask slip and the truth emerge that their ultimate aim remains unchanged, "that the name of Israel be no more in remembrance".

The reference to God's "hidden ones" needs some comment. It means literally, those whom God protects, who are hidden under the shadow of His hand. Some render it "treasured ones" recalling the words of Deuteronomy, "He kept him as the apple of his eye" (32:10).

In this sense we can understand the words as being true of all Israel. However, we recall also the words of David:

"For in the time of trouble he shall hide me in his pavilion: in the secret of his tabernacle shall he hide me; he shall set me up upon a rock."   (Psalm 27:5)

These are the words not of all Israel, but of one of God's faithful servants who has put his trust in God's promises and looks to Him for deliverance. It raises the interesting question as to whether there will be a remnant in Israel holding to the truth of God's purpose in the Lord Jesus Christ when he eventually returns.

Verses 6-8

We have already commented in our opening remarks on the ten nations enumerated here as confederate together. The Edomites were to the south-east of the land of Israel, while the Ishmaelites, a nomadic people, occupied the territory from the east of Egypt to the Persian Gulf (Genesis 25:18). Moab and Ammon were east of Israel on the other side of the Jordan, while the maritime states of the Philistines to the west and Tyre to the north held the western flank. The Hagarenes dwelt to the east of Gilead (see 1 Chronicles 5:10) whereas Gebal was either to the north of Tyre or an area in the mountains of Edom. The Amalekites, of course, were from the south and always implacable foes of Israel.

These were in many respects diverse people with little in common except for hatred of Israel and their God. We believe it would be true to say that although the psalm has had a recurring fulfilment throughout history, it is only in our days that the confederacy has finally emerged in all its fulness.

Verses 9-12

The Psalmist's prayer is that God would deal with this great host as in the past He had dealt with the Midianites (Judges 7,8) and the Canaanites (Judges 4,5). In both these instances the victory was won, not by Israel's military prowess, but by the direct action of God. Both of these opponents of Israel were confederacies of nations. This is not immediately apparent in the case of Jabin, King of Canaan. But he dwelt in Hazor, whereas the captain of his host, Sisera, dwelt in Harosheth of the nations (RV margin, Judges 4:2). There is here a suggestion of other peoples involved which is confirmed by Deborah in her song:

> "Then fought the kings of Canaan in Taanach by the waters of Megiddo." (Judges 5:19)

Although they were "discomfited with the edge of the sword before Barak", it was the Lord who was responsible (Judges 4:15) and it was His direct intervention that gained the victory, for –

> "the stars in their courses fought against Sisera. The river of Kishon swept them away." (verses 20,21)

Endor (Psalm 83:10) is not mentioned in Judges but it is in the same valley as Taanach and Megiddo, and is another instance of the way in which later scripture adds detail to what had previously been revealed. The host of the Canaanites became as dung for the earth (verse 10). Their bodies were left unburied where they had fallen upon the battlefield.

Gideon's victory over the Midianites was also a triumph for God over a confederacy of nations. "The Midianites

650

came up, and the Amalekites, and the children of the east" (Judges 6:3). The Psalmist's plea was:

> "Make their nobles like Oreb, and like Zeeb: Yea all their princes as Zebah and Zalmunna."   (verse 11)

Oreb and Zeeb (their names mean 'raven' and 'wolf') were the nobles, literally the generals of the host. They were the military commanders, whereas Zebah and Zalmunna were the kings of the Midianites (Judges 8:5).

How terrible the slaughter of the Midianites was is perhaps indicated by Isaiah who likens "the day of Midian" to the destruction of Sennacherib's host (9:4) and to the deliverance from Egypt (10:24-26). As in Jehoshaphat's day, that slaughter was accomplished by each other's hands (2 Chronicles 20:23 and Judges 7:22).

The enemies of God said, "Let us take to ourselves the pastures of God in possession" (verse 12, with RV margin). Throughout the Psalms of Asaph we have seen the wonderful figure of the shepherd and the sheep and it is not absent from this last of the group of psalms. Israel were God's flock and they lay down in His land, on His pastures.

Verses 13-18

This last section of the psalm is a continuation of the prayer that God would deal with the enemy as He had with these ancient foes:

> "O my God, make them like a wheel; as the stubble before the wind."   (verse 13)

The word "wheel" is the Hebrew *galgal*, literally, 'a rolling thing'. Some think it refers to the dust caught by the strength of the wind, others to the wild artichoke whose globular heads break off in the autumn, and light as a feather are sent in their thousands scudding across the plains (Thomson, *The Land and the Book,* page 563). The figure however is clear, for like the stubble before the wind, the chaff from the summer threshing floors (Daniel 2:35), they are swept away.

It is the perfect figure of the flight of a defeated, panic-stricken army. Those who can recall the photographs of shoes and other items of clothing cast away in haste by

651

retreating armies at the time of the Six-Day War, will have a literal picture of what the figurative language describes:

"As the fire burneth a wood, and as the flame setteth the mountains on fire; so persecute them with thy tempest, and make them afraid with thy storm."

(verses 14,15)

God's wrath is like a forest fire as it pursues and consumes His enemies. It is like a fire in the dry scrubland on the mountainside. When the wind blows and fire breaks out it spreads from bush to bush with amazing rapidity until the whole mountain is ablaze. So when God manifests Himself in human affairs none can stand before Him, and the hearts of those who have dared to oppose Him tremble with fear:

"Fill their faces with shame; that they may seek thy name, O LORD. Let them be confounded and troubled for ever; yea, let them be put to shame, and perish."

(verses 16,17)

Let them be disgraced, says the Psalmist, in the knowledge that their crafty counsel has been confounded and all their ambitions frustrated. It is his desire that the God of Israel should triumph over His enemies, not just out of a spirit of vengeance, but that in their confusion they might recognise that Israel's God is indeed the only true God and that in consequence, "they might seek thy name, O LORD" (verse 16).

This must ever be the primary object of all God's work but if they will not acknowledge Him in truth, convinced by the force of circumstances, then:

"Let them be ashamed and dismayed for ever; yea, let them be confounded and perish."   (verse 17, RV)

Through the judgements of God they will learn, and not just them but all men, "that (He) whose name alone is JEHOVAH, (is) the most high over all the earth" (verse 18). They will learn that all the gods whom they have worshipped are vanity. There is but one God who alone is sovereign over all the nations of the earth. Their design to bring ruin upon Israel will be turned back upon them, and He who reveals Himself as Yahweh will be acknowledged as the Most High over all the earth.

THE PSALMS OF THE SONS OF KORAH

IT seems appropriate that we should, by way of introduction, consider again the psalms that bear a title attributing them to the Sons of Korah. There are twelve psalms which are thus described, Psalms 42 to 49*, which we have already considered, and Psalms 84,85,87 and 88, although we think it possible that Psalm 89 could be added to this list, making a total then of 13.

The house of Korah had an illustrious place throughout the history of the Kingdom of Judah in the compiling and singing of the songs of the temple. Their musical skill was transmitted from generation to generation and that in spite of the rebellion and destruction of their forbear, whose name they took and which must have been a perpetual reminder to them, and indeed to all Israel, that though Korah had died for his sin (Numbers 16:31-35) his children had been spared (26:10,11).

The sons of Korah were Levites belonging to the family of Kohath (1 Chronicles 6:16,22). Numbered amongst them was Samuel (verse 28) who founded the School of the Prophets and who must have been largely responsible, in those early days, for the development of the music of the tabernacle – a task no doubt brought to a conclusion, as far as the tabernacle was concerned, by David.

Heman (of the house of Korah) whose name appears at the head of Psalm 88 was the grandson of Samuel (1 Chronicles 6:33, RV), and was one of the foremost among those whom "David set over the service of song in the house of the LORD, after that the ark had rest. And they ministered before the dwelling place of the tabernacle of

---

* This assumes that Psalm 43 which bears no title of authorship is to be identified with Psalm 42. Indeed many believe that they are in fact one psalm. Note the recurring phrase, "Why art thou cast down, O my soul?" (Psalm 42:5,11; Psalm 43:5).

the congregation with singing, until Solomon had built the house of the LORD in Jerusalem: and then they waited on their office according to their order" (verses 31,32).

But not only were they singers, they also had responsibility as "keepers of the gates of the tabernacle" (9:19). Presumably this was a duty which they also carried out in respect of the temple. They were also warriors, as were most of the Levites, and they are named amongst those who came to David at Ziklag, "armed with bows, and (that) could use both the right hand and the left in hurling stones" (12:1,2,6).

Heman is named with Asaph and Jeduthun as amongst those who ministered "with trumpets and cymbals ... and with musical instruments of God" when David brought the ark of God to Jerusalem (16:37-43). He is linked again with Asaph and Jeduthun in 1 Chronicles 25 and among his accomplishments is the ability to "prophesy with harps, with psalteries, and with cymbals" (verse 1). He is described as the "king's seer" and he was blessed with fourteen sons and three daughters (verse 5). All these sons and daughters alike –

"were under the hands of their father for song in the house of the LORD, with cymbals, psalteries, and harps, for the service of the house of God, according to the king's order."
(verse 6)

The Sons of Korah were therefore established through Heman in the work of singing and playing psalms in the worship of the sanctuary.

They were still involved in the days of Hezekiah for when he began his reformation (2 Chronicles 29:1-5) two of the sons of Heman are mentioned as prominent in that work (verse 14). A little later:

"He set the Levites in the house of the LORD with cymbals, with psalteries, and with harps, according to the commandment of David, and of Gad the king's seer, and Nathan the prophet: for so was the commandment of the LORD by his prophets."
(verse 25)

As David had Gad and Nathan to guide and instruct him, so Hezekiah had Micah and Isaiah. Isaiah, particularly, would have had association with the Sons of Korah for he himself was a Levite. It is interesting to speculate whether in fact he might have been a member of that family. Do we perhaps have an indication in the description of his vision of the glory of God (Isaiah 6) when, "the posts of the door moved at the voice of him that cried" (verse 4)? Was he a doorkeeper in the house of God?

Now we know that Hezekiah appointed men to copy out the proverbs of Solomon (Proverbs 25:1). We read also that –

"Hezekiah the king and the princes commanded the Levites to sing praise unto the LORD with the words of David, and of Asaph the seer."   (2 Chronicles 29:30)

As scripture implies and Jewish tradition teaches, it is reasonable to suppose that Hezekiah applied himself to the psalms in a similar fashion to David; not only arranging their order for the temple worship but also, in the revival of spiritual feeling, superintending the composition of new songs that sprang out of the circumstances of his life and times. Into this category come the psalms of the Sons of Korah which all bear, we believe, the stamp of the experiences of men of God in the time of Hezekiah and which also have strong verbal and literary links with the prophecy of Isaiah. It was not that Isaiah had the psalms before him, or that the Sons of Korah had read the prophet's writings, but they both sprang out of the same spiritual experiences. It was the same history; the same things that were on the lips of men of God, and the Lord, through His Spirit, caused them to write of those things that were relevant against the background of their times.

As we saw that there were special characteristics associated with the Psalms of Asaph (i.e., God is presented as the judge of His people and of all the earth), so also there are particular features discernible in the psalms of the Sons of Korah. There is an evident emphasis upon God as the King:

"Thou art my King, O God: command deliverances for Jacob."   (Psalm 44:4)

"Thy throne, O God, is for ever and ever: the sceptre of thy kingdom is a right sceptre."   (Psalm 45:6)

The earthly king in this instance is the representative of the Majesty on High. He rules on God's behalf in God's kingdom.

> "For the LORD most high is terrible; he is a great King over all the earth." (Psalm 47:2; see also 6-8)

> "O Lord of hosts, my king, and my God." (Psalm 84:3)

To this emphasis upon God as the king must be added the prominence given to Jerusalem (Zion) which is in the heart of those who long to worship God in His sanctuary (Psalms 42,43,84). It is "the city of God" (Psalm 46:4; 48:1-3,8; 87:1-3). Implicit in this emphasis upon "the city of God" is the fact that it is under the protection of the Lord of Hosts who dwells in the midst of His people and is therefore their King (Psalms 46-48,84,87).

Another feature which should be noticed is the manner in which the title "LORD of Hosts" (*Yahweh Tzvaoth*) is used in the psalms of the Sons of Korah (see Psalm 46:7,11; 48:8; 84:1,3,8,12). The title in this form occurs only once in the Psalms (24:10) outside the psalms of the Sons of Korah, and it is also a characteristic phrase of Isaiah's prophecy, being used there throughout its pages on over sixty occasions.

We sketch briefly the historical background to the psalms of the Sons of Korah that we have dealt with previously in Volume One.

Psalms 42 and 43

Both psalms reflect the longing of a faithful man cut off from the worship of God in Zion (Psalm 42:1,2; 43:3). He is exiled temporarily in "the land of Jordan, and of the Hermonites" (42:6). Cut off from "the house of God" (Psalm 42:4) he longs for the day when he shall come again to God's altar and praise Him upon the harp (Psalm 43:4). The reference to "the altar" and "the harp" seems to identify the writer as a Levite of the house of Korah and he is prevented from travelling to Zion by an "ungodly nation" (Psalm 43:1) who taunt him with the cry, "Where is thy God?" (Psalm 42:3,10, compare with the words of Rabshakeh – Isaiah 36:18-20).

The Assyrians besieged Samaria for three years before they turned their attention to Judah and Jerusalem. In this period it would have been particularly difficult for any Israelite to travel to Jerusalem to keep the feasts, a situation that would have been felt all the more keenly by a Levite who had actively assisted Hezekiah in his reforms.

Psalm 44

The psalm is a lamentation and has much in common with any time of calamity that might have befallen Israel. The events surrounding Sennacherib's invasion, however, seem particularly appropriate. He had, first of all, carried away captive the three tribes on the east of Jordan, followed by the other seven. So the Psalmist could lament that they were scattered "among the heathen" and had become "a byword among the heathen" (verses 11,14). They had become a reproach to their neighbours and a scorn and a derision to those round about (verse 13). They were scorned by the likes of Rabshekah who reproached and blasphemed (verse 16).

Yet although all this had come upon them they had not forgotten God, neither had they dealt falsely in His covenant (verse 17). Such words would have been particularly appropriate to Levites who had dedicated themselves to the service of God when Hezekiah had encouraged them to assist in the work of reformation. In faith they could cry, "Awake, why sleepest thou, O Lord?" (verse 23), words which are echoed in Isaiah's prophecy:

"Awake, awake, put on strength, O arm of the LORD;
awake as in the ancient days, in the generations of old."
(Isaiah 51:9; cp. also Psalm 44:1-3)

Psalm 45

There is an old Jewish tradition that the psalm celebrates the marriage of Solomon and Pharaoh's daughter. Looked at in relation to the Lord Jesus Christ and his bride it might not matter much whose wedding it originally celebrated for the truths expressed would remain the same. In the context of the psalms of the Sons of Korah, however, it seems appropriate to think rather of the marriage of Hezekiah and Hephzibah, particularly given the manner in which Isaiah in his prophecy first uses language that is based on the king's marriage and secondly in his prophecies of the Lord Jesus seems to use the very language of the psalm:

"Thou shalt be called Hephzi-bah ... for the LORD delighteth in thee, and thy land shall be married."

(Isaiah 62:4)

"For as a young man marrieth a virgin, so shall thy sons marry thee: and as the bridegroom rejoiceth over the bride, so shall thy God rejoice over thee."

(Isaiah 62:5)

"He hath covered me with the robe of righteousness, as a bridegroom decketh himself with ornaments, and as a bride adorneth herself with her jewels."

(Isaiah 61:10)

In the psalm the king is described as "fairer than the children of men" (verse 2). Isaiah speaks of one who is "beautiful upon the mountains" (52:7) and describes the joy of those who "shall see the king in his beauty" (33:17). The Psalmist declares that "grace is poured into thy lips", (verse 2), while Isaiah says of the king that he "bringeth good tidings" and "publisheth peace" (52:7). He testifies again that because the spirit of God rests upon him, he shall be "of quick understanding in the fear of the LORD" (Isaiah 11:3).

In the psalm the king rides forth in triumph "because of truth and meekness and righteousness" (verse 4). Isaiah says "righteousness shall be the girdle of his loins" (11:5) and if the arrows of the king are sharp in the heart of his enemies (Psalm 45:5), he shall also "smite the earth with the rod of his mouth, and with the breath of his lips shall he slay the wicked" (Isaiah 11:4). We note also the similarity in the language of God-manifestation: "Thy throne, O God, is for ever and ever" (Psalm 45:6); and the child born who shall be called, "Wonderful, Counsellor, The mighty God, The everlasting Father, the Prince of Peace" (Isaiah 9:6).

Psalm 46

This psalm describes precisely the crisis arising from Sennacherib's invasion. The contrast between the waters that "roar and be troubled" and the "river, the streams whereof shall make glad the city of God" (Psalm 46:3,4)

658

reflect accurately Isaiah's description of the Assyrian invader as the "waters of the river, strong and many, even the king of Assyria, and all his glory" and his contrast with "the waters of Shiloah that go softly" (Isaiah 8:6). Similarly Isaiah's reference to Emmanuel (God with us) is emphasised in the psalm for "God is in the midst of her" (verse 5) and "the LORD of Hosts is with us" (verse 7).

In verses 8 and 9 the Psalmist gives a vivid description of the destruction of Sennacherib's host and the concluding thoughts of the psalm, "Be still, and know that I am God: I will be exalted among the heathen, I will be exalted in the earth" (verse 10) are an echo of Isaiah's language, "the LORD alone shall be exalted in that day" (Isaiah 2:17). "Cease ye from man, whose breath is in his nostrils" (verse 22).

Psalm 47

This short psalm contains few, if any, historical references but it is a song of praise for the victory wrought by Israel's king. In this respect it is very appropriate to celebrate the victory over the Assyrian described in the preceding psalm.

Psalm 48

As one writer said, "Here the coincidences thicken". The holy mountain is "beautiful in elevation, the joy of the whole earth" (verses 1,2, RV). Isaiah (and Micah) speak of the kingdom age:

"The mountain of the LORD's house shall be established in the top of the mountains, and shall be exalted above the hills; and all nations shall flow unto it."   (Isaiah 2:2)

Again we have a wonderful description of the manner in which God despatched the Assyrian host:

"For, lo, the kings were assembled, they passed by together. They saw it, and so they marvelled: they were troubled, and hasted away. Fear took hold upon them there, and pain, as of a woman in travail." (verses 4-6)

The reference in the words that follow to breaking "the ships of Tarshish with an east wind" (verse 7) may present some difficulty in understanding. However, might it not be that reinforcements of some kind, perhaps mercenaries, were being brought by sea and in a disaster not mentioned specifically elsewhere, God destroyed them with a great wind? Isaiah consistently suggests this might be so. He says:

> "The day of the LORD of hosts shall be upon every one that is proud and lofty ... and upon all the ships of Tarshish, and upon all pleasant pictures. And the loftiness of man shall be bowed down, and the haughtiness of men shall be made low."
>
> (Isaiah 2:12-17)

So the call to walk about Zion, to count her towers, to mark her bulwarks and consider her palaces (verses 12,13), would be very apt for a city delivered from the hand of the enemy, and particularly so if the city walls were reconstructed and the fortifications strengthened.

Psalm 49

This psalm is different in character from the others considered. Although true of worldly men in every generation, it is appropriate to the attitude, both in Judah and Israel, that led to God bringing down the Assyrian upon them. The psalm speaks of those "that trust in their wealth and boast themselves in their riches" (verse 6). Again:

> "Their inward thought is, that their houses shall continue for ever, and their dwelling places to all generations; they call their lands after their own names."
>
> (verse 11)

The exhortation of the Psalmist is:

> "Be not thou afraid when one is made rich, when the glory of his house is increased."
>
> (verse 16)

These words can be compared with the following passages from Isaiah and Amos, who both prophesied in the days immediately preceding the Assyrian threat:

> "Woe unto them that join house to house, that lay field to field, till there be no place."
>
> (Isaiah 5:8)

> "And I will smite the winter house with the summer house; and the houses of ivory shall perish, and the great houses shall have an end, saith the LORD."
>
> (Amos 3:15)

This emphasis on wealth and property can be detected in other passages in these prophecies. It was enjoyed during the days of Uzziah of Judah and Jeroboam of Israel and was no doubt perpetuated through the reigns of their successors.

We may note, however, that there was one individual in the days of Hezekiah who had risen in the king's favour, yet was not faithful in his office. So Isaiah was commanded:

"Thus saith the Lord GOD of hosts, Go get thee unto this treasurer, even unto Shebna, which is over the house and say, What hast thou here? and whom hast thou here, that thou hast hewed thee out a sepulchre here, as he that heweth him out a sepulchre on high, and that graveth an habitation for himself in a rock?"
(Isaiah 22:15,16)

Here was a man who, in the spirit of Cain (who called his city after the name of his son), was seeking to perpetuate his name in the earth (cp. Genesis 4:17; Psalm 49:11). To such as Shebna the Psalmist said:

"Their beauty shall consume in the grave from their dwelling." (verse 14)

So Isaiah also testified:

"The LORD will carry thee away with a mighty captivity … and there the chariots of thy glory shall be the shame of thy lord's house" (22:17,18)

Perhaps the promise to Eliakim the son of Hilkiah, "I will clothe him with thy robe, and strengthen him with thy girdle" (22:21) gives a particular relevance to the words of the psalm, "The upright shall have dominion over them in the morning" (verse 14).

Having looked briefly at the historical background of those psalms already dealt with, we leave the question of the historical circumstances of the remaining psalms to our detailed considerations.

PSALM 84

THERE is a very close affinity between this song and Psalms 42 and 43. The language of the one is echoed in the others. For purposes of comparison we set out some of the relevant passages below.

Psalms 42 & 43	Psalm 84
"Let them bring me unto thy holy hill, and to thy tabernacles" (Psalm 43:3).	"How lovely are thy tabernacles, O LORD of hosts!" (verse 1, RV margin)
"My soul thirsteth for God" (Psalm 42:2).	"My soul longeth, yea, even fainteth" (verse 2).
"For the living God" (Psalm 42:2).	"My flesh crieth out for the living God" (verse 2).

(These are the only two places in the Book of Psalms where the phrase "living God" is used)

"When shall I come and appear before God?" (Psalm 42:2).	"Every one of them in Zion appeareth before God" (verse 7).
"For I shall yet praise him" (Psalm 42:5).	"They will be still praising thee" (verse 4).

The connection is not just verbal, however. Reading Psalms 42 and 43, and catching their spirit, will convince the reader that Psalm 84 expresses the same sentiments.

Again, as the suggestion that the writer of Psalms 42 and 43 was a Levite or one of a group of Levites cut off from the house of God by Sennacherib's invasion, was confirmed by the language of the songs, so here in Psalm 84 there is a close affinity with the house of God. There is a personal reminiscence, recalling the sight of birds of the air flying in its precincts and fluttering about its courts (verse 3). Most pointedly these Sons of Korah, who were doorkeepers in the house of God (1 Chronicles 9:19), demonstrated that the words of verse 10 are not vague and indeterminate, but specific and particularly relevant to them:

"I had rather be a doorkeeper in the house of my God, than to dwell in the tents of wickedness."

Whether the author of all three psalms is the same we cannot say with any certainty but, in any event, all three psalms originated from the same Levitical group.

There is no geographical information regarding their enforced exile in Psalm 84, whereas Psalm 42 speaks of the land of Jordan and of Mount Hermon (verse 6). But there is perhaps a clue in Psalm 84:6 where their journey to Zion takes them through the valley of Baca. If, as suggested below, this name is a reference to the balsam tree, then it is interesting to note that naturalists tell us the valley of Jordan, with its deep depressions and tropical climate, was famous for its balsam trees. The fact that their journey took them in this direction is strong corroborative evidence that, as in Psalms 42 and 43, they began their journey on the east of Jordan, perhaps on the slopes of Hermon itself. In any event they too are seen to be Levites, cut off from the worship in which they delighted by the activities of Sennacherib and his army.

If there is any difference in emphasis then it must lie in the fact that Psalm 84 suggests in the tense of the verbs that the pilgrim had arrived. He has completed the journey and is looking back on those experiences that have culminated in his appearing before God in Zion.

The psalm can be divided conveniently into three sections:

1. His longing to dwell in the house of God (verses 1-4).

2. His determination to achieve that end (verses 5-8).

3. His prayer for God to fulfil his desire (verses 9-12).

The stanzas are separated by "Selah" as we are instructed to pause and meditate, but we note also how the final thoughts of each stanza are taken up and reflected in the opening words of the next.

His Longing for Zion (verses 1-4)

"How lovely (RV margin) are thy tabernacles (*Strong*, 'dwelling places'), O LORD of hosts." (verse 1)

The fact that the word rendered "tabernacles" is plural has caused difficulty for some. It is said to be referring to all the temple buildings or to be poetic in form; again, it "may be 'amplificative', expressing the dignity of the house of God" (see *Cambridge Bible*) – what is called elsewhere a "plural of majesty".

We see no difficulty for the inspired word of God is inclusive. It can catch together in this one phrase, although describing the longings of men in Hezekiah's day, all the dwellings of God, for each can be described by the man who longs for them as lovely. It could be the tabernacle of old, or Solomon's temple or, with particular relevance to ourselves, the Lord Jesus Christ. Wherever God is pleased to dwell must appear lovely to those who truly seek Him in the midst of the ugliness of this world of sin and death. We remember that God was in the Lord Jesus Christ, "reconciling the world unto himself" and when we behold the beauty of his holiness, the moral excellence of his character, then we should feel an overwhelming desire to be like him – to be numbered amongst those whom, in him, God will be pleased to call His sons and daughters.

In this respect the psalm, although having a particular historical background, is relevant to all who are "strangers and pilgrims on the earth" (Hebrews 11:13), who look "for a city which hath foundations, whose builder and maker is God" (verse 10).

> "My soul longeth, yea, even fainteth for the courts of the LORD: my heart and my flesh crieth out for the living God."
> (Psalm 84:2)

The verbs are in the perfect tense (*Cambridge Bible*) and thus the sense is rather 'my soul hath longed; yea, even fainted'. The word rendered "longed" means literally 'hath grown pale', and that translated "fainted" more exactly means 'faileth'. It is an expression of the intensity of the longing experienced. Like those who "watch for the morning" (Psalm 130:6), it was as though the tension had been etched on their faces. There was a physical reaction to their inward yearning.

The reference to "the courts of the LORD" seems conclusive in establishing the reference to the temple, and it must be observed that it was not the building itself that was the object of their desire but what it represented. It was the temple of "the living God". That was where He dwelt and there He was to be found. It was the opportunity to worship and meet with Him there, in a way that was not possible anywhere else on earth, that filled their hearts with joy. The verb "crieth out" carries the idea of 'joyous singing' and this pouring forth of the hearts in songs of joy was, no doubt, a characteristic of their pilgrimage and of its consummation when they appeared before God in Zion.

The phrase "living God" is a link with Hezekiah's experiences. As Rabshakeh taunts the king, pointing to the Assyrian victories over surrounding nations, he asks:

"Have the gods of (these) nations delivered them?"

(2 Kings 19:12)

Hezekiah's response was to recognise that their gods were but wood and stone, whereas his trust was in the living God (2 Kings 19:4):

"O Lord God of Israel, which dwellest between the cherubims, thou art the God, even thou alone, of all the kingdoms of the earth; thou hast made heaven and earth. Lord, bow down thine ear, and hear: open, Lord, thine eyes, and see: and hear the words of Sennacherib, which hath sent him to reproach the living God."

(2 Kings 19:15,16)

It was with soul, heart and flesh that the Psalmist desired to worship God. With his natural emotions, his spiritual aspirations and with his body, the total living being was used in praise and worship. It was the dedication of every part; the whole man. We might compare the Psalmist's insight as to what constitutes the whole man with Paul's description of "spirit and soul and body" (1 Thessalonians 5:23). We might reasonably deduce from this comparison that heart and spirit are descriptive of the same quality.

The Psalmist reminisces on the fact that in his exile he had thought of the birds of the air who had unhindered access to the temple and its precincts:

665

"Yea, the sparrow hath found an house, and the swallow a nest for herself, where she may lay her young, even thine altars, O LORD of hosts, my King, and my God."   (verse 3)

No doubt these thoughts would have been very real to the Psalmist as he thought how he was cut off from the temple, whereas the birds had free access to its courts and altars. He would surely have likened himself to the birds, as he longed for a similar freedom, and perhaps this is sufficient reason for us to see spiritual lessons for ourselves. They were two quite different birds: the tiny fluttering sparrow and the graceful swallow, yet they found a place to rest, a place of refuge in God's house. So it is with us. We might be quite different in the natural qualities and abilities we bring but there is room for us all in God's house. It might be noted also that whereas the sparrow was indigenous to the land, the swallow was a migratory bird, and so perhaps we see not only that God's house offers sanctuary to people of all kinds but also to both Jew and Gentile.

There is something very poignant about these words concerning the birds of the air, for the fact that such humble creatures could find rest in the vicinity of God's altars is highlighted by the manner in which the Psalmist speaks of God as "Yahweh of hosts, my king and my God". We know that though "five sparrows (are) sold for two farthings ... not one of them is forgotten before God" (Luke 12:6). We "are of more value than many sparrows" (verse 7). How much greater then the blessing enjoyed by those who seek to dwell in God's house. They are under the protection of the heavenly host (Psalm 34:7), appointed by the One who is our King and our God. Truly the Psalmist could exclaim:

"Blessed are they that dwell in thy house: they will be still praising thee."   (Psalm 84:4)

In Psalm 42 the writer expressed his longing and his confidence "for I shall yet praise him for the help of his countenance" (verse 5). Now in the courts of the temple that longing is fulfilled: his happiness (blessedness) is complete. The verb describing his praise carries the idea of perpetuity; it has the sense of 'again and again'. It is the

666

expression of deep-felt joy, of lasting satisfaction. It is seen in the pouring forth of continual praise.

His Determination (verses 5-8)

"Blessed is the man whose strength is in thee: in whose heart are the ways of them." (verse 5)

The Psalmist reflects on his journey; the manner in which all obstacles had been surmounted and all difficulties overcome. Great is the happiness of such a man whose strength is in God.

It has been observed that both in the Hebrew of the Old Testament and the Greek of the New Testament the exhortation to "be strong" is never in the active voice, but always in the passive voice. Literally it is, 'be ye strengthened'. God is not looking for strong men who could glory in the flesh, but men and women of humble and contrite spirit who tremble at His word, in which they have learned that "(His) strength is made perfect in weakness" (2 Corinthians 12:9).

The word rendered "way" means literally 'highway', and taken at face value the verse says that we must have the highways in our heart. The question we ask is, "What highways?" We have to supply an answer and the translators of the RV have surely shown a true instinct for the meaning of the passage, taking its context into account, by rendering the words, "in whose heart are the highways to Zion".

They were well trodden paths in the days of Hezekiah and, through the word of God, we can travel the same way that all men of God traverse and that will bring us eventually to Zion. No doubt those Levites knew every step of the way and if we treasure in our hearts the pathways that will bring us eventually to "appear before God", then great indeed will be our happiness. However, in the journey to Zion, whether it be literal or spiritual, there are difficulties to be overcome. It is necessary to pass "through the valley of Baca" (verse 6).

The word "Baca" is from a root which means 'to weep'. It is thought to be associated with the balsam tree which exuded 'tears' of gum (*Cambridge Bible*) and flourished in dry and arid valleys. So for the man who treasures the "highways to Zion", even the "vale of tears" becomes "springs" (verse 6, RV) – places of refreshment and healing (the balsam produced the balm of Gilead).

When adversity and tribulation overtake him he is not crushed by the weight but he uses them to his advantage, recognising that "whom the LORD loveth he correcteth" (Proverbs 3:12; Hebrews 12:5,6). All these apparent obstacles serve only to heighten his desire and help to mould his character. The divine initiative is recognised for, "Yea, the early rain covereth it with blessings" (verse 6, RV).

In response to the faith of the pilgrim, who refuses to be daunted by the difficulties of the way, God pours forth His blessings. He sends the early rain (see Joel 2:23, margin, "teacher of righteousness") which, with its soft gentle showers, stands in scripture for the teaching of the word of God (see Deuteronomy 32:2; 2 Samuel 23:4; Isaiah 55:10). It is His doctrine, the sweet influences of the word, that produces the faith that can overcome the obstacles of the way. It is the word of God interacting with the experiences of life that can cause faith to develop and mature so that every difficulty and trial becomes a milestone on the journey to Zion:

"They go from strength to strength, every one of them in Zion appeareth before God."   (verse 7)

Instead of fainting in the way, they derive fresh strength from each experience and gain deeper insight and new vigour, with the vision of their ultimate destination all the clearer and sharper because of the contrast with "the weeping" sometimes associated with the way. Spiritually:

"They that wait upon the LORD shall renew their strength; they shall mount up with wings as eagles; they shall run, and not be weary; and they shall walk, and not faint."   (Isaiah 40:31)

We must not to take the words, "appear before God" too literally. The Psalmist is dwelling upon the pilgrimages made three times each year to celebrate the feasts:

"Three times in the year all thy males shall appear before the Lord GOD."   (Exodus 23:17; 34:23)

The word rendered "appear" is from a root meaning 'to see' (*Strong's*). They were to be seen before God on these special occasions. It is only when we move from the literal background of the psalm to the spiritual experience of those whose pilgrimage takes them through the wilderness of life that the words take on, for us, a deeper and fuller meaning. That we are justified in seeking this deeper significance is evident from the prayer of the Psalmist that concludes this section:

"O LORD God of hosts, hear my prayer: give ear, O God of Jacob. Selah." (verse 8)

That God should be described as the Lord of hosts is appropriate given the host of the Assyrian encamped against Jerusalem. It was a recognition that –

"they that be with us are more than they that be with them." (2 Kings 6:16)

Nevertheless, there is an aptness also about the linking together of the Lord's host of angels and the "God of Jacob", for there is no other man in scripture in whose life the angels of God were more clearly manifest than his (Genesis 28:10-22; 32:1,2,24-32; 48:15,16). It is significant that Jacob should say after one of these experiences, "I have seen God face to face" (Genesis 32:30). He had wrestled with an angel and in the trials and tribulations of life we, likewise, wrestle in prayer and spiritually clasp around the angel, as Jacob did, and echo his words, "I will not let thee go, except thou bless me" (Genesis 32:26). It is as though in the experiences of life we too see the face of God; not literally, of course, but in the recognition of His hand in our lives. It is in the assurance that His presence is with us that we are confident also that eventually we "shall ascend into the hill of the LORD" and "stand in his holy place" (Psalm 24:3), for "this is the generation of them that seek after him, that seek thy face, O God of Jacob" (Psalm 24:6, RV).

Prayer for God to Fulfil His Desire (verses 9-12)

The Psalmist develops the prayer of verse 8:

"Behold, O God our shield, and look upon the face of thine anointed." (verse 9)

669

There are two ways to understand the opening phrase: firstly, as in the AV, to regard God as the shield; secondly, following the RV margin to understand "our shield" as the object of the verb 'behold', and thus to maintain a parallelism with the second clause of the verse, i.e., "behold our shield" and "look upon thine anointed".

Thus the anointed is also described as the shield of his people. Clearly God's anointed is King Hezekiah, and in this context he would also be the shield, the protector and defender of the people. Certainly, throughout the crisis created by the Assyrian invasion, the people had rested upon Hezekiah and it was his faith and example that sustained them. He was also God's representative and as such was a symbol of the divine protection (see Psalm 89:18, RV, where God's anointed King is described as a shield).

The desire that God would behold or look upon Hezekiah with favour is understandable when we remember his sickness and the dreadful depths to which the nation had sunk before the might of Assyria. In a very real sense he had been "the saviour" of his people under the hand of their God.

The little word "for" implies a connection that is not immediately apparent: "For a day in thy courts is better than a thousand. I had rather be a doorkeeper in the house of my God, than to dwell in the tents of wickedness" (verse 10).

There is a suggestion in these words that a specific day is intended, not just any day – in that sense not a day of twenty-four hours as such, but a day of victory and rejoicing. Thus Psalm 118 (a psalm of Hezekiah) speaks of "the day which the LORD hath made; we will rejoice and be glad in it" (verse 24). It is in this context that the Psalmist can think of the joy of dwelling in the courts of the Lord. To be there rejoicing in all that God had done for His people was far better than a thousand days spent elsewhere. Even the meanest position in the house of God, humbly to serve at His threshold, brings far greater joy and satisfaction than anything known by the wicked in their habitations. So for us, our service to God should bring a happiness far beyond anything that this world has to offer:

> "For the LORD God is a sun and a shield: the LORD will give grace and glory: no good thing will he withhold from them that walk uprightly." (Psalm 84:11)

It is striking that the Psalmist should speak of *Yahweh Elohim*. Using statistics derived from *Ellicott's Commentary*, we find that the name and this title are conjoined twenty times between Genesis 2:4 and Genesis 3:24, yet only nine times in the rest of the Old Testament. The accuracy of the figures might be questioned if account is taken of some variant readings, but this does not affect the point being addressed.

The consideration of this psalm is not the place for a detailed examination of the significance of God's name and title, but its use in the record of the creation and fall of man must be a clear indication that its meaning is bound up with God's purpose in man. It must point to Yahweh's ultimate intention to be made manifest in "bringing many sons unto glory" (Hebrews 2:10).

This is one of only two occurrences of the words in apposition in the Book of Psalms (see also 72:18), and its use in this context leads us to conclude that the scripture is pointing to the fact that the deliverance wrought in the life of Hezekiah was in a special sense a type of the work of salvation that God would accomplish in the person of the Lord Jesus Christ.

The Lord God is a sun and a shield; both the provider of light and of protection. Although there are passages that liken Messiah to the sun (see Malachi 4:2), this is the only occurrence in scripture that directly uses the metaphor of God Himself.

Could there be an allusion here to the glory of God that Moses saw (Exodus 33,34)? Is the manifestation of brightness and majesty that he was privileged to behold likened to the sun? When God's glory passed by, Moses was shielded, for "I will put thee in a clift of the rock, and will cover thee with my hand while I pass by" (Exodus 33:22). Admittedly these links are tenuous, but the words that follow are more decisive: "The LORD will give grace and glory".

671

The word rendered "grace" signifies 'favour' and it is the word employed by Moses repeatedly, having first been used of Moses by the Lord Himself:

"Thou hast also found grace in my sight."
(Exodus 33:12)

"If I have found grace in thy sight, shew me now thy way, that I may know thee, that I may find grace in thy sight." (verse 13)

"For wherein shall it be known here that I and thy people have found grace in thy sight?" (verse 16)

"For thou hast found grace in my sight, and I know thee by name." (verse 17)

"If I now have found grace in thy sight, O Lord, let my Lord, I pray thee, go among us." (Exodus 34:9)

The word rendered "glory" is the same Hebrew word (*kabowd*) used in Exodus 33 and 34 but its use here is a warning to us not to use words like mathematical equations. In different contexts they can have different values and it is context that must guide us in our interpretation of their meaning. Thus the word is often rendered "honour" and this seems to be the sense here. The God who shows favour to them that seek Him will give honour to them also. Surely God honoured Moses when He declared His name. Such will finally be vindicated in the sight of men for, "no good thing will he withhold from them that walk uprightly" (verse 11).

The word rendered "uprightly" means literally 'to be entire or complete'. It is often translated "perfect", not in the absolute sense, but descriptive of the man who is single-minded, who maintains his integrity before God. From such our Father in Heaven will withhold no good thing. All blessings flow from Him and the ultimate good is eternal life (cp. Psalm 34:12; 1 Peter 3:10). It is His good pleasure to give us the kingdom (Luke 12:32).

Truly we can say with the Psalmist:

"O LORD of hosts, blessed is the man that trusteth in thee." (Psalm 84:12)

PSALM 85

THE opening words of this psalm have led many to conclude that it belongs to the period after the exile in Babylon. This view overlooks the fact that there was a captivity in the days of Hezekiah that, we might infer from scripture, was far more extensive than that we know took place in the days of Nebuchadnezzar. Not only were the inhabitants of Judah carried away when Sennacherib's army ravaged the land but many would have sought refuge in neighbouring countries. Only eight years previously the Northern Kingdom had succumbed before the might of Assyria and they too had been carried away to a strange land. Isaiah testifies to this captivity:

"Until the cities be wasted without inhabitant, and the houses without man, and the land be utterly desolate, and the LORD have removed men far away, and there be a great forsaking in the midst of the land."

(6:11,12)

Similarly, Hezekiah's ambassadors to the prophet Isaiah request him to "lift up thy prayer for the remnant that is left" (37:4). The clear implication is that not only had the land been desolated but the people carried away captive. There was but a remnant left. That some, at least, of this captivity returned is evident. The references to returning exiles both in the Psalms and in the writings of Isaiah bear powerful testimony to the fact that after the destruction of his army, Sennacherib, if he did not expel them from his sight, at the very least treated them with consideration and allowed any that were disposed to return, to do so.

That the prophecies written against this background, have a future fulfilment at the time of the end is beyond dispute, but we must not ignore the relevance of the passages to the events of those times. For these events

673

formed the basis of both the prophet's and Psalmist's visions of the future. Thus the prophet Isaiah testifies:

"And there shall be an highway for the remnant of his people, which shall be left, from Assyria; like as it was to Israel in the day that he came up out of the land of Egypt." (11:16)

"And it shall come to pass in that day, that the great trumpet shall be blown, and they shall come which were ready to perish in the land of Assyria, and the outcasts in the land of Egypt, and shall worship the LORD in the holy mount at Jerusalem." (27:13)

(see also 35:10; 43:5-6; 48:20; 56:8, etc.)

We note in the latter passage the reference to "the great trumpet" and it is hard to escape the conclusion that this is a reference to the Jubilee trumpet (Leviticus 25:8-13). The two features of the Jubilee that we note in this connection are the release of the captive, for "ye shall return every man unto his possession" and the blessing of the ground which was to bring forth of its increase to sustain them although they had let it lie fallow in obedience to the divine command (see verses 19-21).

The appropriateness of the Jubilee trumpet to the returning captives is obvious, but the blessing of the land is also referred to in connection with the devastation that the Assyrian must have left behind:

"And this shall be a sign unto thee, Ye shall eat this year such things as grow of themselves, and in the second year that which springeth of the same; and in the third year sow ye, and reap, and plant vineyards, and eat the fruit thereof." (2 Kings 19:29)

(see also Isaiah 55:12,13)

Whether it was actually a Jubilee year we cannot say. But if not, God treated them in the deliverance wrought as though it was and they enjoyed the blessings of His hand. We shall return to the theme of the Jubilee in our consideration of the psalm. Notwithstanding what we have written, however, we do not believe that the words of verse 1 are a direct allusion to this return from captivity; although all that we have written we believe to be relevant to the background of the psalm.

There is a difficulty that has been observed by almost all commentaries on this psalm. The opening verses (1-3) speak of God's forgiveness and His favour towards His land. They have experienced this because He has taken away His wrath and turned away the fierceness of His anger. However, verses 4 to 6 are a further plea for God to cause His anger to cease and to revive His people that they may rejoice in Him. The accomplished fact of verses 1 to 3 appears to be contradicted by the prayer of verses 4 to 7. We believe that the explanation lies in the history of the times as outlined above. We have previously drawn attention to the fact that references to "captivity" do not necessarily imply a sojourn in prison or in a foreign land. On occasion the allusion is to deliverance from trouble and calamity. Thus, "the LORD turned the captivity of Job" (Job 42:10; see also Psalm 14:7; 53:6; 126:1,4).

So it was that the Lord delivered Judah out of the hand of the Assyrian. The angel of the Lord went forth and slew Sennacherib's army. In that event and in the days immediately following, the people would have felt in their joy and zeal that God had forgiven them and turned away His wrath from them – as indeed He had. The land was, however, in great distress. There was the danger of famine and disease. The cities of Judah were broken down and, in human terms, they still remained vulnerable to any predators (neighbouring nations) that might seek to prey on them. So after the initial elation there would be conflicting emotions: a realisation that it was only in the continuation of God's blessing that a full recovery could be achieved; the thought of their brethren carried away by the Assyrian would weigh heavily upon them. It is in the realisation of all these factors that the Psalmist presents us, not with a contradiction, but with a reflection of the complementary emotions that would arise in the hearts of the people at this particular time.

The psalm falls easily into two sections:

1. The people's prayer (verses 1-7).

2. The assurance of God's faithfulness (verses 8-13).

God has Forgiven and Blessed His people (verses1-3)

"LORD, thou hast been favourable unto thy land: thou hast brought back the captivity of Jacob. Thou hast forgiven the iniquity of thy people, thou hast covered all their sin. Selah. Thou hast taken away all thy wrath: thou hast turned thyself from the fierceness of thine anger." (verses 1-3)

It is important to appreciate that the things that had befallen Israel and Judah were the consequences of their continued sinfulness. This resulted in God, in wrath and anger, bringing the Assyrian into the land.

We have already commented in the previous introductory chapter on the manner in which the people, generally, came to trust in riches (Psalm 49). The wealth and prosperity enjoyed in the days of Jeroboam II of Israel and Uzziah of Judah are the underlying causes for much of the injustice and oppression of the poor that filled those lands in these days. The Northern Kingdom was, of course, largely given over to idolatry as well (2 Kings 14:23,24), but in the days of Uzziah and Jotham it would appear that Judah maintained an outward form of true worship (2 Chronicles 26:3,4; 27:1,2). We note, however, the comment in this last passage regarding the reign of Jotham: "And the people did yet corruptly".

That the sin of the people was developing and spreading in the days of Uzziah is evident. Isaiah's vision of the glory of God and his obedience to God's call came in the year that King Uzziah died (Isaiah 6:1). It is interesting to note that Isaiah confesses his own sinfulness and acknowledges that of the people in the language of leprosy:

"Then said I, Woe is me! for I am undone; because I am a man of unclean lips, and I dwell in the midst of a people of unclean lips." (Isaiah 6:5)

It was as if, spiritually, the leprosy of the king (2 Chronicles 26:19-23) clave to the people. His pride and arrogance, which led to his presumptuous sin, was a reflection of the attitude of the people generally. Isaiah testified against them:

676

"Ah sinful nation, a people laden with iniquity, a seed of evildoers, children that are corrupters: they have forsaken the LORD, they have provoked the Holy One of Israel unto anger, they are gone away backward." (1:4) Notice again how Isaiah continues in the language of leprosy:

"Why should ye be stricken any more? ye will revolt more and more: the whole head is sick, and the whole heart faint. From the sole of the foot even unto the head there is no soundness in it; but wounds, and bruises, and putrifying sores: they have not been closed, neither bound up, neither mollified with ointment." (verses 5,6)

The moral depravity that had simmered just under the surface was now breaking out (see Isaiah 6:9,10) and it was this disregard for the right ways of God that created the situation in which the grosser, religious sins of Ahaz developed and grew like a canker in the land (2 Chronicles 28:1-4). It was for these reasons that God said:

"O Assyrian, the rod of mine anger, and the staff in their hand is mine indignation. I will send him against an hypocritical nation, and against the people of my wrath will I give him a charge, to take the spoil, and to take the prey, and to tread them down like the mire of the streets." (Isaiah 10:5,6)

Although Hezekiah had cleansed the land of idolatry and false worship, his reform had touched the hearts of only a remnant of the people, and the Assyrian brought home to the nation generally the reality of their sin and the wrath of their God. When therefore the Lord destroyed Sennacherib's host, principally because of Hezekiah's righteousness and intercession, how deeply would the inhabitants of Jerusalem in particular have felt that God had forgiven their sins, and turned away His wrath and indignation from them.

A Prayer for God to Continue to Show Mercy (verses 4-7)

As already intimated, this elation at God's deliverance would be tempered by the realisation that the land was still desolate, the threat of famine very real and the people generally in great distress. This would have brought a realisation that their need for God's continued blessing was a matter of pressing concern and that if they were to receive it they must turn again to the Lord their God. So they cried:

> "Turn us, O God of our salvation, and cause thine anger towards us to cease. Wilt thou be angry with us for ever? wilt thou draw out thine anger to all generations? Wilt thou not revive us again: that thy people may rejoice in thee? Shew us thy mercy, O LORD, and grant us thy salvation."   (verses 4-7)

The consequential distress of the Assyrian invasion was perceived by many as evidence that God's anger had not been completely removed. Hence the plea, "Turn to us (RV margin), O God of our salvation, and cause thine anger towards us to cease" (verse 4). That God was a Saviour was acknowledged. They had recent experience of this fact but the desolation of the land was, in a sense, a reflection of their own spiritual condition. Like the land, they too needed the reviving power of God's word to enable them to bring forth fruit abundantly.

The questions posed are surely rhetorical and there can be no doubt what the answers would be. If God turned to them and they responded to His overtures of mercy, then He would not be angry for ever or draw out His indignation to all generations. He would "quicken" them (verse 6, RV) and they would rejoice in His blessings. So the final sentiments of their prayer:

> "Shew us thy mercy, O LORD, and grant us thy salvation."   (verse 7)

God's mercy (Hebrew, *chesed*) embraces His faithfulness towards His people, the love that He bare them in the bonds of the covenant. In these final words of prayer all that the people desired is encompassed as they looked for His salvation.

God's Answer to Their Prayers (verses 8-13)

Like the prophet Habakkuk (2:1) the Psalmist will hold himself in readiness to hear the answer of God:

> "I will hear what God the LORD will speak."   (verse 8)

His trust is in the word of God, for what He speaks He will perform. As he hears so he communicates to the people:

678

"For he will speak peace unto his people, and to his saints: but let them not turn again to folly."   (verse 8)

Here is the answer to their prayer. He will speak to them in peace and bless them provided they do not turn back to the pride and confidence in self that led to unbelief and disobedience. This had been their folly (Psalm 14:1).

"His people" and "his saints" are complementary terms. The word 'saints' (*chasidim*) is derived from the word *chesed*, rendered "mercy" above. In this context it is clearly intended to describe those who have experienced the lovingkindness of God, who because they "have made a covenant with (him) by sacrifice" (Psalm 50:5) are counted as His "holy ones".

The consequence of the word of peace was that those who feared Him, who were faithful to their calling as saints, would find that His salvation was nigh them and that these blessings would be enjoyed "that glory may dwell in our land" (verse 9).

"Glory" speaks of the presence of God tabernacling amongst them. The word "dwell" is that which describes the abiding of God in the Most Holy Place when His splendour shone from between the cherubim. From this word was derived the term *Shekinah* which is used to represent the presence of God in the temple and the tabernacle. That it has its ultimate fulfilment in the Lord Jesus Christ and the kings and priests of the future age is evident, for it will be said:

"Behold, the tabernacle of God is with men, and he will dwell with them, and they shall be his people, and God himself shall be with them, and be their God."
(Revelation 21:3,4)

God's presence was the token of His blessing, His glory the assurance that He was with them once more. When God's glory was revealed to Moses He described His Name:

"The LORD, The LORD God, merciful and gracious, longsuffering and abundant in goodness and truth, keeping mercy for thousands, forgiving iniquity and transgression and sin, and that will by no means clear the guilty."   (Exodus 34:6,7)

679

These divine attributes, manifest through His name, are now personified in a marvellous way as mercy and truth. His love for His people and His fidelity to the covenant meet together in the salvation of His people. As with a kiss, righteousness and peace have greeted each other in the divine blessing upon His land and His people (verses 9,10). These four divine attributes, indicative of the manifestation of God's name in human experience, are bound together and conspire together in perfect harmony to produce the desired result. These are attributes of the Deity, yet they speak also of the Lord Jesus Christ in whom the Father was manifest. These are the qualities that will appertain on the earth in the day when he sits on the throne of David (Psalm 72:1-3; 89:14; Isaiah 32:16,17). Where these qualities are manifest among men, the result must always be true joy and perfect harmony.

The people of Judah enjoyed this blessing in the days of Hezekiah for:

"Truth shall spring out of the earth; and righteousness shall look down from heaven. Yea, the LORD shall give that which is good; and our land shall yield her increase."   (verses 11,12)

Truth (i.e., faithfulness) shall spring out of the earth as the natural response to heaven's blessing. In the tokens of His presence among them their faith will be renewed, for the picture is of harmony between heaven and earth (see Isaiah 45:8; Hosea 2:21-23).

The language now relates to the passage from 2 Kings that we quoted in the introduction. As in the Jubilee, God blessed the land and, as in other scriptures, the fruitfulness of the ground is a reflection of the spiritual revival of the people. Having described the bountifulness of the harvest (2 Kings 19:29), the Lord speaking through Isaiah says:

"And the remnant that is escaped of the house of Judah shall yet again take root downward, and bear fruit upward."   (verse 30; see Isaiah 37:31)

In the words of the Psalmist:

"The LORD shall give that which is good; and our land shall yield her increase."   (verse 12)

680

There is here an echo from the words of the preceding psalm: "No good thing will he withhold from them that walk uprightly" (84:11). Although not conclusive, it helps to establish the link between the two for these were the things in which the sons of Korah rejoiced and concerning which they would have spoken to each other day by day.

In all these manifestations of His goodness that resulted in the salvation of His people, the Lord had, as it were, gone before them and continuing the personification of the previous verses, "righteousness" had been His herald:

"Righteousness shall go before him; and shall make his footsteps a way to walk in." (verse 13, RV)

In His wonderful works His righteousness had been displayed. They had seen His ways, they had been taught His paths; now the responsibility was theirs to walk in His footsteps, to follow where He led and to embrace in their lives that righteousness so that it might be their experience that righteousness and peace should kiss each other. The result would be that Truth should spring out of the earth.

PSALM 86

THIS is not a psalm of the sons of Korah. It bears the title, "A prayer of David". It is one of only two psalms that bear this title, the other being Psalm 17. It is also the only psalm of David to appear in what is commonly known as the Third Book of Psalms (Psalms 73 to 89), all the other psalms being Levitical in character, that is, associated with the families of either Asaph or Korah.

Commentators have little to say about this psalm, except that most doubt it was written by David. None that we have read addresses the problem why this one psalm should be inserted amongst those as being for the "Sons of Korah" – all of which, we have argued, are associated with the reign of good King Hezekiah. One feature that almost all emphasise is that it lacks any obvious structure and appears to be composed of phrases and allusions drawn mainly from other psalms and also from certain other specific passages of scripture. One writer has called it "a mosaic of fragments" (the *Cambridge Bible*).

An exception to the general view is found in the *Speaker's Commentary* where the writer claims that the poetic form of the psalm follows that of Psalm 85 precisely. This is not a matter on which we feel competent to judge but, if this were so, we might infer a close connection between the two as far as authorship is concerned. Why then does it claim to be a psalm of David? With the aid principally of the *Cambridge Bible*, we have prepared the following table indicating the references to other psalms. Those marked with an asterisk are, we understand, verbatim or almost verbatim quotations from those psalms. It will be observed that every psalm quoted is in fact a psalm of David, so that in effect whoever actually compiled Psalm 86 it could still be described as a prayer of David. We suggest that this psalm is a distillation of the meditations of the Sons of Korah (or of Hezekiah himself) upon the psalms of David, with the words and thoughts of the sweet Psalmist of Israel brought together in such a manner as to make them appropriate to the events and circumstances of their times.

It was truly, in their minds, a prayer of David; yet a prayer that could be repeated meaningfully by their king, Hezekiah.

Psalm 86	Text	Psalms of David	Text
verse 1	Bow down thine ear, O LORD ...	31:2	Bow down thine ear to me.
	for I am poor and needy.	40:17	But I am poor and needy.*
verse 2	Preserve my soul	25:20	O keep my soul.*
verse 3	Be merciful to me, O LORD: for I cry unto thee daily.	57:1,2	Be merciful unto me, O God ... I will cry unto God.
verse 4	For unto thee, O Lord, do I lift up my soul.	25:1	Unto thee, O LORD, do I lift up my soul.*
verse 6	Give ear, O LORD, unto my prayer; and attend to the voice of my supplications.	55:1	Give ear to my prayer, O God; and hide not thyself from my supplication.
verse 7	In the day of my trouble I will call upon thee: for thou wilt answer me.	17:6	I have called upon thee, for thou wilt hear me.
verse 9	All nations whom thou hast made shall come, and worship before thee, O Lord.	22:27	All the ends of the world shall remember and turn unto the LORD: and all the kindreds of the nations shall worship before thee.*

* Verbatim or almost verbatim quotations in Psalm 86

verse 11	Teach me thy way, O LORD;	27:11	Teach me thy way, O LORD* (see also 25:4,5).
	I will walk in thy truth: unite my heart to fear thy name.	26:3	I have walked in thy truth.
		26:11	I will walk in mine integrity (see also 26:1).
verse 12	I will praise thee, O Lord my God with all my heart: and I will glorify thy name.	9:1	I will praise thee, O LORD, with my whole heart.
		50:23	Whoso offereth praise glorifieth me.
verse 13	Thou hast delivered my soul from the lowest hell.	56:13	Thou hast delivered my soul from death.
verse 14	O God, the proud are risen against me	54:3	For strangers are risen up against me.*
	... the assemblies of violent men.	22:16	The assembly of the wicked.
verse 16	O turn unto me, and have mercy upon me.	25:16	Turn thee unto me, and have mercy upon me.
verse 17	Show me a token for good: that they which hate me may see it.	40:3	He hath put a new song in my mouth ... many shall see it and fear.

The quotations and allusions might appear, of themselves, to be very general in character but it must be appreciated that it is the contexts from which they were drawn that would have been in the Psalmist's mind, and a consideration of the background and context of these psalms will reveal how appropriate they are to the circumstances in which Hezekiah found himself.

It will be observed that the only verses in the psalm that have not been identified in some way with a psalm of David are verses 5,8,10,15 and these contain direct quotations or allusions to Exodus 15 and 34. We reproduce these in the following table.

---

* Verbatim or almost verbatim quotations in Psalm 86

Psalm 86	Text	Exodus	Text
verse 5	For thou, Lord, art good, and ready to forgive; and plenteous in mercy unto all them that call upon thee.	34:6,7	The LORD, The LORD God, merciful and gracious, longsuffering, and abundant in goodness and truth, keeping mercy for thousands, forgiving iniquity.
verse 8	Among the gods there is none like unto thee.	15:11	Who is like unto thee, O LORD, among the gods?
verse 10	For thou art great, and doest wondrous things: thou art God alone.	15:11	Doing wonders.
		34:10	Before all thy people I will do marvels.
verse 15	But thou, O Lord, art a God full of compassion, and gracious, longsuffering, and plenteous in mercy and truth.	34:6,7	*see above.*

Exodus 15 is the record of the Song of Moses, which he sang to celebrate the manner in which the God of Israel had triumphed gloriously in destroying the host of Pharaoh, king of Egypt. Its relevance to the destruction of Sennacherib's army needs no further explanation. Of further interest are the words of Hezekiah's prayer when he spread the letter from Rabshakeh before the Lord (Isaiah 37:14):

"O LORD of hosts, God of Israel, that dwellest between the cherubims, thou art the God, even thou alone, of all the kingdoms of the earth: thou hast made heaven and earth." (Isaiah 37:16)

The echoes of Exodus 15 are evident. The references to the occasion when God declared His name to Moses are very relevant to the manner in which God's grace was manifested towards His people, His faithfulness to the covenant that He had made with them.

The thought of God's fidelity to the covenant is emphasised in this psalm. The word rendered "holy" by which the Psalmist describes himself (verse 2) is clearly related to that rendered "saints" in Psalm 85 (verse 8). He is not describing the quality of his life so much as the privilege he enjoys in experiencing, through the covenant, the lovingkindness of his God. The word is closely connected with *chesed* (Psalm 85:7) and this word is used three times in Psalm 86 (verses 5,13,15) to emphasise the love that God had towards His people.

The pertinent comment was made by one writer that, although on occasions the word "saint" is used of individuals in the Old Testament, the equivalent Greek word is never used of an individual, but only of a collective company of believers. This observation makes clear the foolishness of those who, contrary to scripture, seek to canonise individuals who, in their estimation, have lived 'saintly' lives.

One further feature of this psalm needs to be noted. That is the fact that on seven occasions the writer uses the title *Adonai*, translated "Lord", to address God (verses 3,4,5,8,9,12,15). The word describes the sovereignty of God and is particularly appropriate to those who dwell under His special care and protection. It is plural in form and while some would refer again to 'a plural of majesty', we can appreciate that He who is manifest through a host of angels (who minister to the heirs of salvation and work out His will amongst the nations) could most aptly apply the title, in this form, to Himself.

Although in one sense the psalm is all of a piece we might, for convenience divide it as follows:

1. The Psalmist's petitions (verses 1-5).

2. The uniqueness of the God of Israel (verses 6-10).

3. A further prayer for continued blessing (verses 11-17).

Another reason for this division is that each of these sections begins with the name of God, Yahweh only occurring four times in the psalm (i.e., verses 1,6,11 and in the concluding ascription of praise – verse 17).

The Psalmist's Petitions (verses 1-5)

The Psalmist bases his prayer to God upon that which he has shown himself to be by his behaviour before Him. Each petition is followed by the grounds of his plea. Thus:

Bow down thine ear, O LORD, and hear me	... for I am poor and needy (verse 1)
Preserve my soul ... O thou my God, save thy servant.	... for I am holy ... that trusteth in thee (verse 2)
Be merciful unto me, O Lord	... for I cry unto thee daily (verse 3)
Rejoice the soul of thy servant	... for unto thee, O Lord, do I lift up my soul (verse 4)

Compared in this way, the Psalmist's prayer is that God would bow down, hear, preserve, save, be merciful and "rejoice the soul of His servant". The reasons he asks God to show such favour towards him is because he is poor, needy yet holy, and puts his trust in Him. He cries unto Him daily for unto Him alone he lifts up his soul.

He beseeched God to hear and answer his prayer because of the plight in which he found himself. "Poor and needy" describes his condition and it can be seen how fittingly it describes Hezekiah at the time that he was sick unto death, with the Assyrian threatening Jerusalem and dissension amongst his advisors as to what they should do. He rests, however, in the fact that he is holy (AV margin, "one whom thou favourest"). He is one of God's covenant people and receives the divine blessing for his trust in God and this is manifest by the manner in which he continues in prayer daily.

Although he begins by pleading for relief from his own distress, he concludes with a declaration that God alone is the true object of all his aspirations and desires:

"For thou Lord, art good, and ready to forgive; and plenteous in mercy unto all them that call upon thee."

(verse 5)

As the section opens with an address to Yahweh, so also it contains a reference to that name declared (see preceding table) and this feature will be seen to be true of each of the other sections.

The Uniqueness of the God of Israel (verses 6-10)

"Give ear, O LORD, unto my prayer, and attend to the voice of my supplications." (verse 6)

687

That God will hear, the Psalmist is confident, for He will answer his prayer (verse 7). In verse 5 he had spoken of his assurance that God was *willing* to save; now he declares his confidence that God is *able* to save, for:

> "Among the gods there is none like unto thee, O Lord; neither are there any works like unto thy works. All nations whom thou hast made shall come and worship before thee, O Lord; and shall glorify thy name. For thou art great, and doest wondrous things: thou art God alone."   (verses 8-10)

The wonder of His works was seen in the destruction of Sennacherib's host and the marvellous way in which He revived both the people and the land. The words carry us forward to the kingdom age and it is surely against this background that both Isaiah and Micah prophesied (Isaiah 2 and Micah 4).

The Apocalypse describes the consummation of this purpose when they shall sing –

> "the song of Moses [cp. Exodus 15] the servant of God, and the song of the Lamb, saying, Great and marvellous are thy works, Lord God Almighty; just and true are thy ways, thou King of saints. Who shall not fear thee, O Lord, and glorify thy name? for thou only art holy: for all nations shall come and worship before thee; for thy judgments are made manifest."   (Revelation 15:3,4)

The wonderful prophecies of the future were, no doubt, based upon the exaltation of Hezekiah and the manner in which the nations came to honour him and his God (2 Chronicles 32:23). As Rabshakeh had said in his taunting words, the gods of the nations had been unable to deliver them out of Sennacherib's hand (Isaiah 37:8-13). But those who were "called gods" were "no gods", for there was but One who was God alone. He has created all things: He is governor amongst the nations (Psalm 22:27,28). He only is able to hear and save those who put their trust in Him.

A Further Prayer (verses 11-17)

Again the Psalmist begins by addressing Yahweh, the God of Israel:

> "Teach me thy way, O LORD; I will walk in thy truth: unite my heart to fear thy name."   (verse 11)

The emphasis upon the name of God is perhaps another reference to the events of Exodus 33 and 34. Moses said, "If I have found grace in thy sight, shew me now thy way, that I may know thee" (Exodus 33:13). God showed Moses His name (Exodus 34:6,7), the qualities by which He became known among men by the manner in which He acted and reacted to the circumstances of their lives.

It is God's intention that knowing His way we should seek to enter into it, that all the qualities of His life should be seen in ours also. Then we shall walk in His truth, for this is not just something to be believed but it must have a practical expression in our lives. If this is to be true of any man then he must sort out his priorities, for he cannot have a divided loyalty. God is one, and so his heart must likewise be united in its desire to serve. He must maintain his integrity; he must be single-minded in his service, for then:

> "I will praise thee, O Lord my God, with all my heart: and I will glorify thy name for evermore. For great is thy mercy toward me: and thou hast delivered my soul from the lowest pit (RV)."　　　　　(verses 12,13)

The expression "for evermore" need not convey more than "for the rest of my life"; but nevertheless, it is appropriate to infuse it with a deeper meaning, as we look to the blessings of the age to come. Just how apt the words are to the circumstances of Hezekiah's life needs no emphasis. He was sick unto death and God delivered him from the gates of the grave:

> "I said in the cutting off of my days, I shall go to the gates of the grave: I am deprived of the residue of my years."　　　　　(Isaiah 38:10)

The Psalmist turns again to the circumstances of life. Proud and arrogant, the Assyrian had sought Hezekiah's life and blasphemed his God. Nevertheless he trusted in the God who had revealed His name to Moses and who, in contrast to his enemies, had shown Himself to be gracious and longsuffering:

> "O God, the proud are risen against me, and the assemblies of violent men have sought after my soul; and have not set thee before them. But thou, O Lord, art

a God full of compassion, and gracious, longsuffering, and plenteous in mercy and truth." (verses 14,15)

At different times in their lives these words would have been true of both David and Hezekiah. How much more were they true of the Lord Jesus Christ who was pre-eminently the Lord's anointed. It is surely significant that when the apostles prayed concerning the manner in which men had conspired together against the Lord Jesus, they quoted the words of Hezekiah (Isaiah 37:16) and David (Psalm 2; see Acts 4:24-27).

It is the revealed character of God (Exodus 34:6; Psalm 86:15) that is the basis of the Psalmist's concluding prayer:

"O turn unto me, and be gracious unto (RV margin) me; give thy strength unto thy servant, and save the son of thine handmaid. Shew me a token for good; that they which hate me may see it, and be ashamed: because thou, LORD, hast holpen me, and comforted me." (verse 16,17)

The request is that God would respond towards him in a manner consistent with His revealed character. He refers to himself as "the son of thine handmaid", and this could be understood as a synonym for "thy servant" because the word "handmaid" signifies a female slave. We note, however, that it was the word used by Hannah (1 Samuel 1:11) in connection with the birth of Samuel and also appropriated by Mary the mother of the Lord Jesus (Luke 1:38). It occurs again in Psalm 116 (verse 16) which is generally accepted as a psalm of Hezekiah, where he describes himself as "the son of thine handmaid".

Given therefore the close connection between Isaiah's prophecy and the life of Hezekiah, the phrase takes on a deeper significance as we consider this man as a type of the Lord Jesus Christ (see Isaiah 7:10-16; 9:6,7; etc.). Particularly interesting are the words of the Lord spoken to Ahaz through the prophet Isaiah:

"Ask thee a sign of the LORD thy God ... Therefore the Lord himself shall give you a sign; Behold, a virgin shall conceive, and bear a son." (Isaiah 7:11,14)

690

We are aware of the difficulties involved in the chronology of the kings of Judah and Israel at this time. Nevertheless we feel confident that these words had an incipient fulfilment in the events of Hezekiah's life. Is it not significant then that if his birth was a sign to the house of David he should, in the very next words of this psalm, request God to show him a token (same Hebrew word translated "sign") for good? It was a request that in the midst of his distress God would give a manifest and unmistakeable sign that he was His servant; so obvious that all his enemies should be filled with shame. Truly God answered Hezekiah's prayer and in that knowledge he could respond, reflecting once more upon the name of God:

"Thou, LORD, hast holpen me, and comforted me."

(verse 17)

PSALM 87

THE subscription to this psalm reads, "upon Mahalath Leannoth". In *The Titles of The Psalms* (pages 76,77) Thirtle gives reasons for reading *m'holoth*, which means 'dancings'. He interprets the meaning of the subscription as "dancing with singing". This seems most appropriate for the final verse of Psalm 87 reads, "They that sing as well as they that dance shall say ..." (verse 7, RV), and the psalm is clearly a celebration of a birth and of the integration of people of foreign extraction into the citizenship of Zion (verses 4-6). A study of the psalm establishes its relevance to the days of Hezekiah. It might be said of its seven verses that every line is pregnant with historical significance; the prophecy of Isaiah, in particular, supplying background information and allusions that give point and emphasis to the language.

The City of God's Choice

Psalm 86 was seen to have strong links with Exodus 15. In the song which he sang on that occasion Moses said:

"Thou shalt bring them in, and plant them in the mountain of thine inheritance, in the place, O LORD, which thou hast made for thee to dwell in, in the Sanctuary, O Lord, which thy hands have established. The LORD shall reign for ever and ever." (verses 17,18)

Some believe that the reference is to the land of Israel as a whole which God would give to the people He had purchased. We feel, however, that this is to overlook the significance of the references to "the mountain of thine inheritance" and "the place thou ... hast made for thee to dwell in".

The emphasis upon "the mountain" and "the place" is one that runs right through the pages of the Old

692

Testament. When God commanded Abraham to offer Isaac he was told to offer him "upon one of the mountains which I will tell thee of" (Genesis 22:2). He went to "the place of which God had told him" (verses 3,4,9). The place was not some indeterminate spot on some mountain or other, but it was a particular location on a special mountain and the significance of this becomes clear as the scriptures unfold and Moriah became the place where the temple was eventually erected.

Space does not allow a detailed list of references but, if we take the Book of Deuteronomy as an example we shall find that such words as, "But unto the place which the LORD your God shall choose out of all your tribes to put his name there, even unto his habitation shall ye seek, and thither thou shalt come" (12:5), are characteristic of the book (see also 12:11,14,18,21,26; 14:23,25; 15:20; 16:2,6, 11,16; 18:6, etc.). There was a place which, in the outworking of the purpose of God, He was to elevate above all others as the place of His habitation.

Of course, the Lord delighted in all the dwellings of His people. When Balaam beheld the tents of the children of Israel he was moved to cry: "How goodly are thy tents, O Jacob, and thy tabernacles, O Israel!" (Numbers 24:5). The Lord Himself said of their land that it was a land He cared for. His eyes were "always upon it, from the beginning of the year even unto the end of the year" (Deuteronomy 11:12).

None of these dwellings, however, could supercede the place that God had chosen and, when eventually they had been established in the land, "he refused the tabernacle of Joseph, and chose not the tribe of Ephraim: but chose the tribe of Judah, the Mount Zion which he loved" (Psalm 78:67,68). So the Psalmist, reflecting upon these truths could exclaim:

"His foundation is in the holy mountains. The LORD loveth the gates of Zion more than all the dwellings of Jacob."   (Psalm 87:1,2)

This message would have been of great comfort to the captives returning from Assyria and the surrounding countries. Faced with the devastation of the countryside they would see in the deliverance of Jerusalem and the

693

manner in which God exalted Hezekiah a token that He would be faithful to the things He had spoken concerning this place, for "Glorious things are spoken of thee, O city of God" (verse 3).

What 'transports of delight' could be written of God's purpose with this city! It was another of the psalms for the sons of Korah, relating to this same time that had testified:

"Beautiful for situation, the joy of the whole earth, is mount Zion, on the sides of the north, the city of the great King. God is known in her palaces for a refuge."

(Psalm 48:2,3)

David had testified:

"Jerusalem is builded as a city that is compact together: whither the tribes go up, the tribes of the LORD, unto the testimony of Israel, to give thanks unto the name of the LORD. For there are set thrones of judgment, the thrones of the house of David."

(Psalm 122:3-5)

Thus we "pray for the peace of Jerusalem: they shall prosper that love thee" (verse 6), for it is in this place that the Lord will command the blessing "even life for evermore" (Psalm 133:3).

Citizenship of Zion

The thoughts of the Psalmist are still centred on the city of Jerusalem, but now his meditation moves to those who are privileged to be counted as citizens of Zion: who enjoy all the blessings that birth into this illustrious city affords.

Men rejoice in their citizenship. It is to them a source of pride and joy, so at that time to be born of Rahab (Egypt) or Babylon, the two world powers of the day (or of Philistia and Tyre or the more distant Ethiopia) was something of which to take note. How men boasted of their origins, as though this bestowed upon them some special standing in the sight of men!

Yet in contrast to the great nations of this world, there were some who rejoiced to be counted in the divine census, as citizens of Zion – men (and women) of whom the Lord shall say when He completes the register of citizens, "that man was born in her" (verse 3-6). These words have a very

694

real historical background. We have referred to the words of 2 Chronicles 32 on many occasions in our consideration of the psalms associated with Hezekiah. It is the basis of these words also:

"And many brought gifts unto the LORD to Jerusalem, and presents to Hezekiah king of Judah: so that he was magnified in the sight of all nations from thenceforth."
(verse 23)

It is important to appreciate that it was not only the king who was honoured, but also through him, the God of Israel who had wrought this deliverance.

In these circumstances Israel were fulfilling their destiny:

"Ye shall be unto me a kingdom of priests, and an holy nation." (Exodus 19:6)

The function of a priest is twofold. He must reveal God to men and he must bring men to God. Thus Israel as a nation, in fulfilment of this priestly function, were intended to be God's witnesses in the earth (Isaiah 43:1,10,12). So now, in the days of Hezekiah, God had revealed Himself through them by the mighty deliverance He had wrought and men were drawn to worship the Lord God of Israel. Of the statutes and judgements that He had given them, God said:

"Keep therefore and do them; for this is your wisdom and your understanding in the sight of the nations, which shall hear all these statutes, and say, Surely this great nation is a wise and understanding people. For what nation is there so great, who hath God so nigh unto them, as the LORD our God is in all things that we call upon him for?" (Deuteronomy 4:6,7)

It was through these events that centred upon good King Hezekiah and the reaction of the surrounding nations that, by the spirit of God, Isaiah was moved to speak of the age to come, of which the circumstances of Hezekiah's days were but a pale portent:

"Arise, shine; for thy light is come, and the glory of the LORD is risen upon thee. For, behold, the darkness shall cover the earth, and gross darkness the people: but the LORD shall arise upon thee, and his glory shall be seen upon thee. And the Gentiles shall come to thy light, and kings to the brightness of thy rising." (60:1-3)

"For Zion's sake will I not hold my peace, and for Jerusalem's sake I will not rest, until the righteousness thereof go forth as brightness, and the salvation thereof as a lamp that burneth. And the Gentiles shall see thy righteousness, and all kings thy glory." (Isaiah 62:1,2)

"And it shall come to pass in the last days, that the mountain of the LORD's house shall be established in the top of the mountains, and shall be exalted above the hills; and all nations shall flow unto it. And many people shall go and say, Come ye, and let us go up to the mountain of the LORD, to the house of the God of Jacob."
(Isaiah 2:2,3)

Truly the Psalmist could say,

"Glorious things are spoken of thee, O city of God."
(Psalm 87:3)

The reference to the citizens of Zion has, however, an even more precise meaning in the days of Hezekiah. Among the nations who came up to worship and to bring their gifts there were some who stayed, who clave to the God of Israel – proselytes, whose hearts were won by the hope of Israel and who rejoiced to be associated with the worship of the only true God. Isaiah speaks of these:

"Neither let the son of the stranger, that hath joined himself to the LORD, speak, saying, The LORD hath utterly separated me from his people: neither let the eunuch say, Behold, I am a dry tree. For thus saith the LORD unto the eunuchs that keep my sabbaths, and choose the things that please me, and take hold of my covenant; even unto them will I give in mine house and within my walls a place and a name better than of sons and of daughters: I will give them an everlasting name, that shall not be cut off. Also the sons of the stranger, that join themselves to the LORD, to serve him, and to love the name of the LORD, to be his servants, every one that keepeth the sabbath from polluting it, and taketh hold of my covenant; even them will I bring to my holy mountain, and make them joyful in my house of prayer: their burnt offerings and their sacrifices shall be accepted upon mine altar; for mine house shall be called an house of prayer for all people." (Isaiah 56:3-7)

These who delighted to be counted citizens of Zion, denied the cities of their origin and were pleased to be associated with the faithful of old and to sojourn in the land of promise as in a strange country, for they too looked "for a city which hath foundations, whose builder and maker is God" (Hebrews 11:10).

As intimated in the introductory remarks, however, we feel that in the midst of all these circumstances there was another event that evoked the singing and dancing of which the psalm speaks. This was the birth of Manasseh. We must forget what he became and think only of the circumstances of his birth. We know from the scriptural record that he was born about three years after the deliverance of Jerusalem and that he was the fruit of the union between Hezekiah and Hephzi-bah. At the time of his sickness Hezekiah had no heir and if he had died then there would have been no son to continue the line. When therefore Manasseh was born, what rejoicing there must have been in the city and the land. The royal line of David was assured and God's fidelity to His covenant confirmed.

These circumstances are reflected in Isaiah 53 and Hezekiah is shown to be a most remarkable type of the Lord Jesus Christ:

"Who shall declare his generation? for he was cut off out of the land of the living." (verse 8)

Yet:

"He shall see his seed, he shall prolong his days, and the pleasure of the LORD shall prosper in his hand." (verse 10)

That Manasseh's birth was seen to be more than just the birth of a royal son is evident from the words of Isaiah 54 (verse 1), the chapter division clouding the connection:

"Sing, O barren, thou that didst not bear; break forth into singing, and cry aloud, thou that didst not travail with child: for more are the children of the desolate than the children of the married wife, saith the LORD."

Manasseh's birth was seen as a token of the blessing of God, as representative of all those who spiritually were

697

born in Zion. It was the desolate, the spiritual remnant in Judah, who had appeared barren, who now rejoiced as men of other nations were joined to the God of Israel.

It is this spiritual meaning that is most important to us, and that we have not misunderstood the message of the psalm or the words of Isaiah is made clear by the manner in which the Apostle Paul quotes the words of Isaiah 54 in the Epistle to the Galatians:

"But Jerusalem which is above is free, which is the mother of us all. For it is written, Rejoice, thou barren that bearest not; break forth and cry, thou that travailest not: for the desolate hath many more children than she which hath an husband. Now we, brethren, as Isaac was, are the children of promise." (4:26-28)

So we who were once "without Christ, being aliens from the commonwealth of Israel, and strangers from the covenants of promise, having no hope, and without God in the world" (Ephesians 2:12), are now "no more strangers and foreigners, but fellowcitizens with the saints, and of the household of God" (verse 19).

It is Zion, "the mother of us all", that stands for all that God has revealed and promised. Those born in her are those who look to this city for the consummation of all they yearn for. Isaiah testifies again:

"For as soon as Zion travailed, she brought forth her children ... Rejoice ye with Jerusalem, and be glad with her, all ye that love her: rejoice for joy with her, all ye that mourn for her: that ye may suck, and be satisfied with the breasts of her consolations; that ye may milk out, and be delighted with the abundance of her glory. For thus saith the LORD, Behold, I will extend peace to her like a river, and the glory of the Gentiles like a flowing stream: then shall ye suck, ye shall be borne upon her sides, and be dandled upon her knees. As one whom his mother comforteth, so will I comfort you; and ye shall be comforted in Jerusalem." (Isaiah 66:8-13)

These words were true of all faithful men in the days of Hezekiah. They are true also of the spiritual ambience in which we are born and grow, and they will have a wonderful consummation in the future when the Lord shall come.

Writing of the spiritual influences which surround men of God, Brother John Thomas translated the words of Psalm 87 as, "the man, even the man, was developed there" (verse 5). Thus he interpreted the psalm to have reference to the Lord Jesus Christ, but particularly to what we sometimes call "the body of Christ", i.e., the many sons whom God is bringing unto glory (see Hebrews 2:10).

With Singing and Dancing (verse 7)

It should not be thought strange that "singing and dancing" should be an expression of the joy felt at the wonderful things that God had done for His people. We know that when David brought the ark of God to Zion he "danced before the LORD with all his might" (2 Samuel 6:14). We might find it difficult to relate to worship expressed in this way, yet clearly David was moved by deep spiritual emotions to show his zeal and his enthusiasm for the dwelling place of God. A careful reading should convince us that this was not a haphazard, thoughtless act of human exuberance. Already, on the first occasion they had sought to bring up the ark to Zion, God had shown His displeasure at human presumption when Uzzah put forth his hand and touched the ark to steady it. The record tells us that David was afraid of the Lord that day (2 Samuel 6:6-9). It was after prayer and deep meditation upon the word of God that David resolved a second time to bring up the ark to the place he had prepared for it. This time they sought God after the due order (1 Chronicles 15:12-16) and as they travelled, every six paces, David sacrificed oxen and fatlings (2 Samuel 6:13).

It is in this context that David's dancing must be considered. All the rejoicing was tempered by the solemnity of the occasion manifested by the Levites. It was not simply human effervescence that caused him to leap and dance, but deep spiritual spontaneity that expressed itself in this way and was consequently appropriate to the occasion. So it was in the days of Hezekiah, at the birth of his son, when men of spiritual disposition saw in this event a representation of the 'new birth' experienced not just by the strangers who joined themselves to the Lord, but also by the faithful remnant in Israel who saw in

699

Hezekiah and the events of his life a token of the eventual outworking of the purpose of God in the earth.

Conclusion

It is a happy coincidence that when Psalm 68 describes the procession that followed the ark to Zion (verses 24-27), it concludes with words of which Hezekiah's experience is reminiscent. "Because of thy temple at Jerusalem shall kings bring presents unto thee" (verse 29). When David celebrated the coronation of Solomon and looked beyond to the day when his "greater son" should sit upon his throne, he also foresaw this great day:

> "The kings of Tarshish and of the isles shall bring presents: the kings of Sheba and Seba shall offer gifts. Yea, all kings shall fall down before him: all nations shall serve him." (Psalm 72:10,11)

The final thought of Psalm 87 is, "all my fountains are in thee" (verse 7, RV). With the AV ("springs") we might interpret these words as speaking of God from whom living waters flow. But there is at least one occasion where the Hebrew word, in keeping with the theme of the psalm, is used in connection with begettal. If this be accepted, following the RV, then the reference is to those who are born or who spring out of Zion. The connection is again with Psalm 68.

> "Bless ye God in the congregations, even the Lord, ye that are of the fountain of Israel." (verse 26, RV)

The reference is to Jacob from whom the whole nation had issued forth as a stream. So we, whose names are "written in heaven" have all issued forth from Jerusalem which is above, the mother of us all (Hebrews 12:22,23; Galatians 4:26). With joy and confidence we look forward to the day when these things of which Psalm 87 speaks shall be fulfilled in the earth, when "that great city, the holy Jerusalem, (shall descend) out of heaven from God" (Revelation 21:10). Of that city it is recorded:

> "The nations of them which are saved shall walk in the light of it: and the kings of the earth do bring their glory and honour unto it ... And there shall in no wise enter into it anything that defileth, neither whatsoever worketh abomination, or maketh a lie: but they which are written in the Lamb's book of life." (verses 24-27)

PSALM 88

THIS song has been described as the saddest in the whole Psalter, a pathetic cry of despair in the midst of unrelieved suffering (*Cambridge Bible*). This is a sentiment echoed by other commentators and while from a certain perspective one might agree with this assessment, an understanding of its historical associations helps us to appreciate better the reason for the Psalmist's feelings. It would be wrong to suppose, as many have, that this psalm is an indication that the author had no hope of a future life. Resurrection is not within the purview of the song. It is concerned with this life and the death that inevitably follows it, particularly as it had relevance to the circumstances of the life of the writer.

It should be noted that there is a strong Jewish tradition that associates this psalm with the nation of Israel. It is regarded as a national rather than an individual cry of distress. The Targum, for instance, paraphrases verse 6, "Thou hast placed me in exile like the nether world".

There is, however, no indication in the psalm itself that it speaks of anything other than personal catastrophe. The psalm has been variously linked with Job, Uzziah, Hezekiah and Jeremiah and it must be freely admitted, it could legitimately have been written by any of these or indeed, by others not named. Our own conviction is that it was written by Hezekiah or adopted by the Sons of Korah for use in connection with the circumstances of his life. With one possible exception, every verse can be appropriately interpreted in the light of Hezekiah's sickness unto death. The exception (verse 15) states, "I am afflicted and ready to die from my youth up".

It is presumed that the "affliction" is the sickness of which the psalm elsewhere speaks and that consequently not only would it be inappropriate to Hezekiah but also to the other suggestions mentioned above. *Strong* interprets the meaning of the Hebrew word as 'depressed in mind or circumstances', and points out that it has been variously translated as "afflicted", "humble", "lowly", "needy" and "poor".

We do not know how long Hezekiah's sickness lasted but the nature of it (a form of leprosy or possibly elephantiasis) implies that it was gradual in its development and the crisis occurred as the Assyrian threat became apparent and the prophet Isaiah delivered his message to the king. Certainly there is no indication of sickness or poor health in Hezekiah's youth but, noting the varied meanings of the word and particularly its association with depression of mind, we believe that the verse can legitimately be applied to Hezekiah's earlier life.

Because of the wickedness of his father, Ahaz, who "made his son to pass through the fire" (2 Kings 16:3 – was this Hezekiah?) he must have lived through a precarious childhood. On becoming king his sweeping reforms would not have made him universally popular and there must have been factions, of which he was only too well aware, that would have wished him dead.

One reason why Hezekiah is such a marvellous type of the Lord Jesus Christ is that although he himself was a righteous man who "trusted in the LORD God of Israel; so that after him there was none like him among all the kings of Judah, nor any that were before him" (2 Kings 18:5), he still associated himself with the sins of the people. As king he was representative of the nation and he regarded their sin as being his own. Throughout his life this was a burden that he carried and as his sickness developed Isaiah presented it to the people as an affliction that he bore on their account. Thus while the 'servant' passages of Isaiah have their true and real fulfilment in the life and work of the Lord Jesus Christ, they were first presented to the people, and had their initial significance, against the background of the circumstances and life of Hezekiah (see Isaiah 53). We suggest that these factors need to be kept in mind in considering the substance of Psalm 88.

The detail will be noted in our study of the psalm but in general terms there are striking similarities between this psalm and Hezekiah's psalm following his recovery (Isaiah 38:9-20). Whereas Hezekiah's 'writing' was penned after the Lord had told him he should be granted an extension of life, Psalm 88 was written in the midst of the crisis. Might it not be part of the prayer of Hezekiah (Isaiah 38:2,3)? The factors which produced the notes of apparent hopelessness are these:

1. Hezekiah had been told that he should die and not live (Isaiah 38:1). Consequently there remained nothing for him in this life and before him lay the awful prospect of the grave.

2. He had no children; possibly he himself was an only son. There was no heir to sit on David's throne.

3. His personal relationship with God as head of His covenant people would end. He was conscious not only of his own fellowship but also of the manner in which "the people rested themselves upon (his) words" (2 Chronicles 32:8).

4. If, as Isaiah presented it, and as Hezekiah accepted it, his sickness was on account of the sins of the people, then his death could speak only of the wrath of God towards them. In this sense the Jewish tradition that would associate the psalm with the nation of Israel reflects a true instinct.

Note how these factors are reflected in the prayer of Hezekiah (Isaiah 38:1,2); his psalm (verses 38:9-20) and Psalm 88:

1. Hezekiah cried: "I shall go to the gates of the grave: I am deprived of the residue of my years. I said, I shall not see the LORD, even the LORD, in the land of the living: I shall behold man no more when I am among them that have ceased to be" (Isaiah 38:10,11 with RV margin; see also Psalm 88:10-12).

2. The desire for a son was at the heart of his distress: "The living, the living, he shall praise thee, as I do

this day: the father to the children shall make known thy truth" (Isaiah 38:19; see also 53:8,10).

3. The covenant was paramount in his mind as he prayed, "I have walked before thee in truth and with a perfect heart, and have done that which is good in thy sight" (Isaiah 38:3; cp. 1 Kings 9:4,5). The stability of David's throne and kingdom depended upon these qualities. God responded: "Thus saith the LORD, the God of David thy father, I have heard thy prayer" (Isaiah 38:5).

4. So also Psalm 88 declares: "Thy wrath lieth hard upon me" (verse 7); "Thy fierce wrath goeth over me" (verse 16).

The psalm is "a Maschil of Heman the Ezrahite". We have written previously on the identity of Heman. It is included among the psalms of the Sons of Korah, so evidently, even if Heman was not of their company, it was committed to their keeping. "Maschil" indicates that it is 'for instruction' and the lesson of the psalm comes down through the centuries to us. "The living, the living, he shall praise thee, as I do this day", for life is the time to serve the Lord; life is our time of opportunity.

Verses 1-3

"O LORD God of my salvation, I have cried day and night before thee." (verse 1)

The first phrase of the psalm is perhaps the keynote, for it is the only time that the Psalmist acknowledges the Lord as his salvation. All that he subsequently writes must be interpreted against the background of this opening confession, for the Lord is his God and he still speaks of "my salvation". Although in his sadness and despair he has been brought nigh unto the grave (verse 3) and before him there lies but the coldness and stillness of the tomb, his hope is still in God, and in these words, if nowhere else in the psalm, there is expressed the hope of eventual resurrection to life.

Day and night the Psalmist has cried. He repeats the fact later:

704

"But unto thee have I cried, O LORD; and in the morning shall my prayer come before (RV) thee."

(verse 13)

The first and last thought of every day was to pray that God would deliver him from his distress. The construction of the Hebrew is broken in form and Kay (*Notes on the Psalms*) comments: "the broken language corresponds to the weakness of the gasping sufferer".

"Let my prayer come before thee (RV, enter into thy presence): incline thine ear unto my cry." (verse 2)

Of the word rendered "cry" it has been said that it denotes a shrill piercing cry, sometimes indicating joy but, in this instance, expressive of the grief felt – a deep emotional experience in the distress he feels as he is brought to the very brink of death itself.

Verses 4-7

Such was the extremity of his plight that as men looked upon him they considered him in their eyes as though he were already dead:

"I am counted with them that go down into the pit: I am as a man that hath no strength (RV, 'help')."

(verse 4)

He was as though –

"cast away (RV margin) among the dead. Like the slain that lie in the grave, whom thou rememberest no more, and they are cut off from thy hand." (verse 5)

It is interesting to observe that the Hebrew rendered "cast away" (RV margin) is cognate with "the several house" (RV margin, 'lazar house') in which Uzziah lived as a leper (see 2 Chronicles 26:21). It is a further indication of the nature of the affliction that has overtaken the Psalmist (see also verse 8 below). The reference to "the slain" is not to natural death but to those who had fallen in battle and whose bodies were buried in a common grave.

For all his life of service to God and man, even though he was counted, because he was a king, with the privileged and the mighty, in death he would be no better than those who suffered such an ignominious end. In death, all were equal, alike cut off from fellowship with God and from seeing the works of His hand:

> "There the wicked cease from troubling; and there
> the weary be at rest. There the prisoners rest together;
> they hear not the voice of the oppressor. The small and
> great are there; and the servant is free from his
> master."   (Job 3:17-19)

The Psalmist felt that even his God had come to regard
him thus, having brought him to the very gates of the
grave:

> "Thou hast laid me in the lowest pit, in darkness, in
> the deeps."   (Psalm 88:6)

In his mind he was as good as dead, the reference to the
"deeps" being probably a metaphor for the depths of
misery that he endured. It was like the great waters of the
sea enveloping him (Psalm 69:15). Surely this must be a
token of God's anger, not just towards him but also
towards His people of whom he was the representative.
Like waves, as trouble and calamity overtook him, he
thought he must be overwhelmed (Psalm 88:7).

Verses 8-12

> "Thou hast put away mine acquaintance far from me;
> thou hast made me an abomination unto them: I am
> shut up, and I cannot come forth."   (verse 8)

As already intimated, the language of leprosy seems to lie
behind the expressions of this verse. All his "familiar
friends" (Hebrew) had turned from him. He was like a
man alone:

> "All the days wherein the plague shall be in him he
> shall be defiled; he is unclean: he shall dwell alone;
> without the camp shall his habitation be."
>   (Leviticus 13:46)

If we understand the nature of his disease we appreciate
the depth of his despair for it was a living death. Of
Miriam's leprosy Aaron said: "Let her not be as one dead"
(Numbers 12:12). It was regarded as the direct stroke of
God and the Psalmist, with the thrice repeated "thou hast"
(Psalm 88:7,8), acknowledges that all that had overtaken
him was of God.

He was truly as one "shut up" who was unable to "come
forth". Although his suffering was to be seen in the
sunken eyes, nevertheless he remains constant in prayer:

"Mine eye wasteth away (RV) by reason of affliction: LORD, I have called daily upon thee, I have stretched out my hands unto thee."   (verse 9)

His trust remained in the God of his salvation (verse 1) for he knew that, "in death there is no remembrance of thee: in the grave who shall give thee thanks?" (Psalm 6:5). In the unconsciousness of death there could be no fellowship with God, no opportunity to experience the wonders of His hands:

"Wilt thou shew wonders to the dead? shall the dead arise and praise thee? Selah. Shall thy lovingkindness be declared in the grave? or thy faithfulness in destruction? Shall thy wonders be known in the dark? and thy righteousness in the land of forgetfulness?"
(verses 10-12)

It must be remembered that resurrection is beyond the purview of his concern. His thought is about God's covenant with David and the fact that he had no heir. It is about the threat of the Assyrian invader and the danger to his people. To die with these issues unresolved was for him the very depths of despair, for he knew that in death God's wonders could not be seen, His faithfulness could no longer be appreciated. It was "the land of forgetfulness" and all those things that pertained to his mortal life were forever gone in the stillness of the tomb. Thus Hezekiah testified:

"I shall go to the gates of the grave: I am deprived of the residue of my years. I said, I shall not see the LORD, even the LORD, in the land of the living: I shall behold man no more when I am among them that have ceased to be (RV margin) ... For the grave cannot praise thee, death cannot celebrate thee: they that go down into the pit cannot hope for thy truth. The living, the living, he shall praise thee, as I do this day: the father to the children shall make known thy truth."
(Isaiah 38:10,11,18,19)

It was not death itself that he feared, but its consequences for the kingdom of Judah. This perplexed and overwhelmed him with a sense of despair. In the oblivion of death there was, for him, no resolution to these problems, no hope of a satisfactory outcome. So he turns again to prayer.

Verses 13-18

As already indicated, the words of verse 13 repeat the thoughts of verse 1. The first and last thought of each day was prayer. There is an emphasis in the Hebrew text that is not apparent in the AV. Literally, "but as for me unto thee, O LORD, have I cried". In effect he is contrasting himself with the dead. While life remains, in the face of all his adversity, he will not cease from prayer. He cries:

"LORD, why castest thou off my soul? why hidest thou
thy face from me? (verse 14)

This is a familiar theme in the psalms (see 10:1; 13:1; 22:1 etc.). Faced with an apparent lack of response from God the Psalmist feels that He has forsaken him. His prayers seem unable to penetrate to God's presence; it is as if He has hidden His face. This is an experience that comes to all men of God in their lives. It is a perplexing experience that is a part of our spiritual training.

Sometimes our lives seem barren and unfruitful. God seems to have left us and we feel bereft of His help. We are conscious of a desolating sense of separation from Him. At such times we might be moved to express our emotions in the words of the Psalmist. However, it is in the midst of such experiences that God looks for that resolute and steadfast spirit that will not let go of the eternal treasures He has committed to our trust. It is part of the chastening of the Lord, one of the ways in which He tries us and puts us to the proof to see if we will keep His word; that He might know all that is in our hearts (see Deuteronomy 8:2; 2 Chronicles 32:31).

The Psalmist expands on the reasons for this questioning that arises within his heart:

"I am afflicted and ready to die from my youth up:
while I suffer thy terrors I am distracted. Thy fierce
wrath goeth over me; thy terrors have cut me off. They
came round about me daily like water; they compassed
me about together." (verses 15-17)

We have already commented in the introductory remarks to this psalm on the appropriateness of verse 15 to the life of Hezekiah. In the face of all his troubles that had "distracted" him, he had continued "instant in prayer". In

708

the midst of all life's suffering, he had never ceased from pleading with God for deliverance. The word rendered "distracted" occurs only on this one occasion in scripture. It appears to describe the mental anguish that would ensue after prolonged wrestling with the difficulties of life; a kind of mental exhaustion and confusion of spirit (*Speaker's Commentary*).

Previously the writer has spoken of waves of tribulation sweeping over him. Now he describes them as like fiery waves as he feels that God's wrath is upon him. Two different words are translated "terrors" in these verses. The first can more literally be rendered 'horrors', describing the feeling that sprang up in his heart as he contemplated his situation. The second means 'alarms', as if each wave of tribulation that overwhelmed him caused him alarm as it alerted him to the deteriorating circumstances in which he found himself. Like a flood they had encompassed him and he felt like a man about to drown with no one to hold out a hand to rescue him (verse 17).

The last verse of the psalm expresses the desolation that he felt:

"Lover and friend hast thou put far from me, and mine acquaintance are darkness."

(verse 18, with RV margin)

In place of friends and acquaintances there is only darkness. In the light of the message, "thou shalt die and not live" (Isaiah 38:1), there remained but the coldness and stillness of the tomb with no ray of light to penetrate that gloom he felt, and to bring the solutions he longed for before he died. By God's grace, we know that his prayers were answered. The Lord had not forsaken him and in the extension of his life all his anxieties were resolved; he saw God's wonders performed and His lovingkindness declared in the land of the living.

The psalm stands as an exhortation for us to learn that life is our time of opportunity, and that in all its difficulties and trials our God will not forsake us; though He try and prove us He will not turn away His face from us, and if we hold fast to the things committed to our trust then we shall come forth as purged gold.

PSALM 89

IT needs only a superficial examination of this psalm to appreciate that, broadly speaking, it falls into two parts. The first (verses 1-37) speaks of the never failing faithfulness and lovingkindness of God; the surety of the covenant that He made with David. The second (verses 38-45) speaks of the disasters that have overtaken the king, the Lord's anointed, and the manner in which the kingdom has been overthrown by enemies who now rejoice in their triumph.

Some have been concerned by the boldness and forthright manner in which the writer addresses God in this second part of the psalm. He seems almost to challenge His faithfulness and lovingkindness, as though the realities of the situation indicated that God had forsaken His anointed, His people and His land. The *Cambridge Bible* comments: "The audacity of the expostulation scandalised many ancient Jewish commentators". However, we need not concern ourselves overmuch with this extreme Jewish reaction. The boldness of the Psalmist is born of faith. It springs from the heart of a man whose meditations have brought him into close proximity with his God, and the two sections of the psalm must be read in conjunction with each other to retain a proper balance. It is because he believes so firmly, and with such passion, that he is overwhelmed, humanly speaking, by the tragedy that has overtaken God's kingdom. In the multitude of his thoughts, assailed by doubt, he beseeches God for an answer. This is a natural human reaction and one that is reflected in the experience of first century believers, and was answered by God in the Book of Revelation by the use made of this psalm.

It is clear that the Apocalypse was addressed to a persecuted community. The writer introduces himself:

"I John, who also am your brother, and companion in tribulation, and in the kingdom and patience of Jesus Christ ..."   (Revelation 1:9)

The letters to the seven ecclesias of Asia also emphasise this fact (see 2:9,10; 3:10). Those who endured such cruel persecution must surely have been assailed with similar doubts and fears as those expressed by the writer of Psalm 89. It is therefore significant that when John introduces the Lord Jesus in Chapter 1 he should do so in the language of the first section of Psalm 89:

"... from Jesus Christ, who is the faithful witness, the firstborn of the dead, and the ruler of the kings of the earth."   (Revelation 1:5, RV)

The use of these titles is not arbitrary. The Spirit has chosen them from the context of Psalm 89 because they are particularly appropriate to the circumstances of those who first received the book.

The title appears in Psalm 89:27: "I will make him my firstborn, higher than the kings of the earth"; and verse 37, "As the moon which is established for ever, and as the faithful witness in the sky" (RV and margin). The title "firstborn" was an assurance that they too would be included in the many sons that God was bringing to glory (see Hebrews 2:10). The fact that he was "higher than the kings of the earth" spoke of his ultimate victory over all those who persecuted them, and as a "faithful witness in heaven" (the sign of the Son of man in heaven?) there was divine assurance that His word would surely be fulfilled.

There is another possible reference to the psalm. In the concluding section of the song the Psalmist cries:

"How long, LORD? wilt thou hide thyself for ever? shall thy wrath burn like fire?   (verse 46)

We are reminded of the souls under the altar who were slain for the word of God and for the testimony which they held, who when the fifth seal was opened –

"cried with a loud voice, saying, How long, O Lord, holy and true, dost thou not judge and avenge our blood on them that dwell on the earth?"   (Revelation 6:10)

Not only is the cry of "How long?" echoed but the Lord is described as "holy and true". The words are derived from

711

our psalm, for "Once have I sworn by my holiness that I will not lie unto David" (verse 35). The word "true" encapsulates the remarkable emphasis upon the faithfulness of God in this psalm (see below). God is true – that is, He is faithful.

Authorship and Background

In the last analysis the message of the psalm remains unaffected by questions of authorship and the precise circumstances of the historical background. Nevertheless it is a matter of interest and, as we have commented previously, historical circumstances help to enlarge our understanding of the words.

As to historical background there is a wide diversity of suggestions from various writers (both Christadelphian and orthodox commentators). Amongst them are the following:

1. The rebellion of Absalom and the flight of David.
2. Shishak's invasion in the days of Rehoboam.
3. The Assyrian invasion in the days of Hezekiah.
4. Manasseh carried away by the Assyrian army.
5. The overthrow of Jehoiachin and his imprisonment in Babylon.
6. Israel in exile bewailing their lot.

With the exception of number 6, which we find untenable, there is something to be said for all of the other suggestions.

The question of authorship has some bearing upon the time it was written. It bears the heading, "Maschil of Ethan the Ezrahite". We have seen in previous studies that Ethan, together with Heman and Asaph were leaders of the temple music and choirs (1 Chronicles 15:17-19). From a comparison of this passage with others (1 Chronicles 16:41,42; 25:1) it has been inferred that he was also called Jeduthun. It is evident that choirs were formed that carried the names of these men beyond their lifetimes, right through the history of the kingdom of Judah. Especially in the case of Asaph (and Korah), psalms were written for these choirs and produced by members of these guilds of singers to commemorate particular historical events. For suggestions 3 to 5 to be appropriate we would need to understand the heading in terms of a guild of singers that bore his name. As far as suggestions 1 and 2 are concerned, he was a contemporary of David, and, presumably, of Solomon (see 1 Kings 4:31). From the context of Psalm 89 the writer appears to be an old man. He writes in a spirit of despair, concerned that he might not live to see God's deliverance of His people:

"Remember how short my time is: for what vanity hast thou created all the children of men! What man is he that shall live (i.e., shall live on) and shall not see death, that shall deliver his soul from the power of the grave?" (verses 47,48, RV with margin)

In these circumstances it is possible that Ethan was still alive when Shishak invaded Judah in the days of Rehoboam. The *Speaker's Commentary* argues for this background as indeed it does for Psalms 74 and 79. In those instances we rejected the argument, because of the internal evidence of the psalms, in favour of a background involving Manasseh's captivity. Although we feel the language of Psalm 89 could easily apply to Manasseh, we lean in this instance to the invasion of Shishak. We do so because not only is the writer contemporary with the disasters that have overtaken Judah, but he appears also to have been associated with David when the promises were made to him. Our personal feeling is that there is an immediacy about the language of the first part of the psalm that implies a close proximity with the words spoken. He had known of these things, through David, at the time that God made the covenant and he had rejoiced with David in the thing revealed. Consequently we believe that the aged Ethan was the author. The historical record that provides the background is found therefore in 2 Chronicles 12:1-12:

1. Rehoboam and all Israel forsook the law of the Lord (verse 1).

2. In Rehoboam's fifth year, Shishak came up against Jerusalem (verse 2).

3. He took the fenced cities that pertained to Judah (verse 4).

4. They become the servants of Shishak (verse 8).

5. He took away the treasures out of the house of the Lord and out of the king's house.

So God was angry with Rehoboam (Psalm 89:38) and his throne was dishonoured in the sight of the nations (verses 38,41,42). His frontiers had been broken down and all his strong cities destroyed (verse 40). The glory of the kingdom had departed (verse 44).

Structure

We stated that the psalm, broadly speaking, could be divided into two parts. That remains true, but within this overall assessment the use of "Selah" indicates that there are four stanzas with a concluding prayer. The second and longest stanza (verses 5-37) can be divided again for, as the use of the pronouns indicate, verses 19-37 are the words of God Himself, whereas the earlier words are the reflections of the writer. Thus:

(a) verses 1-4   Introductory Song of Praise.

(b) verses 5-18   The incomparable greatness of the Lord.

(c) verses 19-37   God reiterates and expounds His covenant with David.

(d) verses 38-45   Judah's throne and kingdom profaned.

(e) verses 46-48   The Psalmist's personal anxiety.

(f) verses 49-51   Concluding prayer.

Introductory Song of Praise (verses1-4)

"I will sing of the mercies of the LORD for ever: with my mouth will I make known thy faithfulness to all generations."   (verse 1)

Immediately we are introduced to the key words of the psalm: God's faithfulness and His lovingkindness. The word translated "mercies" (lovingkindnesses) is the Hebrew *chesed* and it is associated throughout the scriptures with the love that God showed to His covenant people. It has been rendered "covenant love" (N. Snaith – *Distinctive Ideas of the Old Testament,* pages 94-130; see also *The Teaching of the Master*, Brother L. G. Sargent, pages 55,56 – 1981 edition). The word is used seven times in the psalm (verses 1,2,14,24,28,33,49).

Perhaps even more distinctive is the emphasis upon the faithfulness of God. This word is also used seven times (verses 1,2,5,8,24,33,49) but in addition, the word "faithful" occurs twice (verses 24,37) and the psalm emphasises God's faithfulness in its confident declarations.

"I have made a covenant with my chosen, I have sworn unto David my servant." (verse 3)

"... will I establish for ever, and build up thy throne." (verse 4)

"My mercy will I keep for him for evermore, and my covenant shall stand fast." (verse 28)

"My covenant will I not break, nor alter the thing that is gone out of my lips." (verse 34)

"Once have I sworn by my holiness that I will not lie unto David." (verse 35)

"His seed shall endure forever." (verse 36)

On these two qualities, faithfulness and loving-kindness, rested all the hopes of God's people. Because of this the Psalmist would sing His praise continually. The words "for ever" could be speaking of his perpetual praise to God during his life but might they not, with more meaning, speak of his assurance that, in God's kingdom he would sing with renewed strength the praises of Him who in vindication of His faithfulness and lovingkindness had fulfilled the word He had spoken? The Psalmist's thoughts were carried forward to that day:

"For I have said, Mercy shall be built up for ever: thy faithfulness shalt thou establish in the very heavens." (verse 2)

Although the king had been humbled and his throne cast down (verse 44), God would build it up again. This truth was established in the heavens themselves. There is a sense in which the heavens speak of the unchanging and never failing will of God as compared with the ever changing scene on earth:

"For ever, O LORD, thy word is settled in heaven." (Psalm 119:89)

But again, might we not see a deeper perspective; for the Lord Jesus risen and exalted to his Father's right hand, a faithful witness in heaven, is the assurance that God has given to all men that He has appointed a day in which He will judge the world in righteousness (Acts 17:31).

In this short introductory section, having spoken of his own conviction, the writer now introduces the grounds of it; the covenant with David, upon which the Lord Himself expounds later in the psalm (verses 19-37):

"I have made a covenant with my chosen, I have sworn unto David my servant, Thy seed will I establish for ever, and build thy throne to all generations."

(verses 3,4)

The use of the same words "for ever" and "to all generations" spoken here of the everlasting covenant lends support to the view expressed above that the Psalmist was thinking of the praise he should offer in the day when God fulfilled His promise.

These two verses contain the sum of the things that God promised David. Almost every word is drawn from the context of 2 Samuel 7. For reference see: "David my servant" (verses 5,8,26).

David uses the words:

"thy servant"	verses 19,20,27,28,29
"establish"	verses 12,13,16,26
"for ever"	verses 13,16,24,26,29
"seed"	verses 12,13,16
"throne"	verses 12,13,16
"build"	verse 27

(The above list is reproduced from data in the *Cambridge Bible,* page 533).

Further comment on God's covenant with David we defer to our examination of verses 19-37.

It is our privilege to share the Psalmist's hope and to seek to emulate his faith. We do so in the confidence that God has said of those who incline their ears to hear:

"I will make an everlasting covenant with you, even the sure (faithful) mercies (lovingkindnesses) of David."

(Isaiah 55:3)

716

The Greatness of God (verses 5-18)

The certainty of any promise being fulfilled depends not only upon the faithfulness of the one who has promised but also upon his ability to perform what he has spoken. It is therefore most appropriate that having introduced the twin qualities of faithfulness and lovingkindness, on which the hope of all God's people rests, the Psalmist's thoughts should turn to His power and might. God's faithfulness can be trusted implicitly because not only is He true to the things that He has spoken, but He also has the power to perform them. Thus the Psalmist dwells upon the might of God manifest in creation and on behalf of His people in delivering them from their enemies (verses 5-14). It is because of this that the people who dwell in covenant relationship with Him are truly happy because the light of His countenance shines upon them (verses 15-18).

This section which emphasises the uniqueness of the God of Israel, His omnipotence and omniscience to whom none can be likened, would stand also as a testimony against the gods of the nations to whom the people of Judah had turned their thoughts:

"And the heavens shall praise thy wonders, O LORD: thy faithfulness also in the congregation of the saints. For who in the heaven can be compared unto the LORD? who among the sons of the mighty can be likened unto the LORD? God is greatly to be feared in the assembly of the saints, and to be had in reverence of all them that are about him." (verses 5-7)

We must be guided by the context. The Psalmist is not thinking of the congregation of the faithful upon earth, but rather he is contrasting the assembly of the angels in heaven who, though themselves holy and mighty in Him, cannot be compared with the majesty and power of the great Uncreate who towers above them in all His wonder. Note that the word translated "wonders" in verse 5 is actually singular not plural. It is as if in this one word the Spirit has caught up together all that He is that makes Him "other than" any to whom men might seek to compare Him.

717

There are two points of exhortation that we do well to dwell upon. Firstly, if angels, so great in power and might, so holy – for they stand in the congregation of heaven itself – recognise His majesty and wonder and worship in fear and reverence, then how much more it becomes us who are made lower than the angels to worship Him with trembling and fear. There is a danger that we might treat God in a casual fashion, both in the way we speak of Him and also in the way we approach Him. We must never take Him for granted; we must never presume upon His mercy by assuming in our complacency that everything will be alright in the end. It is not just a matter of the words we use but it has to do with our hearts and minds: how we feel about God; how we have come to appreciate His greatness and the great privilege we enjoy in being able to address our prayers to Him, who is pleased to be called our Father.

The second point of exhortation is one that should fill us with wonder and awe for, acknowledging the need for us to worship God with due reverence and fear, what we must never forget is that "unto the angels hath he not put in subjection the world to come" (Hebrews 2:5). It is not these "sons of the mighty" who stand in the congregation of heaven that God will exalt in the age to come, but it is man whom He created in His image and likeness. Truly we can say with the Psalmist: "What is man, that thou art mindful of him? and the son of man, that thou visitest him? (Psalm 8:4).

From the recognition of God's greatness amongst the army of heaven, the Psalmist turns to a consideration of the way in which He manifested His power to deliver His people:

"O LORD God of hosts, who is a strong LORD like unto thee? or to thy faithfulness round about thee? Thou rulest the raging of the sea: when the waves thereof arise, thou stillest them. Thou hast broken Rahab in pieces, as one that is slain; thou hast scattered thine enemies with thy strong arm." (Psalm 89:8-10)

The title "LORD God of hosts" is particularly appropriate given the preceding verses which have spoken so eloquently of the angelic host. The Psalmist is recalling the words of Exodus 15 when Moses sang his song of victory to celebrate the destruction of the Egyptian army:

"Who is like unto thee, O LORD, among the gods? who is like thee, glorious in holiness, fearful in praises, doing wonders?" (verse 11)

The similarity of thought and language between the psalm and the words of Moses is evident. Note also that the Psalmist uses the same appelative for God as Moses (see Exodus 15:2): "Who is a mighty one like unto thee, O JAH? and thy faithfulness is round about thee" (Psalm 89:8, RV). The Psalmist dwells upon God's faithfulness and might, the two qualities that give us the assurance that His promises will be fulfilled. Faithfulness is spoken of as though it had a separate existence. It is not personification, but rather it is spoken of as surrounding God; as though it were the very atmosphere in which He dwells.

There is no need to fear the nations, in this instance Shishak and the Egyptians, for God rules in the kingdom of men. To illustrate the point the Psalmist describes the raging of the sea, that most turbulent and formidable of powers, used so often in scripture to describe the madness of the nations in their fury against God's people (see Psalm 46:3; 65:7; etc.). At the Red Sea, God demonstrated His sovereignty over both the raging of the waves and the fury of the people, for there He broke Rahab in pieces; Rahab of course, being another name for Egypt (see Psalm 87:4; Isaiah 51:9) – again so appropriate in the context of this psalm.

The sovereignty of the God of Israel is beyond dispute:

"The heavens are thine, the earth also is thine: the world and the fulness thereof, thou hast founded them. The north and the south, thou hast created them: Tabor and Hermon rejoice in thy name." (verses 11,12, RV)

Some suggest that Tabor and Hermon geographically stand for west and east, thus standing in apposition to the north and south. This may well be so but the naming of the mountains, the most conspicuous of all the natural features of the land, taken with the rendering of the RV, carries us a stage further, for these mountains rejoice. It is as if by their very grandeur they speak of the awesome

719

power and might of the One who created them and rejoice in the manner in which they fulfilled this purpose (see Psalm 19:1).

The language of the psalm in verse 13, "Thou hast a mighty arm", echoes the words of Moses in Exodus 15 (see verse 16). Similarly: "Strong is thy hand" (see Exodus 15:9) and "high is thy right hand" (see verses 6,12). By the use of these words (arm, hand, right hand), we are assured that God not only possesses this power but also is prepared to use it, as indeed He had done when He destroyed Pharaoh and his host. His power, however, is not used in an arbitrary fashion, but it is directed always by those qualities in which He has made Himself known:

"Justice and judgment are the habitation of thy throne: mercy and truth shall go before thy face."

(Psalm 89:14)

Here the qualities for ever associated with Israel's God are emphasised. Righteousness and judgement are the foundation (see RV) on which His throne is established. Lovingkindness and truth are personified as if they were angels attending in His presence ready to do His bidding; to go before His presence in the performance of His will. Truly happy are the people who have such a God as this and whose king sits as His representative on the throne of David:

"Blessed is the people that know the joyful sound: they walk, O LORD, in the light of thy countenance. In thy name do they rejoice all the day: and in thy righteousness are they exalted." (verses 15,16, RV)

The reference to the joyful sound (Hebrew, *teruah*) recalls the blowing of the trumpets on Israel's festive occasions. In Numbers 10 the silver trumpets were to be blown:

"In the day of your gladness, and in your set feasts, and in the beginnings of your months ... over your burnt offerings, and over the sacrifices of your peace offerings; and they shall be to you for a memorial before your God." (verse 10, RV)

Only those who enjoyed this privilege of worshipping the Lord God could know the joyful sound. They were truly blessed, happy above all other peoples. We find it

720

interesting that the emphasis is not upon hearing the sound but upon knowing it. There are three trumpets referred to in the Old Testament scriptures: the silver trumpet, the ram's horn (*shofar*) and the jubilee trumpet. The sounds were distinctive; they were not just a noise, but they gave information and by them the people were instructed. Thus in Numbers 10 the various soundings of the silver trumpets were intended to advise the people whether the congregation should be called together, whether the princes only should come, whether the camp should take their journey or whether an alarm should be sounded to alert the people (see verses 2-7).

In these circumstances, for Israel, the trumpet represented the voice of God – a fact emphasised in other scriptures:

> "God is gone up with a shout, the LORD with the sound of a trumpet." (Psalm 47:5)

> "And when the voice of the trumpet sounded long, and waxed louder and louder, Moses spake, and God answered him by a voice." (Exodus 19:19)

No doubt many in Israel would have wished to sound the trumpets, but this was clearly impracticable. The priests only (and later the Levites) were to sound the trumpets. They were God's representatives for He spoke through them, but they also represented the people of Israel, because they were a kingdom of priests (Exodus 19:6). For it was not only to the priests but to all the people that God had revealed Himself. Blessed indeed were the people who knew the joyful sound, who had heard and understood the things that God had revealed concerning Himself and His purpose. These and these only should walk in the light of His countenance. There seems to be a clear allusion to the priestly blessing of Numbers 6:

> "On this wise ye shall bless the children of Israel, saying unto them, The LORD bless thee, and keep thee: the LORD make his face shine upon thee, and be gracious unto thee: the LORD lift up his countenance upon thee, and give thee peace. And they shall put my name upon the children of Israel; and I will bless them." (verses 23-27)

Interestingly, this blessing follows the instructions regarding the Nazarite vow, which any Israelite, either man or woman, could make. Now the Nazarite vow was an opportunity for an individual to enter, in a measure, into the privileges and responsibilities of the high priest (verses 5-8 compared with Leviticus 10:9,11; 21:5,10-12). Those who took this vow were recognising that the high priest, in his office, was representative of the nation of Israel as a whole, for they were a kingdom of priests and shared a collective responsibility, living as they did under the divine favour, to show forth the light of truth to those about them. Thus, continuing his meditation upon the blessing of Numbers 6, the Psalmist writes, "In thy name shall they rejoice all the day: and in thy righteousness shall they be exalted" (Psalm 89:16).

We too enjoy these blessings and can pray with the Psalmist: "LORD lift thou up the light of thy countenance upon us" (Psalm 4:6). In the confidence that we walk in the sunshine of His favour we can say: "Thou hast put gladness in my heart, more than they have when their corn and their wine are increased" (verse 7). Because they walk in the light of His countenance and rejoice in His name they are exalted; because He is righteous that promised, He will fulfil His word.

"For thou art the glory of their strength: and in thy favour our horn shall be exalted. For our shield belongeth unto the LORD; and our king to the Holy One of Israel."   (verses 17,18, RV)

God alone is their strength; that which they have accomplished is through His power. The glory was not theirs but His and their strength was confirmed when in humility they acknowledged God's hand and took no pride in their own wealth and power.

The horn is the symbol of power and strength (see Psalm 75:5,10) and it is only in God's favour that their horn shall be exalted. The emphasis upon possessing "their horn" suggests that the reference is to their king in whom God's power resides. Consistent with this view the RV, correctly we believe, changes the sense suggested by the AV (see Kay, *Psalms with Notes, Cambridge Bible* etc.). "Shield" and "king" stand in what has been termed "synonymous parallelism". Both refer to the Lord's anointed and it is, in effect, a declaration that the kingdom of the Lord was founded and sustained by His hand. The king, if faithful, would be a shield to his people and he owed his status and authority to the one who had anointed and exalted him.

This verse is one of the decisive factors, in our view, in establishing the background of the psalm. The kingdom is still in existence (it cannot refer to the exile). The king still sits upon his throne (it cannot refer to David or Manasseh). It is recorded that Shishak "took away all the shields of gold which Solomon had made" (1 Kings 14:26) but, says the Psalmist, "our shield belongeth unto the LORD". While God maintained him, no earthly power could overthrow him, whatever limited success God permitted them to have.

God's Faithfulness to His Covenant (verses 19-37)

The reference to the king in verse 18 is the trigger that leads to the declaration anew of the covenant that God made with David. It reiterates the divine decrees (see 2 Samuel 7 and 1 Chronicles 17) and in a most interesting manner expands the things that had been previously revealed. Particularly relevant, given the historical circumstances that form the background to this psalm, are verses 30-32, for they give us an insight into the initial fulfilment of the promises and reflect the Psalmist's appreciation of why God had allowed the Egyptians to triumph over His anointed in the way they had (see below).

As the Psalmist remembers the promises he says, in an evident allusion to 2 Samuel 7 (verses 4-17):

"Then thou spakest in vision to thy holy one, and saidst, I have laid help upon one that is mighty; I have exalted one chosen out of the people."   (verse 19)

Clearly it was Nathan the prophet who had the vision. "Thy holy one" can be identified as David who was the recipient of the message. There is some textual evidence for the words being plural and not singular – consequently the RV has "thy saints". If this were the true rendering, then the reference would be to Israel as a nation on whose behalf David received the covenant. It surely has to be said, however, purely on the emphasis in scripture itself, that the covenant is presented as being made with David as an individual and not with Israel as a nation, although undoubtedly they were involved and shared the blessings that were promised. On these grounds, with no decisive evidence one way or another as far as the text is concerned, we consider that the singular, referring to David himself, is more appropriate. This is in harmony with verse 3: "I have made a covenant with my chosen."

God has laid help upon one that is mighty who has been chosen from among the people. The idea behind the word translated "laid", which has a wide variety of uses, appears to be 'conferred'. The same word is used in Psalm 21 where it is said of the king, "honour and majesty hast thou laid upon him" (verse 5). He is king by divine appointment. God has helped him that he might help His people and he is identified as one that is mighty, a phrase used elsewhere of David because of his exploits (2 Samuel 17:10). God had found David. He had identified him and acknowledged him as His servant. He had been anointed with holy oil. On that occasion it was necessary for Samuel to be reminded:

"Look not on his countenance, or on the height of his stature; because I have refused him: for the LORD seeth not as man seeth; for man looketh on the outward appearance, but the LORD looketh on the heart."

(1 Samuel 16:7)

God had provided Himself a king from among the sons of Jesse (1 Samuel 16:1) and reflecting upon this incident and the words of God recorded concerning David, the Apostle Paul testified to the Jews in Antioch in Pisidia, concerning him:

"I have found David the son of Jesse, a man after mine own heart, which shall fulfil all my will."

(Acts 13:22)

The words spoken to Nathan the prophet and revealed by him to David (verse 19) are here in this psalm recorded in more detail than in the historical books of 2 Samuel and 1 Chronicles. God's hand and His arm were seen as evidence of His power in action (verse 13). The allusions

724

were to the deliverance from Egypt memorialised in the Song that Moses and all Israel sang (Exodus 15). This hand and this arm were now to be manifest in the experience of David himself in establishing and strengthening him on the throne (verse 21). The enemy should not prevail against him nor the wicked triumph but God would smite all them that hated him (verses 22,23).

God's faithfulness and mercy were assured and in God's name his horn would be exalted (verse 24). There is a subtle change of emphasis here that turns our thoughts away from David himself to his seed. His horn (i.e., strength), would be perpetuated in his seed. Thus another psalm testifies, "There will I make a horn spring forth unto David" (Psalm 132:17, *Amplified Bible*).

Thus the covenant language is now enlarged to embrace Solomon in whom the promise had an incipient fulfilment and more appropriately the Lord Jesus Christ in whom it was finally realised. Thus "I will set his hand also in the sea and his right hand in the rivers" (verse 25). The sea is the Mediterranean and the rivers, the river of Egypt and the Euphrates. Thus is described the boundaries of the kingdom promised to Israel in the covenant that God made with Abraham (Genesis 15:18). This was the dominion enjoyed by Solomon and his sovereignty was the basis of Psalm 72, which looked beyond him to David's greater Son who "shall have dominion from sea to sea, and from the river unto the ends of the earth" (verse 8).

God had declared of David's seed, "I will be his father, and he shall be my son" (1 Chronicles 17:13). So, "He shall cry unto me, Thou art my father, my God, and the rock of my salvation" (Psalm 89:26). Not only does he acknowledge his filial relationship but he recognises Him as the rock of his salvation. The words are reminiscent of Psalm 18 which David sang when the Lord delivered him from all his enemies. Four times in that psalm (verses 1,2 (twice), RV; verses 31,46) David speaks of the Lord as his rock and his language echoes the Songs of Moses (Deuteronomy 32) and Hannah (1 Samuel 2). The link with the song of Hannah is particularly appropriate for it becomes the basis of Mary's song when the angel announced the birth of the Lord Jesus Christ (Luke 1:46-55). To the king's cry acknowledging God as his father, his rock and his salvation, the Lord responds:

"I will make him my firstborn, higher than the kings of the earth. My mercy will I keep for him for evermore, and my covenant shall stand fast with him."

(verses 27,28)

God had said of Israel, "Thus saith the LORD, Israel is my son, even my firstborn" (Exodus 4:22). Thus God's representative upon the throne of Israel, in whom all Israel's privileges and responsibilities met (for he was their representative too), was elevated to the rank of firstborn with all that was implied in that title. Of every king, anointed with holy oil, who sat upon the throne of David, there was a sense in which it could be said on his accession to the throne, "Thou art my Son; this day have I begotten thee" (Psalm 2:7 with Acts 13:32-37). This in no way detracts from the fact that the Lord Jesus was uniquely the only begotten of the Father. By birth his Davidic right was divinely established and God would give him "the heathen for thine inheritance, and the uttermost parts of the earth for thy possession" (Psalm 2:8). Once more these twin attributes of lovingkindness (mercy) and faithfulness (shall stand fast) are emphasised. Because of these qualities his seed will endure for ever.

It is at this point that the psalm gives us an insight into the covenant God made that we might not otherwise have appreciated:

"If his children forsake my law, and walk not in my judgments; if they break my statutes and keep not my commandments; then will I visit their transgression with the rod, and their iniquity with stripes."

(verses 30-32)

The language is a clear reference to the words of 2 Samuel 7: "If he commit iniquity, I will chasten him with the rod of men, and with the stripes of the children of men" (verse 14), but here it is expounded to cover all his children. How appropriate and how necessary were these words at this time given the disobedience of Rehoboam. He had been chastened with the rod of men, for God had used Shishak to punish him and in the understanding of these verses was God's answer to all the fears and anxieties of the Psalmist. Given that Rehoboam's experience would have been the first time that God had chastened the king in this manner (although subsequently repeated frequently), the words of explanation were particularly needful to allay the concern of faithful men.

A close reading of 2 Samuel 7 and 1 Chronicles 17 reveals, we believe, a different emphasis. The record in Samuel embraces Solomon and all the royal seed whereas the record in Chronicles, which does not record these particular words about "chastening for iniquity", is more particularly about the Lord Jesus Christ.

Having this knowledge God would have them to understand:

"Nevertheless my lovingkindness will I not utterly take from him, nor suffer my faithfulness to fail. My covenant will I not break, nor alter the thing that is gone out of my lips. Once have I sworn by my holiness that I will not lie unto David. His seed shall endure for ever, and his throne as the sun before me. It shall be established for ever as the moon, and as a faithful witness in heaven." (verses 33-37)

There are passages of scripture that defy comment and this surely is one. What words of ours can add to its significance or improve its clarity? God's word is irreversible and His promise inviolate.

There is perhaps just one point that we can make. His throne is to endure as the sun and to be established for ever as the moon. The last phrase regarding the faithful witness is taken by some to refer to the moon, by others to refer to the rainbow, but surely it is God Himself who is the faithful witness in heaven. The *Speaker's Commentary* says, "and the Witness in heaven is faithful". How significant then that the title should be appropriated to the Lord Jesus Christ (Revelation 1:5) in whom God was pleased to manifest Himself, and in whom all His promises are yea and amen (2 Corinthians 1:20).

Judah's Throne Cast Down (verses 38-45)

This latter part of the psalm stands in stark contrast to the emphasis upon the faithfulness and lovingkindness of

God in the earlier verses, for the reality of the situation seems to contradict everything that God has spoken. It is a problem for the Psalmist and as he wrestles with it he pleads with God to demonstrate that He has not, and will not, cast off His anointed and His throne for ever:

"But thou hast cast off and abhorred, thou hast been wroth with thine anointed. Thou hast made void the covenant of thy servant: thou hast profaned his crown by casting it to the ground."   (verses 38,39)

There is an emphasis in the original text upon the word "thou" that can perhaps be best expressed by repeating the word: "But thou, thou hast cast off." It was God who had done all these things; God who had promised. The vehemence of the language springs out of faith; an utter conviction that what God had spoken was true and that consequently He must respond to the cries of His servant.

He sees not just the king but the people of Judah involved in the punishment. In words that recall the description of Israel as a vine (Psalm 80:8-13) he cries:

"Thou hast broken down all his hedges; thou hast brought his strong holds to ruin. All that pass by the way spoil him: he is a reproach to his neighbours. Thou hast set up the right hand of his adversaries; thou hast made all his enemies to rejoice."   (verses 40-42)

Shishak took the fenced cities (i.e., the hedges) that pertained to Judah (2 Chronicles 12:4). The Lubims, the Sukkiims and the Ethiopians (12:3), they that passed by, spoiled him. Rehoboam and the men of Judah had no power to stand against the enemy: "Thou hast also turned the edge of his sword, and hast not made him to stand in the battle" (Psalm 89:43).

The result was that all the glory of the kingdom ceased, for Shishak carried away all the treasures out of the house of the Lord and out of the king's house, including the shields of gold that Solomon had made (2 Chronicles 12:9). "Thou hast made his brightness to cease, and cast his throne down to the ground" (Psalm 89:44, RV). It appears that the experience was such that Rehoboam became prematurely old: "The days of his youth hast thou shortened: thou hast covered him with shame" (verse 45). We remember that Rehoboam at the beginning of his reign

disregarded the counsel of the old men and listened rather
to the advice of the young who had grown up with him (2
Chronicles 10:8-14). In his folly there seems something
particularly apt that he should have grown old before his
time on the invasion by Shishak in Rehoboam's forty-sixth
year; the fifth year of his reign (see 2 Chronicles 12:1-13).

The Psalmist's Anxiety (verses 49-51)
The Psalmist makes his appeal that God would now
withdraw his anger, that this apparent contradiction
should not continue, for his days could not be extended
much longer and the enemies, not only of Israel, but of her
God, were taunting and rejoicing in her shame:

"How long, LORD? wilt thou hide thyself for ever?
shall thy wrath burn like fire? Remember how short my
time is: wherefore hast thou made all men in vain?
What man is he that liveth, and shall not see death?
shall he deliver his soul from the hand of the grave?
(verses 46-48)

We have commented on these verses in the earlier part of
our study on the psalm. It seems as if the Psalmist is
dwelling upon the fleeting nature of his own life and the
transience of all human experience. If God is not true to
His word then surely all men are created but for vanity, for
the grave would eventually claim all. This was of course
not the Psalmist's true conviction. It arose from the
musings of his heart, faced with the calamity that had
overtaken Judah's king and throne.

Concluding Prayer (verses 49-51)
So he cries:

"LORD, where are thy former lovingkindnesses, which
thou swarest unto David in thy truth? Remember, Lord,
the reproach of thy servants; how I do bear in my bosom
the reproach of all the mighty people; wherewith thine
enemies have reproached, O LORD; wherewith they have
reproached the footsteps of thine anointed."
(verses 49-51)

He pleads with God to manifest openly once more those
qualities upon which the covenant was founded. In the
present circumstances the enemies, not just of the king,

but of God Himself, found reason to rejoice and to reproach the king and all faithful men who had trusted God's word. The Psalmist shared the reproach of all the people, as the enemy taunted that God could not or would not help them, because they had misplaced their trust. This mockery they directed particularly at the king. It was as though every step he took they were watching and directing their insults.

There is no answer from God. But the first section of the psalm is the assurance that God will fulfil His word and that whatever the difficulties and adversities of life that might seem to contradict His faithfulness, those who truly seek Him need not fear or be discouraged. For, "My covenant will I not break, nor alter the thing that is gone out of my lips. Once have I sworn by my holiness that I will not lie unto David" (verses 34,35).

This psalm concludes what is commonly known as the Third Book of Psalms. It has the usual benediction with which each of the Books closes, and it stands as an appropriate postscript to the wonderful theme of Psalm 89:

"Blessed be the Lord for evermore. Amen and Amen."
(verse 52)

PSALM 90

THIS song begins what is commonly known as the Fourth Book of Psalms, 90–106 (see Introduction to Volume 1). The prefix to the psalm says, "A prayer of Moses the man of God". Moses is not alone in being honoured by such a title (Samuel, David, Elijah and others), but he is thrice described elsewhere in this way (Deuteronomy 33:1; Joshua 14:6; Ezra 3:2). It is an expression of the closeness of his relationship with God and of the affinity that he had with the things that God had revealed.

Not surprisingly some 'orthodox' commentators doubt the Mosaic authorship, but many others feel the song breathes a spirit that is most appropriate to the great lawgiver and we believe that the substance of the psalm confirms beyond any reasonable doubt that Moses was the author. Thus Psalm 90 has to be recognised as the most ancient of all the songs in this collection of inspired writings.

We intend to show that this is a psalm of the wilderness. It speaks of that generation that perished because of their unbelief. It is appropriate at this juncture that we draw attention also to the two psalms that follow (91 and 92). They bear no indication of authorship but it has been said that where a psalm has no title, as a 'rule of thumb' it can be presumed that it was written by the author of the previous psalm. This principle certainly holds good for Psalm 91 for that also is clearly a psalm of the wilderness. Whereas Psalm 90 speaks of the generation that perished, we show when dealing with Psalm 91 that it is addressed specifically to Joshua who lived through all the privations of the wilderness to enter the land. What is particularly striking is that while Psalm 92 bears no indication of authorship, the superscription says "a Psalm or Song for the sabbath day". What could be more appropriate? – the generation that perished, Joshua who entered the land and the rest that remained for the people of God (Hebrews 3:7-11; 4:1-10). It is a remarkable trilogy of psalms.

As far as the structure of the psalm is concerned we divide it for purposes of exposition in the following way:

1. God the Eternal   (verses 1,2)
2. Man the ephemeral   (verses 3-6)
3. Man under wrath   (verses 7-12)
4. An appeal to God's grace   (verses 13-17)

The word "prayer" used in the title is a translation of the Hebrew word *tephillah,* which means 'intercession, supplication' (*Strong*). The underlying purpose of the psalm is therefore Moses' desire to seek the good of the people of Israel as a whole, notwithstanding the unbelief that had resulted in a whole generation perishing.

God the Eternal

> "Lord, thou hast been our dwelling place in all generations. Before the mountains were brought forth, or ever thou hadst formed the earth and the world, even from everlasting to everlasting, thou art God."
>
> (verses 1,2)

It is not the covenant name that is used to address God but the title *Adonay* which speaks of His sovereignty; His rulership over all the works of His hands. He had been a dwelling place to successive generations (Hebrew, 'generation and generation'). It is Moses who wrote:

> "Remember the days of old, consider the years of many generations (same Hebrew word): ask thy father, and he will shew thee; and thy elders, and they will tell thee."   (Deuteronomy 32:7)

This passage is an appeal to consider God's past dealings with His people and the words of the psalm are also built upon the record of past experience: "thou hast been", literally, 'thou hast proved thyself to be'; not just a statement of what God is but an acknowledgement of what His servants had come to know Him to be in all generations – a "dwelling place" or, more literally, 'a home'.

There is a certain poignancy to read these words from the pen of Moses; a man who was, humanly speaking, never settled. He was forty years in the land of Egypt, a stranger in a strange land; forty years in the land of Midian, separated from his people; and forty years in the wilderness, only to die with the vision of the land before him. Yet he could say, "Lord, thou hast been our home". As one has put it, "Moses warmed himself at the fires of God". This, of course, had been true of successive generations of God's people and of none more so than Abraham, Isaac and Jacob who had no fixed dwelling place but "sojourned in the land of promise, as in a strange country, dwelling in tabernacles" (Hebrews 11:9), for they "confessed that they were strangers and pilgrims on the earth" (Hebrews 11:13).

The teaching of the psalm is carried forward into the New Testament in John 14:

"In my Father's house are many mansions (literally, 'abiding places')."   (verse 2)

"Jesus answered and said unto him, If a man love me, he will keep my words: and my Father will love him, and we will come unto him, and make our abode (Bede, in a forthright manner 'our home') with him."
                                                    (verse 23)

This wonderful figure of the home taken from the depths of human experience, speaks to our hearts. It is a most searching word of exhortation, knowing that God is with us, to ask, Do we feel at home with Him? Are we comfortable with Him? for that, of course, is what home means. It is our place of rest, our place of refreshing, our place of refuge; nowhere do we feel more comfortable and at ease, and that is how we should feel with God. The word translated "dwelling place" is closely related to another meaning 'refuge'. Some would substitute the second word for the first in this instance, but there are no serious grounds for doing so. The association of ideas that links refuge and dwelling place together is none the less sound and in this respect the words of the psalm once more echo the words of the Book of Deuteronomy:

"The eternal God is thy refuge (RV, dwelling place), and underneath are the everlasting arms." (33:27)

Men may wrestle with the concept of the reality of God, for His timelessness is beyond our comprehension. They may study the theory of relativity in an endeavour to understand the mystery of time. They may talk of astrophysics as they struggle with the complexity of the universe, but nowhere could it have been expressed with such simplicity, yet with a majesty and grandeur, transcending mere human thought. The psalm cuts through scientific terminology and gives us an insight into the nature of God that a thousand human scientific journals could never equal.

"Before the mountains were brought forth, or ever thou hadst formed the earth and the world, even from everlasting to everlasting, thou art God." (verse 2)

The mountains stood in men's eyes as symbols of eternity and strength (see Genesis 49:26; Deuteronomy 33:15). The word translated "earth" is the usual word for the earth at large. It means literally, 'firm' – what we today would describe as *terra firma*. The word rendered "world" is different. The Hebrew *tebhel* describes the fruitful, cultivated earth which is inhabited by man (e.g., Proverbs 8:31).

The translation, "thou hast formed" hides a startling and dramatic figure in the Hebrew text. Literally, 'didst travail in birth with' or as the RV margin, "gavest birth to". This is a figure used also in the Book of Job, chapter 38:

"Who shut up the sea with doors, when it brake forth, as if it had issued out of the womb?" (verse 8)

"Out of whose womb came the ice?" (verse 29)

These facts might be of purely academic interest, except perhaps that they tell us of the close affinity that God has with the work of His hands. However, the words of the psalm and of the Book of Job prompt another connection. The same Hebrew word is used of Israel in Deuteronomy 32:

"Of the rock that begat thee thou art unmindful, and hast forgotten God that gave thee birth." (verse 18, RV)

Thus we read in Exodus 4:

"Israel is my son, even my firstborn."   (verse 22)

Although the figure was not used of the creation of man when he "was formed (moulded) from the dust of the ground" (Genesis 2:7), surely the idea is latent in scripture and for this reason God could say of Adam, "which was the son of God" (Luke 3:38).

"From everlasting to everlasting thou art God". The Hebrew word *olahm* signifies literally 'a hidden time': thus from 'hidden time', from an indefinite past to an indefinite future. We have expressed the idea of unlimited time backward and forward to describe the reality of the One who is without beginning or end of days.

In the most sublime terms the opening section of this psalm teaches us that the eternity of God, His changelessness, His permanence, is the answer to all our rootlessness and homelessness. Even transient creatures of the dust, such as we, can find a home and feel comfortable and at ease with Him who is from everlasting to everlasting. This is the foundation on which the remainder of the psalm is built.

Man the Ephemeral (verses 3-6)

The contrast between the opening verses and this section of the psalm is stark:

"Thou turnest man to destruction; and sayest, Return, ye children of men"   (verse 3)

But it is not simply a contrast between the eternity of God and the transience of man. The opening address acknowledged God as sovereign and recognised Him as ruler. So now it is emphasised that man's life is absolutely at the disposal of God.

The Hebrew word translated "destruction" is from a root meaning 'to crush', hence powder or dust. Significantly the RV margin says, "Thou turnest man to dust". The word used for "man" is the Hebrew *enosh*. It means 'frail or feeble' and stands in this context for the mortal nature which man experiences because of the fall. The word "return" linked with the "children of men (literally, 'Adam')" is clearly an echo of the divine sentence passed upon Adam, as indeed is the verse in its entirety.

735

"In the sweat of thy face shalt thou eat bread, till thou return unto the ground; for out of it wast thou taken: for dust thou art, and unto dust shalt thou return." (Genesis 3:19)

Another psalm recalls both the words of Genesis 3 and those of Psalm 90:

"Thou hidest thy face, they are troubled: thou takest away their breath, they die, and return to their dust."
(Psalm 104:29; see also Ecclesiastes 12:7)

The precise connection between verse 3 and the verse that follows may not be immediately apparent:

"For a thousand years in thy sight are but as yesterday when it is past, and as a watch in the night."

We must not presume that the Psalmist is saying that one day equals a thousand years. Rather the emphasis is upon the rapidity of time as experienced by men. For man it was nevertheless measurable. It had its hours and its minutes in which events took place. But with God there is no such measurement of time whereby He is bounded. Indeed, not only is a thousand years like yesterday when it is past, a fleeting impression upon the mind of man, but also like a watch in the night through which men would normally sleep, unconscious of its passing. The night in ancient times was divided into three watches, but in New Testament times, in accordance with Roman practice, into four (see Judges 7:19 and Mark 13:35). Thus is expressed the relationship of the Eternal to time, that which sets the boundaries of human existence and experience.

Nevertheless there is a connection, we believe, between verses 3 and 4. For if the first speaks of the divine sentence upon Adam, the second carries us forward to the patriarchal age to demonstrate the reality of man's transience. Methuselah enjoyed the longest recorded life. He lived for 969 years, almost a thousand years. What then if a man should outlive Methuselah? It would still be, relatively speaking, no more than yesterday when it is past or a watch in the night, impossible to compare with the nature of the great Uncreate.

Methuselah was the son of the prophet Enoch. His name means 'at his death it shall be sent'. He died in the year of the Flood. So the connection is carried forward, remembering that all human life is at God's disposal:

"Thou carriest them away as with a flood." (verse 5)

Such is the transitory nature of human life and the manner in which successive generations are carried away.

These thoughts and ideas come together in Peter's Second Epistle:

"Whereby the world that then was, being overflowed with water, perished ... But, beloved, be not ignorant of this one thing, that one day is with the Lord as a thousand years, and a thousand years as one day ... But the day of the Lord will come as a thief in the night." (3:6-10)

(see Matthew 24:43 for the idea of the watch)

So the ephemeral nature of man is described further.

"They are as a sleep: in the morning they are like the grass which groweth up ... In the morning it flourisheth, and groweth up; in the evening it is cut down, and withereth." (Psalm 90:5,6)

Once swept away, as a consequence of the divine edict in Eden, they are as a sleep, lost in the unconsciousness of death from which they can only be released by God's saving grace. Is this a play on the "watch" in the night?

They are like the grass. It is hard for us, with our green fields, to appreciate the aptness of the figure. We have to enter into the everyday experiences of those who lived in the land of Canaan. Although there were undoubtedly different kinds of grasses, the meaning is clear. Watered by the dew of heaven, the grass would spring up and flourish in the early morning sun. However, scorched by the fierceness of the midday heat it would wither and die as the evening drew on. Again, remembering that for the Israelite the day began with the evening, we wonder if this is a play upon "yesterday when it is past".

The grass would, of course, renew itself in the morning and so it was a continuing cycle, ever renewing, ever fading. Such is human life in its successive generations and the early promise, in the flourishing of youth, serves only to emphasise the frustration of all human endeavour, as the withering of age so quickly follows (see also James 1:10,11).

Man Under Wrath (verses 7-12)

The transitory nature of human life is now given a more precise application:

> "For we are consumed by thine anger, and by thy wrath are we troubled." (verse 7)

The development of thought to this point has been general – the ephemeral nature of human life contrasted with the changeless nature of the Everlasting God. But He is not angry with us simply because of our nature. His wrath does not abide on us simply because we are what we are, transitory, mortal creatures of the dust. God's anger is directed against the unbelief and sin of men. So the passage speaks of actual experience: "we are consumed"; "by thy wrath are we troubled".

We have come specifically to that generation that perished in the wilderness because of their lack of faith. They were consumed in the wilderness and lived in perpetual anxiety because of impending death. Yet as we consider this section of the psalm we do well to remember that there is a sense in which that generation lived out their natural span. The punishment was:

> "Surely they shall not see the land which I swear unto their fathers." (Numbers 14:23)

> "Your carcasses shall fall in this wilderness." (verse 29)

We recognise that for them all to die within the thirty-eight year period it would be necessary for God to accelerate the process, yet very many of them would have lived their normal lifespan before they fell. We make this point to establish the fact that it is, consequently, correct to apply some of these verses to our own experience and expectancy of life, as indeed we often do (e.g., Psalm 90:10). So Moses, having observed all that befell the generation among whom he lived, acknowledged that:

> "Thou hast set our iniquities before thee, our secret sins in the light of thy countenance. For all our days are passed away in thy wrath: we spend our years as a tale that is told." (verses 8,9)

738

God had not turned away His face from their iniquity but they lived their lives with all their secret sins revealed. Literally the word rendered "light" means a 'luminous body', hence something that illuminates. It is the word used in Genesis 1, there also rendered "light(s)":

"And God said, Let there be lights in the firmament of the heaven ... to give light upon the earth ... And God made two great lights; the greater light to rule the day, and the lesser light to rule the night."   (verses 14-16)

So the sun of God's countenance shines into all the crevices and shadowy abysses of man's darkness, revealing all his hidden sins.

There is a like figure in the New Testament where we are exhorted to "keep the feast ... with the unleavened bread of sincerity and truth" (1 Corinthians 5:8). The word rendered "sincerity" is a compound of two Greek words. It means literally 'to judge by sunlight' and William Barclay in *New Testament Words* (page 67) describes a vivid background that illuminates the word.

In an eastern bazaar, goods would be displayed in all the dark corners and shadowy recesses of the ill-lit shops. If we were to purchase a piece of pottery, for example, then we should bring it out into the full glare of day. We should examine it by sunlight to discover what flaws it contained or what cunning attempts had been made to disguise its imperfections.

The words of Moses (and Paul) are as relevant for us today as when they were first written. How should we feel if all the secrets of our lives, all the things we hide in the dark corners of our minds, and the shadowy recesses of our hearts, were dragged out into the full light of day? Would those who think they know us best still recognise us? But God does not need to drag them out, for the light of His countenance shines with revealing light into every crevice of our being and if we love the light then we shall eradicate from our lives every thing that would offend.

Elsewhere (Numbers 6:24-26; Psalm 16, etc.), "the light of God's countenance" denotes the bestowal of the divine favour. The word for 'light' in these instances, although closely related, is different from the illuminating light of Psalm 90 and Genesis 1. Surely there is a word of comfort here, for that light which reveals will also forgive when the sin is acknowledged and repented of. This is the great responsibility and the privilege of those who live in the light of His countenance.

"All our days", says Moses, "are passed away in thy wrath". This does not mean that throughout their years in the wilderness the wrath of God was abiding on them. In fact Numbers 14:20 tells us very clearly that in response to Moses' prayer, God pardoned the sin of this people. They could not, however, escape the punishment for their sin; they still had to live with the consequence of their actions. So that which God decreed in His wrath was something they lived with until the divine edict had been fulfilled. The question is sometimes asked, 'Had that generation proved themselves unworthy of eternal life?' We suggest that the events recorded do not preclude individuals, who might have been included in the sin of the nation at that time, from subsequently showing the qualities in which God delights. Consequently the facts are not incompatible with the thought that some who died in the wilderness may yet obtain eternal life.

Interestingly, the thought of "yesterday when it is past" lingers on. The word translated "passed away" means literally 'to turn' (*Strong*). It has specific reference to what is described as 'the turn of the day', that is the onset of evening which heralds the passing of the day (see Jeremiah 6:4, "the day declineth", RV). So the brevity and fleeting nature of human life is emphasised. It is as Moses says, "as a tale that is told". If we simply accept the words of the AV translation, then the older we get the more we can relate to the words of the psalm. Our life is like a story, so quickly told, so soon forgotten. As we look back it is so difficult sometimes to appreciate how many years have passed since the events we store in our minds occurred.

There are, nevertheless, other suggested renderings, all of which adequately express the truth concerning the transitory nature of human life – a word, a sigh, a murmur, a thought or a meditation. We do not know what authority it has, but we particularly like the aptness of the Chaldee Version: "like the breath of the mouth in winter".

This is a figure we all readily understand: a puff of breath appearing as vapour, then caught away by the breeze:

"What is your life? It is even a vapour, that appeareth for a little time, and then vanisheth away." (James 4:14)

"The days of our years are threescore years and ten; and if by reason of strength they be fourscore years, yet is their strength labour and sorrow; for it is soon cut off, and we fly away." (Psalm 90:10)

This is not a precise definition of the length of human life but a general assessment of the experience of men; true of us today as it was for Israel of old. Medical research might have extended the boundaries a little but no one can doubt the truth of the words. If life is extended to "four score years", or even beyond, it serves only to emphasise that human vanity, the strength in which it delights, ends in the travail and misery that so often advancing years brings. Truly life swiftly passes and we fly away.

"Who knoweth the power of thine anger, and thy wrath according to the fear that is due unto thee?"
(verse 11, RV)

To know, or to understand the intensity of God's anger against sin will, if a man is exercised by this knowledge and lays it up in his heart, produce a reverence and fear of God that will act as a deterrent to further offence:

"So teach us to number our days, that we may apply our hearts unto wisdom." (verse 12)

Of no other generation could it be said, more appropriately, that they could number their days. They knew the limit that God had imposed beyond which they could not live. With the passing of the years those that remained would become more acutely aware of how limited was the time that remained. The fact, that they could "get us an heart of wisdom (RV)" is in itself an indication that their unbelief in not going up to inherit the land was not an irrevocable sin:

"The fear of the LORD is the beginning of wisdom."
(Proverbs 9:10)

The exhortation was – learn from your experiences. Through them get a heart of wisdom and, accepting God's judgements, look beyond the land which because of their unbelief *they* could not enter, to "the rest that remains for the people of God". In all our weakness, in the manner in which we too sometimes fail to rise to the greatness of our calling, we must seek to learn from our experiences, conscious always of the transitory nature of our life. We cannot literally number our days for we do not know what the next hour will bring, but we know the boundaries, the limits of human life, and the importance of grasping the opportunities while time remains:

"LORD, make me to know mine end, and the measure of my days, what it is; that I may know how frail I am. Behold, thou hast made my days as an handbreadth; and mine age is as nothing before thee: verily every man at his best state is altogether vanity."

(Psalm 39:4,5)

An Appeal to God's Grace (verses 13-17)

There was no way that God's decision regarding the generation that died in the wilderness could be changed. The Levites, of course, were not subject to this condemnation (see Numbers 26:57-62). Also the little ones (Numbers 14:31) would live through the privations of the wilderness and enter the land. It is interesting to reflect upon this new generation. Their time in the wilderness was the direct result of the sin of their fathers (see Numbers 14:33). Looked at from a national perspective there was no alternative and God turned this period of time to advantage by training and chastening them that they might enter the land a mature and disciplined people. In this respect the generation that perished, if they accepted God's will for them, had a part to play for the good of the nation as a whole. This larger perspective helps us to understand how, although there was no future for the generation that sinned, Moses could pray on behalf of Israel as he reflected not only on the demise of the older generation but also on the effect this might have upon those who lived with their condemnation. Moses' prayer is, therefore, a plea that God would gladden the hearts of those who should not enter the land and encourage those who would, by manifesting His grace in such a way as to assure them that His purpose with this people remained inviolate.

742

"Return, O LORD, how long? and let it repent thee concerning thy servants. O satisfy us early with thy mercy; that we may rejoice and be glad all our days."

(verses 13,14)

The tone of these words suggests, we feel, that the psalm was written earlier rather than later in the forty-year period. The fact that Moses is praying for all the people, not just for those who would enter the land, is an indication of the part they could yet play in the outworking of God's purpose.

Moses, the "Man of God" had seen His glory and heard His name proclaimed. He had a keen insight into the nature of God and an understanding of His character. He knew that God's anger would not burn for ever, that His wrath could be turned away. Not, of course, that God could regret His actions, but in the outworking of His purpose He "remembered that they were but flesh; a wind that passeth away, and cometh not again" (Psalm 78:39).

Such words as, "Return (literally, 'turn again'), O LORD ... let it repent thee" are characteristic of Moses. The psalm echoes his words recorded in Exodus (32:12) and repeated in Deuteronomy (32:36). His plea was that this cloud that hung over the nation might be lifted, that the night of trouble might pass and the morning (RV) of God's mercy dawn upon this people. It is not, we believe, a prayer for the day when they shall enter the land, but for God to so bless the people in the wilderness that they might be able to rejoice all the days of their life. Let this joy, says Moses, be found "according to the days wherein thou hast afflicted us, and the years wherein we have seen evil" (verse 15).

In effect Moses says, 'Help us to learn that in our affliction, in these days of evil, you have not abandoned us'. This becomes apparent when we appreciate that the word rendered "afflicted" is the same as that translated "to humble thee" in Deuteronomy 8:

"And thou shalt remember all the way which the LORD thy God led thee these forty years in the wilderness, *to humble thee*, and to prove thee, to know what was in thine heart, whether thou wouldest keep his commandments, or no. And he humbled thee, and

743

suffered thee to hunger, and fed thee with manna ...
that he might make thee know that man doth not live
by bread only, but by every word that proceedeth out of
the mouth of the LORD."   (verses 2,3)

Through all their experiences God was still at work for "as
a man chasteneth his son, so the LORD thy God chasteneth
thee" (verse 5).

That they might know that this was Moses' concern:

"Let thy work appear unto thy servants, and thy
glory unto their children. And let the beauty of the LORD
our God be upon us: and establish thou the work of our
hands upon us; yea, the work of our hands establish
thou it."   (Psalm 90:16,17)

When Moses speaks of God's work his thoughts are
dominated by the promises that He made to Abraham.

"He is the Rock, his work is perfect: for all his ways
are judgment: a God of truth and without iniquity, just
and right is he."   (Deuteronomy 32:4)

Ultimately it was in the inheritance of the land that God's
work was to be brought to fruition. That work, however,
depended in part upon the cooperation of all the people.
Therefore, "establish thou the work of our hands". In the
everyday enterprises of life, as we too seek the greater
good of 'the nation' and the outworking of God's purpose
we also pray that He add His blessing that we may
prosper. It is as true for us today as it was for Israel in the
wilderness.

In this way God would give that assurance to all His
people, "thy servants" and their children, that He was
faithful who had promised. They would see His glory, not
necessarily in its physical manifestation, but in the
declaration of His character through His works among
them. They would appreciate anew the beauty (literally,
the 'pleasantness' – see Psalm 27:4) of their God and
rejoice in His grace and kindness, manifest not only to the
children but also to that generation that perished in the
wilderness.

PSALM 91

A S we intimated in our consideration of Psalm 90, both Psalms 91 and 92 are linked with it in a remarkable trilogy of songs. They are all psalms of Moses and they deal respectively with the generation that perished in the wilderness (Psalm 90), Joshua who lived through the privations of the wilderness to enter the land (Psalm 91) and the rest that remained for the people of God (Psalm 92).

The key to understanding Psalm 91, we believe, lies in a proper appreciation of its use of pronouns. The opening verses consist of a general statement (verse 1), followed by an affirmation by the author of his faith in God (verse 2). In verse 3 the writer proceeds by addressing another person, "Surely he shall deliver thee", and continues this discourse through to verse 9 – the whole section being characterised by the use of the pronouns, 'thee', 'thou', 'thy' and 'thine'. In verse 9 there is a brief reference to the author's personal conviction, "Because thou hast made the LORD, which is my refuge, even the most High, thy habitation", before the address is continued to the end of verse 13. In the final three verses (14-16) of the psalm, God Himself speaks to the one addressed assuring him of deliverance and length of days.

As we have already indicated we believe that the author of the psalm is Moses and the person addressed, Joshua, the son of Nun, who lived through all the hardships of the wilderness, witnessing the destruction of the generation that perished, finally to enter the land in fulfilment of the word of God. The appropriateness of the language to Joshua will become apparent when we look in more detail at the substance of the psalm. Unquestionably it speaks in a marvellous way of the providence of God, the way in which He can preserve in safety the life of one who puts

745

his trust in Him. It is an interesting reflection upon the language of the psalm that during the Second World War it was known to many brethren and sisters in the U.K. as "the air raid psalm", i.e., "thou shalt not be afraid of the terror by night" (verse 5).

"There shall no evil befall thee, neither shall any plague come nigh thy dwelling. For he shall give his angels charge over thee, to keep thee in all thy ways."
(verse 10,11)

The aptness of the language to those who suffered the terror of night bombing of the cities in which they lived can be appreciated, but some brethren and sisters were killed in the air raids and in reality the message of the psalm, although providing comfort for the time of trial, had no real relevance to that situation. In a similar vein the *Speaker's Commentary* points out that in the *Talmud* the psalm is referred to as "a song of accidents". The application of the psalm to our pilgrimage will be discussed later in this chapter.

The Secret Place

"He that dwelleth in the secret place of the most High shall abide under the shadow of the Almighty. I will say of the LORD, He is my refuge and my fortress: my God; in him will I trust." (verses 1,2)

We notice first that in these two verses there are four different words used to describe the great Uncreate. He is called the Most High (*El Elyon*) for He is supreme, exalted above all others. He is the Almighty (*El Shaddai*), the all-sufficient one, the all-sufficing. By His name *Yahweh* (the LORD) has He made Himself known, both through His word and through His actions and, finally, He is my God (*Elohim*). The use of the divine name and three different titles in these two introductory verses serves to emphasise the supremacy of God manifest in different ways that combine together to express the wonder of His omnipotence. This is seen so marvellously in the providential care that was shown towards Joshua (and Caleb) throughout his wilderness pilgrimage.

What is "the secret place of the most High"? A series of quotations from other psalms helps us to understand:

"One thing have I desired of the LORD, that will I seek after; that I may dwell in the house of the LORD all the days of my life, to behold the beauty of the LORD, and to enquire in his temple. For in the time of trouble he shall hide me in his pavilion: in the secret of his tabernacle shall he hide me; he shall set me up upon a rock"

(Psalm 27:4,5)

"Thou shalt hide them in the secret of thy presence from the pride of man: thou shalt keep them secretly in a pavilion from the strife of tongues." (Psalm 31:20)

"Thou calledst in trouble, and I delivered thee; I answered thee in the secret place of thunder: I proved thee at the waters of Meribah." (Psalm 81:7)

There are several ideas that emerge:

1. That God hides those who put their trust in Him in His secret place, described as His pavilion (*Strong*, His covered place or booth) or tabernacle.
2. It is the secret place of His presence. It is a place where God dwells, a place where He can be found.
3. Such a place was Sinai, the secret place of thunders where Moses entered into the presence of God and saw His glory (Exodus 33 and 34).

God's "secret place" is established to be then, (a) a place of safety and protection, and (b) a place where He may be found, where He reveals Himself and where men can have fellowship with Him.

The references to "he shall set me up upon a rock" (Psalm 27) and "the secret place of thunder" are particularly relevant. When Moses went up into the mount he entered "the secret place of the most High". There he had fellowship with God and spoke with Him. There God revealed His will and purpose for Israel. But we notice also the reference to the tabernacle (Psalm 27:5) for all these ideas come together in Exodus 33 and 34. First of all, following the sin of Israel in the matter of the golden calf (Exodus 32):

"Moses took the tabernacle, and pitched it without the camp, afar off from the camp, and called it the Tabernacle of the congregation. And it came to pass, that every one which sought after the LORD went out

747

unto the tabernacle of the congregation, which was without the camp." (Exodus 33:7)

This tabernacle, of course, is not that for which Moses had received the pattern in the mount, for that tent with its furniture had not yet been constructed (Exodus 35 to 40). This tent was the place where God met with Moses and spake with him "face to face, as a man speaketh unto his friend" (Exodus 33:11). Significantly this passage tells us also that "his servant Joshua, the son of Nun, a young man, departed not out of the tabernacle".

It was in this tabernacle that Moses asked God, "I beseech thee, show me thy glory" (verse 18). The Lord's response was –

"there is a place by me, and thou shalt stand upon a rock: and it shall come to pass, while my glory passeth by, that I will put thee in a clift in the rock, and will cover thee with my hand while I pass by." (verses 21,22)

So Moses ascended into the mount and "the LORD ... stood with him there, and proclaimed the name of the LORD" (Exodus 34:5).

Another psalm expresses the truth of the matter:

"The secret of the LORD is with them that fear him; and he will shew them his covenant." (Psalm 25:14)

There is much exhortation in these events for us. We know that God is "the King eternal, immortal, invisible, the only wise God" (1 Timothy 1:17). When Moses forsook Egypt "he endured, as seeing him who is invisible" (Hebrews 11:27). Although God is everywhere present by His spirit, those who seek Him must appreciate the fact that He dwells in secret (see again Exodus 33:7) beyond the visible material things that He has created. To know Him we have to enter the "secret place". We have to withdraw ourselves from all distractions, from the things that would intrude, into a realm where the standards of men no longer exist. There, in secret, we shall be true to ourselves and true to God, for we shall be alone with God and it is from such a relationship that our fellowship with Him will develop and our understanding of Him and His ways grow.

It was to these truths that the Lord Jesus directed us when he said:

748

"But when thou doest alms, let not thy left hand know what thy right hand doeth: that thine alms may be in secret: and the Father which seeth in secret himself shall reward thee openly."   (Matthew 6:3,4)

And again:

"But thou, when thou prayest, enter into the closet, and when thou hast shut thy door, pray to thy Father which is in secret; and thy Father which seeth in secret shall reward thee openly."   (verse 6)

So, "He that dwelleth in the secret place of the most High shall abide under the shadow of the Almighty".

In the experience of Moses, God stood by him on the rock and covered him with His hand as He revealed His name. For all men of faith, like Joshua, who expressed his desire by "departing not out of the tabernacle", this must be a continuing experience. For those who abide in this relationship there is the assurance that they will be afforded divine protection. Their lives will be governed by His providential hand. Although in Moses' experience God overshadowed him with His hand, there appears to be an extension of the idea in the psalm, for "He shall cover thee with his feathers, and under his wings shalt thou trust" (verse 4).

Once again the psalms provide a rich tapestry of background:

"Keep me as the apple of the eye, hide me under the shadow of thy wings."   (Psalm 17:8; also 36:7)

"Because thou hast been my help, therefore in the shadow of thy wings will I rejoice."   (Psalm 63:7)

It is possible that the allusion is to the overshadowing wings of the cherubim above the mercy seat. There God dwelt in the midst of His people and it was a token of the fact that "I will walk among you, and will be your God, and ye shall be my people" (Leviticus 26:12).

The figure of the bird and his wings occurs also in Deuteronomy, although it is expressed in a different way from the Psalms:

"As an eagle stirreth up her nest, fluttereth over her young, spreadeth abroad her wings, taketh them, beareth them on her wings: so the LORD alone did lead him, and there was no strange god with him."

(32:11,12)

It is because of these truths that Moses can declare, "I will say of the LORD, He is my refuge and my fortress: my God; in him will I trust" (Psalm 91:2).

The *Speaker's Commentary* suggests that the translation should more properly be, "I say to the LORD", thus making it a direct address and acknowledgement of His care and protection. Dwelling with God, He becomes a refuge, a shelter, a place of safety. He is a fortress for in Him we are defended from all the vagaries of life that would destroy our spiritual life. It is important to realise that the psalm is not talking about a kind of insurance policy that would protect us from the ills that are common to men, but rather of those things that would cause us to stumble and fall on our journey to the kingdom. This is a theme to which we shall return before we conclude this study.

Moses Addresses Joshua (verses 2-8)

"Surely he shall deliver thee from the snare of the fowler, and from the noisome pestilence. He shall cover thee with his feathers, and under his wings shalt thou trust: his truth shall be thy shield and buckler."

(verses 3,4)

The change of pronoun indicates that the author (Moses) is now addressing another individual (Joshua) and the protection promised is of a very real and literal kind, for it was an assurance to Joshua that nothing could prevent him from entering the land. God would be true to the things that He had promised.

Nevertheless the "snare of the fowler" is still a figure of speech. Both the words translated "snare" and "fowler" are from the same root. The one means 'a net' and the other 'the entangler'. It is the figure of the hunter who snares animals, and when used of the wicked describes those who seek to cause harm and injury to their fellow men by their wiles.

"Keep me from the snares which they have laid for me, and the gins of the workers of iniquity."

(Psalm 141:9)

750

Literally, the word "noisome" means 'eagerly to covet or rush upon' (*Strong*), particularly in the sense of seeking to ruin or destroy. By a kind of personification the pestilence is presented as rushing to destroy men but, from every kind of evil, Joshua would be protected. We have already commented upon the manner in which God would overshadow Joshua as a bird would hover over its young, but in addition the assurance is given that "His truth shall be thy shield and buckler". Both the shield and the buckler describe large shields that would protect the whole body, the entire man. What protected Joshua was God's truth, that is His faithfulness to His promises. His word can be trusted implicitly and because of that Joshua had nothing to fear. He could have complete and absolute confidence that he would inherit the land.

Perhaps the appropriateness of the language of the psalm to Joshua can best be appreciated by contrast with the generation that perished. The message was:

"Thou shalt not be afraid for the terror by night; nor for the arrow that flieth by day; nor for the pestilence that waketh in darkness; nor for the destruction that wasteth at noonday. A thousand shall fall at thy side, and ten thousand at thy right hand; but it shall not come nigh thee." (verses 5-7)

How they must have feared for the arrow, the pestilence and the destruction, for they knew, every one of them, that they would die in the wilderness.

Once again note the use of personification: the pestilence that "walked" and the destruction that "wasted" are spoken of as though they had an existence of their own, thus giving dramatic force to the language. As it had been with Israel, "they saw the Egyptians dead upon the sea shore" (Exodus 14:30,31), so it was also true of Joshua's experience for:

"Only with thine eyes shalt thou behold and see the reward of the wicked." (Psalm 91:8)

The Most High's Providential Care (verses 9-13)

It is at this point in the psalm that the author refers to his own experience once again and establishes links with the first verse of this psalm and also with the first verse of the preceding psalm (Psalm 90:1):

> "Because thou hast made the LORD, which is my refuge, even the most High, thy habitation ..."
>
> (verse 9)

The change in pronouns establishes the point. Moses affirms that "the LORD is my refuge", the One in whom he found security. Because Joshua had made the Most High his habitation, he was assured of His continuing care in the exercise of His providential hand. Some commentators, finding difficulty with the change of pronouns, seek to alter the construction of the text (see for instance the RV margin), but there do not appear to be any strong textual grounds for doing so and the historical background suggested rests easily, we believe, on the change of pronoun to be found in the text of the AV.

The word rendered "habitation" is the same as that used in Psalm 90 (verse 1): "LORD thou hast been our dwelling place (literally, 'our home') in all generations". Like Moses, Joshua was at home with God (see previous chapter). The measure of his comfort in the presence of God is seen in the passage already quoted:

> "Joshua, the son of Nun, a young man departed not out of the tabernacle."   (Exodus 33:11)

In other words, he remained there and that is the precise meaning (i.e., 'to remain', *Strong*) of the Hebrew word translated "dwelleth" in verse 1: "He that dwelleth (remaineth) in the secret place of the most High".

Because of this abiding relationship with God, "because he had another spirit with him, and hath followed (God) fully" (Numbers 14:24):

> "There shall no evil befall thee, neither shall any plague come nigh thy dwelling. For he shall give his angels charge over thee, to keep thee in all thy ways. They shall bear thee up ... lest thou dash thy foot against a stone."   (Psalm 91:10-12)

The affirmation of God's protection is declared even more emphatically. No *evil* would befall him, and the word encompasses every form of calamity for nothing could prevent him from entering the land. No plague would come nigh his dwelling – literally 'his tent', emphasising the fact of his pilgrimage through the wilderness.

The word "plague" is commonly used to express 'the stroke' of God's hand as in the case of leprosy. It was particularly apt to describe the fate of so many in the wilderness. But Joshua need not fear, for God would give his angels charge concerning him.

The work of angels in the life of a believer is a fascinating and absorbing topic which should be a comfort to us all (see Genesis 28:12-15; 32:1,2; Psalm 34:7; 2 Kings 6:13-18; Hebrews 1:13,14). In this instance Joshua is assured that the angels would encamp around him to ensure that God's promise would be fulfilled. They would keep him in all his ways lest he dash his foot against a stone. Nothing would cause him to stumble and fall.

There is an interesting parallel between the words of the psalm and the record in Exodus 23.

EXODUS 23	PSALM 91
"Behold, I send an Angel before thee, to keep thee in the way, and to bring thee into the place which I have prepared" (verse 20).	"For he shall give his angels charge over thee, to keep thee in all thy ways" (verse 11).
For mine Angel shall go before thee, and bring thee in" (verse 23).	
"He shall bless thy bread, and thy water: and I will take sickness away " (verse 25).	"Thou shalt not be afraid ... for the pestilence ... the destruction" (verses 5,6).
	Neither shall any plague come nigh thy dwelling" (verse 10).
"The number of thy days I will fulfil" (verse 26).	"With long life will I satisfy him" (verse 16).

What could have been true for Israel if they had been faithful, remained true for Joshua, who embodied within himself everything that Israel should have been. He would enter the land as they could have if they had obeyed the word of the Lord, and in this he was a type of the Lord Jesus Christ who in an even more meaningful way was the Israel of God. The angels would bear him up in their

753

hands. As in the figure of the bird already considered (verse 4; Deuteronomy 32:11) the angels would (figuratively) carry him to the promised land. As God had blessed Israel so He would bless Joshua.

> "Ye have seen what I did unto the Egyptians, and how I bare you on eagles' wings, and brought you unto myself." (Exodus 19:4)

Even the beasts of the field would pose no threat for, "Thou shalt tread upon the lion and adder: the young lion and the dragon shalt thou trample under feet."

> (Psalm 91:13)

For accuracy and general interest we give the precise meanings of the Hebrew words identifying the beasts referred to as found in *Strong's Concordance*:

The Lion	From a root to roar, hence a fierce lion.
The Adder	From a root to twist, hence an asp.
The Young Lion	A young lion.
The Dragon	A marine or land monster. A sea serpent or a jackal. Translated "serpent" (Exodus 4) and "whale" (Jonah).

All these animals should pose no threat to Joshua. Indeed he would tread them under foot, recalling the curse on the serpent (Genesis 3:15). These words had a literal meaning for Joshua but they also spoke figuratively of the fact that no power of evil, no form of human wickedness, would prevail against him to prevent him from entering the land.

God Speaks (verses 14-16)

In this final section of the psalm, God Himself addresses His servant Joshua to assure him of His blessing:

> "Because he hath set his love upon me, therefore will I deliver him: I will set him on high, because he hath known my name. He shall call upon me, and I will answer him: I will be with him in trouble; I will deliver him, and honour him. With long life will I satisfy him, and shew him my salvation." (verses 14-16)

When men love God it is because He has first loved them. Thus it was recorded of God's love towards His people Israel:

"The LORD did not set his love upon you, nor choose you, because ye were more in number than any people."
(Deuteronomy 7:7)

"Only the LORD had a delight in thy fathers to love them, and he chose their seed after them."
(Deuteronomy 10:15)

As God had delighted in His people, so Joshua delighted in his God. He had found true joy and happiness in his knowledge and understanding of Him. It is for this reason that God will deliver (literally, 'set free' or 'enable to escape') him from every kind of danger. He will lift him up; exalt him; set him in a high place beyond the reach of those who would do him harm:

"The LORD hear thee in the day of trouble; the name of the God of Jacob set thee on a high place."
(Psalm 20:1 with AV margin)

These things God will do because he has known His name; because he has entered into the "secret place of the most High" and has developed a knowledge and understanding of all the things that are comprehended by His name. This, of course, is not simply an intellectual knowledge but it is an experiential knowledge. He had come to know the things of the name by the manner in which God had revealed Himself to His people and, on a personal level, worked in his life. The name of God, Yahweh, is a verbal noun meaning, "He who will be". It is a name of purpose, a name that is revealed in action. So to this man who has known His name God gives the assurance of His blessing in a six-fold play upon the meaning of that name. "Therefore *will I* deliver him: *I will* set him on high ... *I will* answer him: *I will* be with him ... *I will* honour him ... *I will* satisfy him."

The God who was to assure His people in a later psalm (46:1) that He would be a very present help in time of trouble, would answer when he called and be with him in times of trouble. He would deliver (literally, 'rescue') him and honour him; exalt him in the eyes of the people as a leader and a saviour because he in his life had honoured God (1 Samuel 2:30).

The ultimate blessing of long life in the land of promise should be his:

> "For with long life will I satisfy him, and shew him my salvation." (Psalm 91:16)

So for Joshua the words would be fulfilled:

> "For he is thy life, and the length of thy days: that thou mayest dwell in the land which the LORD sware unto thy fathers, to Abraham, to Isaac, and to Jacob, to give them." (Deuteronomy 30:20)

The words, of course, have a larger spiritual significance, for they look forward to the eternal inheritance, that rest that remaineth for the people of God (Hebrews 4:9) of which Joshua is assured and of which his experiences were a type and a shadow.

The Lord Jesus Christ

The psalm is beyond question Messianic in character for it speaks also of the Lord Jesus Christ who bore the same Hebrew name as his illustrious predecessor; a name in which was enshrined the message of salvation that was to be found in Yahweh, God of Israel. Truly in a deeper, fuller sense than with Moses and Joshua, the Lord Jesus would have entered into "the secret place of the most High" and consequently the protection of God's providential hand would be afforded to him as it had been to Joshua.

The circumstances of his life were, however, different. The detail of the psalm reflects the experience of Joshua, but its message remains true for the life of the Lord Jesus. It has particular relevance to his temptation in the wilderness, for –

> "The devil taketh him up into the holy city, and setteth him on a pinnacle of the temple, and saith unto him, If thou be the Son of God, cast thyself down: for it is written, He shall give his angels charge concerning thee: and in their hands shall they bear thee up, lest at any time thou dash thy foot against a stone." (Matthew 4:5,6; see also Luke 4:9-11)

Commentators, particularly those who believe in a supernatural devil, make much out of the fact that the quotation does not correspond exactly with the words of the psalm. Particularly, they draw attention in Luke's account to the omission of the words, "in all thy ways" (verse 11) claiming it is a deliberate misquotation designed to ensnare the Lord Jesus.

This is not the place to discuss, in detail, the Lord's temptation. Sufficient to say at this juncture that the real issue which confronted the Lord in the wilderness was the question of the cross and the crown. The Lord's response to the temptation helps in the understanding of its nature. "Jesus said unto him, It is written again, Thou shalt not tempt the Lord thy God" (Matthew 4:7). The reference is to the book of Deuteronomy: "Ye shall not tempt the LORD your God, as ye tempted him in Massah" (Deuteronomy 6:16).

The events at Massah are recorded in the Book of Exodus (chapter 17). There the people chided with Moses and tempted the Lord, asking:

"Wherefore is this that thou hast brought us up out of Egypt, to kill us and our children and our cattle with thirst?" (verse 3)

What they did was to attempt to put God to the test. The question they asked was, "Is the LORD among us, or not?" (verse 7). In effect they said, 'Prove that you are true to your word. Give us water to drink that we may know that you will bring us into the land'.

So the temptation of the Lord Jesus was not about giving the people some spectacular sign that would prove he was the Son of God, but rather it was about putting God to the test. It was about the cross. How could he be sure that God would be true to His word and raise him from the dead? Well, put Him to the test and see if His angels would indeed bear him up. Interestingly, if we consider the temptation in this way, the omission of the words "in all thy ways" is particularly pointed.

The issue for Joshua was long years facing the dangers and privations of the wilderness; but for the Lord Jesus in his temptation, it was focused on one issue alone – that of the cross and his three days in the coldness of the tomb. It seems appropriate that the words describing a more diverse providential care should be omitted in order to place the emphasis on the one issue – the salvation of the Lord Jesus from death. Hence, "to keep thee".

That angels did indeed "keep him in all his ways" is emphasised, for at the conclusion of the temptation, "angels came and ministered unto him" (Matthew 4:11). The temptation is only recorded in detail in Matthew and Luke. Mark's Gospel is, however, particularly interesting:

"And immediately the Spirit driveth him into the wilderness. And he was there in the wilderness forty days tempted of Satan; and was with the wild beasts; and the angels ministered unto him." (1:12,13)

Mark's record seems to encapsulate the message and language of the psalm: "He was with the wild beasts", for:

"Thou shalt tread upon the lion and adder: the young lion and the dragon shalt thou trample under feet."

(Psalm 91:13)

We have already noted the allusion to the curse on the serpent but may there not also be here a reference to the divine commission in creation?

"And God said, Let us make man in our image, after our likeness: and let them have dominion over the fish of the sea, and over the fowl of the air, and over the cattle, and over all the earth, and over every creeping thing that creepeth upon the earth." (Genesis 1:26)

This dominion over the works of God's hand will eventually be achieved through the victory of the Lord Jesus over sin. There in the wilderness as the Lord wrestled with the great issues that confronted him, this truth was emphasised as Mark's record, by implication, speaks of his supremacy over the beasts of the field:

"Thou madest him to have dominion over the works of thy hands; thou hast put all things under his feet. All sheep and oxen, yea, and the beasts of the field."

(Psalm 8:6,7)

Mark sums up the whole message of Psalm 91 when he adds the pertinent comment, "And the angels ministered unto him".

The Message For Us

What then is the message of the psalm for us today? We know that faith in God is not like an insurance policy that protects us from all the ills to which the flesh is heir. We suffer the common lot of all men, although we believe that God's providential hand works through these everyday things of life for our spiritual good. How then do we apply the psalm to our experiences? The message for Joshua was that nothing could prevent him from entering the land, for God was faithful who had promised.

So it is with us. If we have the spirit of Joshua, God will ensure that no spiritual disaster will overtake us that would prevent us from entering the kingdom. Only our own foolishness, our stubbornness and self-will can prevent God from fulfilling His will in us.

We "are kept by the power of God through faith unto salvation ready to be revealed in the last time" (1 Peter 1:5). God's providence is at work in our lives to ensure that that end will be accomplished. The message is:

"Fear not, little flock; for it is your Father's good pleasure to give you the kingdom."   (Luke 12:32)

PSALM 92

AS we have already indicated, this psalm bears the superscription "A Psalm or Song for the sabbath day" and is, consequently, appropriately placed following the two psalms of the wilderness, Psalm 90 and 91.

It has no indication of authorship and the question may well be asked, 'Is the superscription the work of the author or of some later hand when the psalms were compiled and arranged for temple worship?' It appears that the psalm was sung on the sabbath day in the services of the second temple. Edersheim comments in his work *The Temple, Its Ministry and Services as they were at the Time of Jesus Christ*:

> "When the drink-offering of the ordinary morning sacrifice was poured out, the Levites sang Psalm 92 in three sections, the priests drawing, at the close of each, three blasts from their trumpets and the people worshipping." (page 188)

Perceptively, one school of Rabbis said of this psalm: "A Psalm or Song for the sabbath-day i.e., A Psalm or Song for the future age (the age of the Messiah) all of which will be sabbaths". The question remains, of course, did they sing it at this time merely because of the superscription placed there by an editor, arranging the psalms for liturgical purposes, or because it had always, from the time it was first written, been associated with the sabbath day in the mind of the author, whether or not he himself placed the superscription at its head?

Another interesting factor is that J. W. Thirtle (*Old Testament Problems*) believed that this psalm and the five which follow (93–97) are all one psalm, mistakenly divided into six, and then followed by one shorter psalm (98 and 99), also designed for the sabbath but embodying passages

760

from Psalm 96 (page 325). He relates all these psalms to the circumstances and events of Hezekiah's day; Hezekiah, in his view, being the compiler of these psalms but not necessarily the author of them.

It is a fact that after Psalm 92 none of the following psalms (93 to 99) have any superscription or indication of authorship. Nevertheless we do know, on the authority of scripture, that David was the author of two of them. Psalm 96 with certain minor variations is part of the anthem that David sang when he brought the ark to Zion (see 1 Chronicles 16:7-36. Compare particularly Psalm 96 with verses 23-35). Also the Epistle to the Hebrews quotes Psalm 95 (verse 7) with the introduction: "Again, he limiteth a certain day, saying in David ..." (4:7).

It has to be admitted that in looking at this group of psalms, like others, we conjecture as to their authorship. However, we shall endeavour before we consider each song in detail, to show that there is a common thread that binds Psalms 93-99 together, and as we know that David wrote two of these songs it does not seem unreasonable to assume that he wrote them all. The theme that binds them together is the reign of God; His sovereignty, recognised and acknowledged by all the earth. In other words, they speak of the millennium rest that God has prepared. If this can be established, what is more appropriate than that David, having written these songs, should then associate them in the Psalter with Psalms 90 to 92. Indeed it is reasonable to suppose that although Hezekiah might have been responsible for the final editing and arranging of the psalms for liturgical purposes, there must first have been some arrangement for their use in the temple when Solomon constructed it. Who better than David who prepared with all his heart for the house of God to have undertaken this task and to have brought Psalms 93 to 99 into relation with Psalm 92, perhaps placing the superscription at its head? Who then wrote Psalm 92? It is certainly a matter of conjecture, but could it not have been Joshua himself to whom Psalms 90 and 91 would almost certainly have been delivered first.

Although it might not be considered conclusive, we believe that there are certain points of contact between

Psalm 92 and Psalms 90 and 91 in both language and thought that make the possibility of Joshua writing the psalm a realistic option. We give below some of the connections that we believe can be identified.

We shall consider the relevance of the allusions to each other when we come to the substance of the psalm.

Psalm 92	Psalms 90,91
"O Most High" (verse 1).	"The secret place of the most High" (91:1). "Even the most High, thy habitation" (91:9).
"I will triumph" (literally, 'shout for joy' verse 4).	"That we may rejoice and be glad" (90:14).
"To show forth thy loving-kindness in the morning, and thy faithfulness every night" (verse 2).	"In the morning it flourisheth, and groweth up; in the evening it is cut down" (90:6). "O satisfy us early (in the morning) with thy mercy" (90:14).
"For thou, LORD, hast made me glad through thy work: I will triumph in the works of thy hands. O LORD, how great are thy works!" (verses 4,5).	"Let thy work appear unto thy servants, and thy glory unto their children" (90:16).
"When the wicked spring as the grass" (verse 7).	"In the morning they are like grass which groweth up" (90:5).
"Mine eye also shall see my desire on my enemies" (verse 11).	"Only with thine eyes shalt thou behold" (91:8).
"They shall still bring forth fruit in an old age" (verse 14).	"With long life will I satisfy him" (91:16).

Structure

The grand theme of the psalm is the sovereignty of God, finally acknowledged and recognised in the blessing of His servants and the destruction of His enemies. There appears to be no consensus among scholars as to the strophical arrangement of the psalm. Purely from a personal point of view we find the suggestion of Perowne (*The Psalms,* Volume II) to be attractive. He writes:

"I believe that we have two principal divisions, verses 1 to 7, and verses 9 to 15, each division consisting of seven verses, separated by a verse (the eighth), which, unlike all the rest, is comprised in a single line. Each seven is again subdivided into a three and four. The whole scheme, therefore, stands thus: 1 to 3; 4 to 7; (8) 9 to 11; 12 to 15."   (page 178)

Thus verse 8 becomes the pivot of the psalm, declaring the truth around which all the other thoughts and ideas revolve. "But thou, LORD, art most high for evermore". The words "most high" are not a repetition of the title used in verse 1 of this psalm and Psalm 90 (verses 1,9), although, of course, the ideas expressed are closely related. The basic idea is that of height: God in the heights or, as it is expressed elsewhere, "God in heaven". God's sovereignty and authority being acknowledged, the pretensions of the wicked are seen to be without foundation (verses 4-7) and they vanish away (verses 9-11).

In our consideration of the psalm we follow the structure outlined above.

It is Good to Give Thanks (verses 1-3)

"It is a good thing to give thanks unto the LORD, and to sing praises unto thy name, O most High." (verse 1)

Literally, it is a 'delightful thing'. The Hebrew word translated "good" also carries the idea of 'lovely' or 'beautiful'. It is good in that it offers to God the tribute that is His due, but also in the sense that it fills the heart of man with the joy that is to be found in fulfilling its highest aspirations.

The word rendered "to sing" means literally 'to make melody'. It can mean either to play an instrument or to sing. It is the root from which the word translated 'psalm' is derived. In this instance it probably has reference both to singing and the playing of instruments. Thanks and praise are rendered to God because by His name, He has shown Himself to be sovereign, governor among the nations – the Most High.

The Psalmist's songs of praise dwell on the qualities of God's name, His lovingkindness and His faithfulness. He sings that he might "shew forth thy lovingkindness in the

morning, and thy faithfulness every night" (verse 2).
These are the divine characteristics that have particular
reference to His covenant, for:

"I will sing of the mercies of the LORD for ever: with
my mouth will I make known thy faithfulness to all
generations ... I have made a covenant with my chosen,
I have sworn unto David my servant."   (Psalm 89:1-3)

There is here a play (verse 2) upon the words of Psalm 90.
There the generation that perished were like the grass
which flourished in the morning, but in the evening it was
cut down and withered away (verses 5,6). In contrast
those, like Joshua, who abode under the shadow of the
Almighty, were reminded constantly of their standing
before Him, for they themselves, through His goodness
which they had experienced in their lives were living
testimonies to His lovingkindness in the morning and His
faithfulness at night. The allusion to Psalm 90 linking
God's lovingkindness with the morning also embraces
verse 14 of that psalm, and we consider this connection
below with verses 4 and 5.

The Psalmist's praise, however, is not confined to
singing his song; it is also expressed through the
instruments that were used:

"Upon an instrument of ten strings, and upon the
psaltery; upon the harp with a solemn sound." (verse 3)

There is doubt over the number of instruments referred to.
Some see as many as four and others only two. Four is
arrived at by reading; a ten-stringed instrument, a lute
(psaltery), a *higgaion* (translated 'solemn sound') and a
harp. Alternatively two is stressed by reading; "a ten
stringed lute and a harp of solemn sound". Of more
abiding interest is the use of these instruments (two, three
or four) in giving praise to God. We have commented
previously upon the fact that the sons of Asaph, Heman
and Jeduthun prophesied with harps, psalteries and
cymbals (e.g., 1 Chronicles 25:1-3). This is a concept that
we might find difficult to understand, but the effect of
appropriate music upon the hearts and minds of men in
bringing them 'in to tune' with God is something perhaps
to which we do not give sufficient thought. Remember that
when David played with his harp, "Saul was refreshed,

and was well, and the evil spirit departed from him" (1 Samuel 16:23). Note also that the word *higgaion*, translated "solemn sound", is elsewhere translated as "meditation" (Psalm 19:14). We can offer silent praise to God in the meditations of our hearts, and the way in which music was used in past ages to aid and encourage such thoughts is, perhaps, one of the factors that lie behind the words of the Psalmist.

The Work of God's Hands (verses 4-7)

Fulfilment and satisfaction had been achieved for the Psalmist because "thou, LORD, hast made me glad through thy work" (verse 4). It is a further reflection upon the words of Psalm 90:

"Let thy work appear unto thy servants, and thy glory unto their children. And establish thou the work of our hands upon us; yea, the work of our hands establish thou it." (verses 16,17)

Joshua's joy was to be found in the fact that God had completed the work for which Moses had prayed on behalf of the people. God's providential care and His visible hand among them had brought them safely into the land. But further reflection upon the words of Psalm 90 reveals a truth that we all need to learn: "Let thy work appear unto thy servants ... and ... establish thou the work of our hands." God's work is carried forward by our work. If God is to work in our lives and accomplish His purpose then we must play our part. We must do what we can and in faith leave the outworking of God's purpose to Him, knowing that He is faithful who has promised.

Moses had prayed, "O satisfy us early with thy mercy; that we may rejoice and be glad all our days" (Psalm 90:14). Literally, 'satisfy us in the morning with thy lovingkindness' and now that the night of sorrow was past, Joshua and all those of like mind could rejoice in the rest that God had provided. But even in the wilderness they had been given the assurance that God would be true to His word, for every morning they had experienced His mercy in the provision of manna. The record in Exodus 16 emphasises the point:

765

"In the morning ye shall be filled with bread ... and in the morning the dew lay round about the host."

(verses 12,13)

"And they gathered it every morning, every man according to his eating."

(verse 21)

Moses had continued his prayer: "Make us glad according to the days wherein thou hast afflicted us" (Psalm 90:15), and the word translated "afflicted" is that which is rendered to "humble thee" in Deuteronomy 8:

"And he humbled thee, and suffered thee to hunger, and fed thee with manna, which thou knewest not, neither did thy fathers know; that he might make thee know that man doth not live by bread only, but by every word that proceedeth out of the mouth of the LORD doth man live."

(verse 3)

So they had learned the lesson and rejoiced in His lovingkindness, for they had seen all His work amongst them brought to fruition. So Joshua could exclaim:

"I will triumph (shout for joy, *Strong*) in the works of thy hands."

(Psalm 92:4)

It should, perhaps, be noted that in the Hebrew text there are two quite different words which have been translated 'work' and 'works' in the AV. The first refers to the providential work of God amongst His people and all the inhabitants of the earth. The second, a more general word, is used of God's creative work (see Genesis 2:2,3). It is this difference that led some rabbis to refer the psalm to the 'rest' of Messiah's reign and others to the creative works of Genesis 1 and the original establishment of the sabbath.

The truth of the matter is that both ideas are connected. The one (creation) is the pattern for the other (the kingdom) and the works of Genesis 1 are the foundation of the purpose that will find their fulfilment in the age to come. This pattern of thought can be identified elsewhere:

"By the word of the LORD were the heavens made; and all the host of them by the breath of his mouth."

(Psalm 33:6)

"For he spake, and it was done; he commanded, and it stood fast."

(verse 9)

766

"The council of the LORD standeth for ever, the thoughts of his heart to all generations."   (verse 11)

The power of God's word in creation is shown to be still active through the operation of that word among men (see verses 10,12,13, etc.). Truly the Psalmist could write:

"O LORD, how great are thy works! and thy thoughts are very deep. A brutish man knoweth not; neither doth a fool understand this."   (Psalm 92: 5,6)

The contemplation of the works of God will always fill the heart of the believer with wonder and admiration. The more we strive to understand God and His ways, the more we come to appreciate how unfathomable are His designs to the human mind. His "judgements are a great deep" (Psalm 36:6).

"For who hath known the mind of the Lord? or who hath been his counsellor?"   (Romans 11:34)

Such things, the deep things of God, are beyond the understanding of faithless, worldly-minded men. A "brutish man", literally, a 'stupid man' in the sense that he cannot raise his mind above the natural things of life, is like the beasts of the field, incapable of discerning spiritual things. Like the fool who says in his heart, "There is no God" (Psalm 14:1), he is incapable of recognising the truths that are readily apparent to the eyes of faith. They fail to perceive the lesson of Psalm 90 (verse 5) and consequently, "When the wicked flourish as the grass, and when all the workers of iniquity do flourish", they do not appreciate that "it is that they shall be destroyed forever" (verse 7). It is as though the message is, the wicked may flourish but they are but ripening and maturing for judgement. Other psalms express the truth in different ways:

"I have seen the wicked in great power, and spreading himself like a green bay tree. Yet he passed away, and, lo, he was not: yea, I sought him, but he could not be found."   (Psalm 37:35,36)

"Surely men of low degree are vanity, and men of high degree are a lie: to be lain in the balance, they are altogether lighter than vanity."   (Psalm 62:9)

It is only the eye of faith that has been into the sanctuary (the secret place of the Most High) that can truly understand their end (Psalm 73:17).

God on High (verse 8)

Exalted above all the machinations of evil men and all the trouble and adversity that can afflict the righteous, the truth that God is in control is the foundation of faith for all His servants. It is in the day when all the works of God are finally consummated in the things that He has promised, and His sovereignty recognised and acknowledged, that the righteous man's faith is finally vindicated.

The Destruction of the Wicked (verses 9-11)

This section of the psalm presents us with a contrast between the wicked, the enemies of both God and His people, and the righteous who are blessed by God:

"For, lo, thine enemies, O LORD, for, lo, thine enemies shall perish; all the workers of iniquity shall be scattered. But my horn shalt thou exalt like the horn of an unicorn: I shall be anointed with fresh oil."

(verses 9,10)

The word "lo" is a form of invitation to behold, to see now the end of the wicked. Perhaps there was a particular instance to which the words refer, but they are true also of the ultimate fulfilment of God's purpose:

"Those mine enemies, that would not that I should reign over them, bring hither, and slay them before me."

(Luke 19:27)

The reference to scattering is not strictly the idea of scattering as of seed. Rather the root meaning is 'to break through', resulting in the dispersal of the various parts. The picture is of the wicked (the kingdom of men) as a unified force (literally, a 'great image', *one* great image; Daniel 2:31) broken in pieces (as with the stone cut out of the mountain) and its constituent parts dispersed abroad:

"Then was the iron, the clay, the brass, the silver, and the gold, broken to pieces together, and became like the chaff of the summer threshingfloors."   (Daniel 2:35)

In contrast, the Psalmist speaks of his horn being exalted like the horn of an unicorn (literally, 'wild ox'). The original text implies an accomplished fact. The height of the animal's horn was understood to represent the measure of its power and strength. The word rendered 'exalt' is from the same root as that used to describe God as "the most High" (verse 8). When God is exalted in the earth then His people are lifted up and set on high. This was true when Israel first entered the land, but the ultimate fulfilment will be in the sabbath of rest in the kingdom age.

The final phrase of verse 10 reads more appropriately, "I *am* anointed with fresh oil". The principal idea seems to be that of restoration of strength and vigour. Interestingly there is a suggested alternative rendering arising from a change in the vowel points that supports this meaning: 'My failing strength is restored with fresh oil'. Behind the words is the figure of an old man whose powers are invigorated by the anointing of oil.

How appropriate this idea is to this psalm becomes apparent when we remember that both Joshua and Caleb were old men when they entered the land. If we take Caleb as an example, then his words recorded in Joshua 14 illustrate the point:

"Forty years old was I when Moses the servant of the LORD sent me from Kadesh-barnea." (verse 7)

"And now, behold, the LORD hath kept me alive ... these forty and five years ... and now, lo, I am this day fourscore and five years old. As yet I am as strong this day as I was in the day that Moses sent me: as my strength was then, even so is my strength now ... therefore give me this mountain, whereof the LORD spake in that day." (verse 10-12)

Once again the Psalmist's words echo the thoughts of the two previous songs:

"Only with thine eyes shalt thou behold and see the reward of the wicked." (Psalm 91:8)

This was true of Joshua in the wilderness as he lived amongst the generation that perished. But it was true also of the situation that existed when they entered the land. The Psalmist had exclaimed, "O LORD ... lo, thine enemies shall perish" and God's enemies were his also. So "Mine eye also hath seen (its desire) upon them that laid wait for me: Mine ear heard (its pleasure) of them that rose up against me" (verse 11, *Cambridge Bible*).

It is not personal vindictiveness that causes God's servants to speak in this way. Rather they look with longing to the day when the sinners will be consumed out of the earth and the wicked shall be no more (Psalm 104:35).

In contrast: "The righteous shall flourish like the palm tree: he shall grow like the cedar in Lebanon" (verse 12). The evergreen foliage of both trees speaks of life – not the brief flourish of the wicked, who are like the grass, ephemeral and transient, but solid, abiding, continuing life. Both trees have life spans that extend over hundreds of years and consequently speak to us not just of the longevity of mortal life, lived under the blessing of God, but also of eternal life. The palm was known particularly for its fruitfulness and the cedar for its fragrance. Such is the outcome of the righteous flourishing in the earth. Fruitful works ascend as a sweet savour before the Lord.

Planted in the House of God (verses 13-15)
The thought of the palm and the cedar is extended into this final section of the psalm.

> "Those that be planted in the house of the LORD shall flourish in the courts of our God." (verse 13)

It might be thought that the reference is to the temple and that the psalm is consequently of a much later date than that we have suggested. This is, however, not necessarily so. The tabernacle (God's house) and all that pertained to it spoke of Israel established in their land and God dwelling in their midst. Speaking of Israel restored, enjoying the blessings of the covenant Ezekiel writes:

> "And they shall dwell in the land that I have given unto Jacob my servant, wherein your fathers have dwelt; and they shall dwell therein, even they, and their children, and their children's children for ever: and my servant David shall be their prince for ever. Moreover I will make a covenant of peace with them; it shall be an everlasting covenant with them: and I will place them,

and multiply them, and will set my sanctuary in the midst of them for evermore." (37:25,26)

What will be true in the future was also in part true of the past, and God planted them in His land:

"Thou shalt bring them in, and plant them in the mountain of thine inheritance, in the place, O LORD, which thou hast made for thee to dwell in, in the Sanctuary, O Lord, which thy hands have established."
(Exodus 15:17)

"Moreover I will appoint a place for my people Israel, and will plant them, that they may dwell in a place of their own, and move no more." (2 Samuel 7:10)

"For the vineyard of the LORD of hosts is the house of Israel, and the men of Judah his pleasant plant."
(Isaiah 5:7)
(see also Psalm 80:8,15; Jeremiah 11:17; 12:2)

Israel are thought of as the planting of the Lord, flourishing and taking root under His tender care. In this sense the language is figurative and speaks not only of Israel planted in their land but also of the millennium rest to which we look. David, in a psalm composed about Doeg the Edomite, before the temple was built, wrote "I am like a green olive tree in the house of God" (Psalm 52:8).

Looking to the outworking of the ministry of the Lord Jesus Christ in the lives of believers, the prophet Isaiah writes:

"To appoint unto them that mourn in Zion, to give unto them beauty for ashes, the oil of joy for mourning, the garment of praise for the spirit of heaviness; that they might be called trees of righteousness, the planting of the LORD, that he might be glorified." (Isaiah 61:3)

The passage quoted above (Joshua 14:7-12) concerning Caleb in his old age, amply illustrates the truth of the continuing emphasis upon the palm and the cedar:

"They shall still bring forth fruit in old age; they shall be fat and flourishing." (Psalm 92:14)

Again the allusion is there to the previous psalm, "with long life will I satisfy him" (Psalm 91:16), and the fruitfulness of the palm which on occasion would produce hundreds of pounds of dates. Continuing the figure, "they would be full of sap and rich in verdure" (*Speaker's Commentary*). The word rendered "flourishing" (verse 14) is the same as that translated 'fresh' in verse 10. Thus is expressed the vigour of the righteous in old age and the conclusion of the matter is:

"To shew that the LORD is upright: he is my rock, and there is no unrighteousness in him."   (verse 15)

The verse refers back to verse 2, "to shew forth thy lovingkindness ... and thy faithfulness". The verb rendered "to shew forth" and here "to shew" is the same, and the "no unrighteousness" of verse 15 is the exact equivalent of the faithfulness of verse 2 (*Speaker's Commentary*). The words of Moses in Deuteronomy 32 unite the two verses of the psalm. He is "a God of truth and without iniquity" (verse 4). The word rendered "truth" is the same as that translated "faithfulness" in verse 2, and the word rendered "iniquity' differs only slightly from that translated "unrighteousness" in verse 15.

Thus God's righteous rule over all the earth will finally be established and recognised. The wicked will no longer flourish; their prosperity will be seen to have been but for a moment. The joy of the righteous, however, will be forever and in it the final vindication of God's righteousness in that sabbath of rest that remains for the people of God. Truly the Psalmist can say of his God, He is "My rock" (see Deuteronomy 32:4,15,18,30,31).

INTRODUCTION TO PSALMS 93–99

WE have already expressed our conviction that all the psalms in this section were written by David around the theme of the sabbath and associated by him with Psalms 90,91, and in particular Psalm 92. Psalm 100 could be included in this group, but although we do not doubt its close connection with these songs, we are not convinced that it belongs with them in the sense that they all have the sabbath background as their theme. If perhaps we could think of Psalm 92 as the prologue to this group of songs, then Psalm 100 is the epilogue. It is appropriate that the total number of psalms in this group is seven. This of itself would impress upon us the thought of the "sabbath of rest".

Two grand themes come together in these psalms and are wrought together in the framework of the songs. Both speak to us in their own way of God's sabbath; the one of its original institution and the other of its ultimate fulfilment in the kingdom age. The thought of God, the Creator, exalted over all, manifesting His power in the midst of the works of His hands, is described in dramatic fashion for all nature joins in the chorus of praise. The seas roar, the rivers clap their hands, the hills are joyful together, the field and all that is therein, together with the trees of the wood, join in the glad song (see Psalm 93:3,4; 95:4-6; 96:11,12; 98:7,8). They sing with all the nations of the earth because God manifests Himself as the righteous judge (Psalm 94:2,15; 96:10,13; 98:4,9; 99:4) as His sovereignty is recognised by all that His hands have made in that day to which the sabbath pointed forward, when His kingdom should be established (Psalm 93:1,2; 95:3; 96:10; 97:1; 98:6; 99:1). The interplay of these various threads of thought will become more apparent as we examine the context of the psalms.

Before we do so it is pertinent to consider briefly when these psalms might have been written. Because of the lack of superscriptions and subscriptions we are totally dependent, for most of the psalms, upon their content and this will inevitably lead to some conjecture. As we have already indicated, however, we do know on the authority of scripture that David wrote two of the psalms (95 and 96) and that the second of these was written to celebrate bringing up the ark to Zion (1 Chronicles 16:23-33). With Psalm 96 as our yardstick we investigate the possibility that all these psalms were written by David as reflections upon that occasion when he brought the ark of God to the tabernacle he had prepared. It was "the ark of the covenant of the Lord of all the earth" (Joshua 3:11,13). How appropriate then that throughout these psalms there should be an emphasis upon the fact that His sovereignty and authority is recognised by all people and nations.

Again "the ark of the covenant" was the symbol of God's presence in the midst of His people. From the mercy seat between the cherubim He reigned as king. Significantly, a psalm (24) almost universally accepted among us as associated with David bringing up the ark to Zion, speaks of the triumphal procession:

"Lift up your heads, O ye gates; and be ye lift up, ye everlasting doors; and the King of glory shall come in. Who is this King of glory? The LORD strong and mighty, the LORD mighty in battle." (verses 7,8)

So the picture that emerges after the ark has been successfully brought to Jerusalem is of God reigning in the midst of His people, typifying the day when God's kingdom will extend from "sea to sea, and from the river unto the ends of the earth" (Psalm 72:8). When manifest in His son "all kings shall fall down before him: all nations shall serve him" (Psalm 72:11). Thus the theme of the Theocracy runs throughout this group of psalms:

"The LORD reigneth." (Psalm 93:1; 97:1)

"For the LORD is a great God, and a great King above all gods." (Psalm 95:3)

"Say ye among the heathen that the LORD reigneth." (Psalm 96:10)

774

"Make a joyful noise before the LORD, the King."
(Psalm 98:6)

"The LORD reigneth ... he sitteth between the cherubims." (Psalm 99:1)

That which was foreshadowed by both the sabbath and the ark of the covenant will finally meet in the reality of the kingdom age. We suggest, however, that the language of the Old Testament concerning the ark of God has strong sabbatical overtones. Consequently it is even more appropriate than we might at first have thought, that David should have linked the two threads together when he associated this group of psalms composed about the bringing of the ark to Zion with Psalm 92, "a Psalm or Song for the sabbath day".

When the ark set forward Moses said:

"Rise up, LORD, and let thine enemies be scattered; and let them that hate thee flee before thee. And when it rested, he said, Return, O LORD, unto the many thousands of Israel." (Numbers 10:35,36)

Note that the ark "rested". It is one of a group of synonyms used to describe the sabbath day.

"For in six days the LORD made heaven and earth, the sea, and all that in them is, and rested the seventh day." (Exodus 20:11)

(note the word used in Genesis 2:3 is different)

Significantly the passage from Numbers 10 is quoted in two other psalms written concerning the journey of the ark to Zion. Psalm 68, which begins with the words of Moses: "Let God arise, let his enemies be scattered" (verse 1), describes the manner in which God led His people: "O God, when thou wentest forth before thy people, when thou didst march through the wilderness" (verse 7), until finally He is enthroned in Zion.

"Sing unto God, ye kingdoms of the earth; O sing praises unto the Lord." (verse 32)

Psalm 132, in words reminiscent of some of the language of psalms 93 to 99, says:

"We will go into his tabernacles: we will worship at his footstool. Arise, O LORD, into thy rest; thou and the ark of thy strength ... For the LORD hath chosen Zion;

775

he hath desired it for his habitation. This is my rest forever: here will I dwell; for I have desired it."

(verses 7,8,13,14)

In addition to the main theme there are numerous verbal links between these psalms and the three preceding songs.

PSALM 93

IN keeping with the ideas already expressed, this psalm was sung in the second temple on the day before the sabbath. Jewish tradition (the *Mishnah*) said: "because God on the sixth day had finished His work, and begun to reign over His creatures."

The Septuagint, with what authority we cannot say, prefaces the psalm in a similar way: "When the earth was peopled with living creatures." Both quotations serve to emphasise the fact that the tradition associating this psalm (and those succeeding it) with the sabbath is of ancient origin.

The key to this and the following psalms in the group is to be found in the pivotal verse of 'the Psalm for the Sabbath day' with which they have become connected. "But thou, LORD, art most high for evermore" (Psalm 92:8). This psalm clearly refers to some event in close proximity to the time it was written. Verse 1 says, "The LORD reigneth". Literally, 'He now reigns' or 'hath become king'. His sovereignty has been established and His authority acknowledged. He has, as it were, literally ascended His throne and proclaimed Himself King. We can appreciate how David would have thought in these terms and seen them in a very real sense as being fulfilled in bringing the ark to Zion. How much more so, however, are the words true of the kingdom age, when the Lord Jesus shall come to sit on David's throne for ever.

Because He is supreme, Creator and King of all that His hands have made, all nature must obey and acknowledge Him and the ragings of men who would exalt themselves against Him, of which the overflowing rivers and roaring seas are but figures, must ultimately submit (verses 3,4) for His word is faithful. His declared will and purpose will be carried out for His "testimonies are very sure" and "holiness becometh (His) house" (verse 5).

The psalm is all of a piece and there is no need to sub-divide it in any way.

> "The LORD reigneth, he is clothed with majesty; the LORD is clothed with strength, wherewith he hath girded himself." (verse 1)

It is always good to be reminded of first principles and the Old Testament affirms in a positive manner that God was the King of Israel. Moses acknowledged the fact in the song he sang after they had crossed the Red Sea. "The LORD shall reign for ever and ever" (Exodus 15:18). He "was king in Jeshurun, when the heads of the people and the tribes of Israel were gathered together" (Deuteronomy 33:5). When the people desired a king like the nations about them God reminded Samuel:

> "They have not rejected thee, but they have rejected me, that I should not reign over them." (1 Samuel 8:7)

And when David spoke before the assembled princes of Israel, he said:

> "And of all my sons, (for the LORD hath given me many sons,) he hath chosen Solomon my son to sit upon the throne of the kingdom of the LORD over Israel."
> (1 Chronicles 28:5)

It was God's kingdom and God's throne and he who sat on it was but the representative of the Most High. It remains true, even of the Lord Jesus Christ, although because he is the only begotten Son of God he sits on that throne as God's heir:

> "I shall give thee the heathen for thine inheritance, and the uttermost parts of the earth for thy possession."
> (Psalm 2:8)

We await the day when the truth will be proclaimed:

> "The kingdom of the world is become the kingdom of our Lord, and of his Christ: and he shall reign for ever and ever." (Revelation 11:15, RV)

In that day the opening words of the psalm will have achieved their ultimate reality.

Throughout these opening sentences of the psalm the verbs, which are in the perfect tense, express not merely a fact but an act (*Cambridge Bible*). God ascended His throne and proclaimed Himself King. He has girded Himself with the royal insignia (majesty) and put on strength like a warrior, clothed for the battle.

For so long it might have appeared to men, particularly those who lacked faith, that God had abdicated His power and authority. The ark had been taken by the Philistines; it had not rested in the tabernacle of the Lord for many years, even after the Philistines had returned it:

"And it came to pass, while the ark abode in Kirjath-jearim, that the time was long ... and all the house of Israel lamented after the LORD."

(1 Samuel 7:2)

Although we believe that Psalm 44 was written at a later date, its spirit expresses perfectly how the faithful in Israel must have felt at that time:

"We have heard with our ears, O God, our fathers have told us, what work thou didst in their days, in the times of old." (verse 1)

"In God we boast all the day long, and praise thy name for ever. But thou hast cast off, and put us to shame; and goest not forth with our armies."

(verses 8,9)

"Awake, why sleepest thou, O Lord? arise, cast us not off for ever. Wherefore hidest thou thy face, and forgettest our affliction and our oppression?"

(verses 23,24)

"Arise for our help, and redeem us for thy mercies' sake." (verse 26)

Now arrayed in His royal garments and girded with power, the people were reminded how "he (had) triumphed gloriously" (Exodus 15:1) when He had overthrown the chariots of Pharaoh for "the LORD is a man of war: the LORD is his name" (verse 3). Note that the words rendered "majesty" (Psalm 93:1) and "glorious" (Exodus 15:1) are from the same cognate verb. When the ark came to Zion they had cried from the walls of the city, "Who is this king of glory?". David had responded, "The LORD strong and mighty, the LORD mighty in battle ... he is the King of glory" (Psalm 24:7-10). As a result of His reign, the exercise of His power and authority, it could now be said:

> "The world also is stablished, that it cannot be moved. Thy throne is established of old: thou art from everlasting." (Psalm 93:1,2)

The former words are repeated in Psalm 96 (verse 10) emphasising the cohesion of thought that binds these songs together. Because God reigned the world was secure. He was in control and the truth behind the words is expressed by the Epistle to the Hebrews which speaks of "the removing of those things that are shaken ... that those things which cannot be shaken might remain. Wherefore we receiving a kingdom that cannot be moved ..." (12:27,28). The word rendered "world" signifies the inhabited world (*Speaker's Commentary*); that order of things that exists upon it. These things will ever be subject 'to shaking' until God's rule is finally established and recognised. For David in the days of the first kingdom, the words doubtless referred to the kingdom of Israel no longer subject to the vagaries of human ambition and opposition. In the great day to come, it speaks of the moral authority that will quell all human rebellion and injustice when "a king shall reign in righteousness" (Isaiah 32:1).

The psalm speaks of the future establishment of God's kingdom when Messiah shall reign over a subjugated earth. This will be realised only because God has always been in control. His purpose, unchanging, can never be frustrated by human rebellion, however it might sometimes appear to the eyes of men, for: "Thy throne is established of old: thou art from everlasting".

In vain therefore do men arraign themselves before God:

> "The floods have lifted up, O LORD, the floods have lifted up their voice; the floods lift up their waves. The LORD on high is mightier than the noise of many waters, yea, than the mighty waves of the sea." (verses 3,4)

The word translated "floods" generally means 'rivers', although on occasions it is linked with the waves of the sea. Here the physical features of the natural world, which are all subject to God, are used to represent the powers of this world which vainly imagine that they can challenge the supremacy of God. Rivers in flood, threatening to inundate the surrounding land are familiar figures for nations which are in the ascendancy. The classic example is the Euphrates used to represent the power of Assyria:

> "Now therefore, behold, the Lord bringeth up upon them the waters of the river, strong and many, even the king of Assyria, and all his glory: and he shall come up over all his channels, and go over all his banks: and he shall pass through Judah; he shall overflow and go over, he shall reach even to the neck." (Isaiah 8:7,8)

The same figure is used of the Nile to represent Egypt (see Jeremiah 46:7,8) and again of the Euphrates in the Assyrian conquest of Egypt (see Jeremiah 47:1,2). In these words (Psalm 93:4,5) is reflected the pattern of human history, but all human endeavour is vain when directed against the Lord on high who is mightier than the noise of many waters.

We have already noted connections between this psalm and the language of Exodus 15 and we have a further allusion in verse 4. The words translated "mightier" and "might" carry a deeper significance. They suggest grandeur and magnificence as well as power (*Cambridge Bible*). A cognate word occurs in Exodus 15 where again there is a connection with the roaring of the seas, but God is mightier than all the assumed power and magnificence of men.

> "Thy right hand, O LORD, is become glorious in power ... Who is like unto thee, O LORD, among the gods? who is like thee, glorious in holiness, fearful in praises, doing wonders?" (Exodus 15:6,11)

God's supremacy was manifest for "Thou didst blow with thy wind, the sea covered them: they sank as lead in the mighty waters" (verse 10).

Note again in Psalm 93 (verse 4) the reference to "the LORD on high" linking this song with Psalm 91 (verse 1) and 92 (verse 1). The transition from the sovereignty of God revealed in nature and history to the faithfulness of His word is sudden and abrupt.

> "Thy testimonies are very sure: holiness becometh thine house, O LORD, for ever." (Psalm 93:5)

All that of which the psalm speaks will be fulfilled because His word is sure. If we were to attempt in a very rough and ready way to transliterate the Hebrew word translated "sure" into English, then we would say the word is "amen". It is faithful and true and can be trusted implicitly.

There is a striking verbal similarity between these words (Psalm 93:5) and Psalm 19 (verse 7). That psalm also is marked by a like transition between the grandeur of God's works in creation (verses 1-6) and the unity and perfection of His word (verses 7-14). In Psalm 19 also the description of God's glory manifest in the heavens has a symbolic meaning (see Romans 10:18). The two are wrought inextricably together: God's work in creation and His work among the children of men, and both are the product of His word.

It is interesting to note that the three psalms which begin with the declaration, "The LORD reigneth" all end in similar fashion with an emphasis upon the holiness of God (Psalm 93:1,5; 97:1,12; 99:1,9).

Psalm 24, to which we have referred twice previously, speaks undoubtedly of David bringing the ark to Zion, and the question was asked:

> "Who shall ascend into the hill of the LORD? or who shall stand in his holy place?" (verse 3)

The answer was:

> "He that hath clean hands, and a pure heart; who hath not lifted up his soul unto vanity, nor sworn deceitfully." (verse 4)

He it is who shall dwell with the devouring fire. He will dwell on high (Isaiah 33:14-16). "(His) eyes shall see the king in his beauty" (verse 17) for he shall dwell in the house of the Lord for ever.

PSALM 94

THIS psalm does not ring with the majestic tones of the preceding psalm or of others within the group we have identified which emphasise the truth that "the LORD reigneth". Nevertheless the fact that God is the King is implicit in David's expressions of faith that eventually God will triumph over all who persecute His people, and will take vengeance on those that oppress the poor. Some have thought that the oppressors referred to are foreign nations that, having achieved ascendancy over Israel, persecute the people. We do not believe that the tone and content of the psalm is consistent with this idea (see verses 4,6-8,20). Those condemned know the God of Israel but choose to ignore Him in the pursuit of their own ambition for power and wealth.

The question might then be asked, What place has this psalm in a group that celebrates the sabbath and God enthroned in Zion? The answer lies in the fact that the psalm expresses the longing of God's people for deliverance. It is a plea for God to manifest Himself on their behalf; to take vengeance on all those who, ignoring His righteousness, have oppressed the poor and helpless amongst their brethren. It is a cry from the midst of sorrow and affliction for God to enter into His rest and openly assume His royal dignity. In this respect Psalm 94 repeats the theme of Psalm 92.

Notwithstanding these considerations, the psalm has links both in vocabulary and style with the two preceding songs. Note for instance the figure of 'rhetorical repetition' (*anadiplosis*) common to all three psalms.

"For, lo, thine enemies, O LORD, for, lo, thine enemies shall perish."   (Psalm 92:9)

"He is clothed with majesty; the LORD is clothed with strength"   (Psalm 93:1)

783

> "O LORD God, to whom vengeance belongeth; O God, to whom vengeance belongeth."
>
> (Psalm 94:1; see also verses 3,23)

The same terms are used to describe those who doubt God's sovereignty; they are brutish and fools (Psalm 92:6; 94:8). Similar language is used of the oppressors of the people. They are "workers of iniquity" (Psalm 92:7; 94:16) and the fact that God is his rock is the basis of his faith (Psalm 92:15; 94:22).

As far as the construction of the psalm is concerned it will be noted that there are three sections in which the Lord is addressed (verses 1-7; 12,13; 18-20) and each of these is followed by the reflections of the writer arising from his plea to God (verses 8-11; 14-17; 22,23). These form an appropriate framework in which to consider the psalm.

The Oppression of the Wicked (verses 1-7)

> "O LORD God, to whom vengeance belongeth; O God, to whom vengeance belongeth, shew thyself. Lift up thyself, thou judge of the earth: render a reward to the proud." (verses 1,2)

The word rendered "vengeance" is plural, indicating what some call 'the intensive plural' so used to describe the completeness of the act. It can be compared with the words of Jeremiah who speaks of "the LORD God of recompences" (51:56). The longing is for God to manifest Himself and the language of the psalm reflects the spirit of the song of Moses (Deuteronomy 32):

> "To me belongeth vengeance, and recompence; their foot shall slide in due time: for the day of their calamity is at hand, and the things that shall come upon them make haste." (verse 35)

It is this conviction, that ultimately God will judge the wicked and triumph over them, that is the basis of the Psalmist's thought. It is true also for all those who wait patiently for God to come in His kingdom:

> "Dearly beloved, avenge not yourselves, but rather give place unto wrath: for it is written, Vengeance is mine; I will repay, saith the Lord." (Romans 12:19)

The wrath to which we "give place" is the wrath of God, for we must seek no redress on our own behalf, but must commit ourselves to Him who judgeth righteously, knowing that vengeance belongeth unto Him and that He will repay in whatever manner is appropriate.

So "in due time" (Deuteronomy 32:35) God will "lift up Himself", exalt Himself above all judges of the earth and "will render to the proud their desert" (Psalm 94:2, RV). The Psalmist is convinced that God will act, that He will ascend His throne and be recognised and acknowledged by His people and, ultimately, by all the earth, but:

> "LORD, how long shall the wicked, how long shall the wicked triumph? How long shall they utter and speak hard things? and all the workers of iniquity boast themselves?" (verses 3,4)

While they appear to have the supremacy, they utter (literally, 'pour forth, like a stream') their hard sayings (literally, 'wantonness' or 'defiance') for they appear to stand in fear of neither God nor man. They boast themselves (i.e., 'they carry themselves high'), they behave in a proud and arrogant manner. This is seen specifically not just in their lack of concern for their poor brethren, but by the manner in which they actively oppress and persecute them:

> "They break in pieces thy people, O LORD, and afflict thine heritage. They slay the widow and the stranger, and murder the fatherless. Yet they say, The LORD shall not see, neither shall the God of Jacob regard it."
> (verses 5-7)

Literally, 'they crush thy people' and the use of the verb in other scripture serves to emphasise that the oppressors are domestic rather than foreign.

In Isaiah's prophecy the Lord enters into judgement with the ancients of His people and the princes thereof. He asks, "What mean ye that ye beat my people to pieces (i.e., 'crush my people') and grind the faces of the poor?" (Isaiah 3:15; see also Proverbs 22:22). The root from which the verb is taken appears also in Psalm 93 (verse 3) where it is translated "lifted up", establishing another verbal link with that psalm.

They had forgotten that this people were God's heritage, for He took them "out of the iron furnace, even out of Egypt, to be unto him a people of inheritance" (Deuteronomy 4:20). They showed their contempt both for the people and their God by the manner in which they took advantage of the most vulnerable and defenceless classes, the widow, the orphan and the stranger, saying that the Lord would not see or regard it. This does not mean that they blatantly and openly blasphemed the God of Israel. More probably they maintained an outward form of worship but in their hearts they denied Him. By their conduct they showed that effectively they were practising a form of atheism (see Psalm 14:1).

The Folly of The Wicked (verses 8-11)

The Psalmist's thoughts turn to the perpetrators of these acts of treachery and those who supported them, for can they not see the foolishness of their ways?

> "Understand, ye brutish (literally, 'stupid') among the people: and ye fools, when will ye be wise? He that planted the ear, shall he not hear? he that formed the eye, shall he not see? (verses 8,9)

It has always been true of human nature that men will be influenced by those whom they perceive to be the 'great and the good'. They will almost instinctively associate themselves with those who are powerful and influential. So there was a need to appeal not just to these men themselves who, in any event were unlikely to listen, but to the people generally who allowed them to prosper. Did they really believe that He who formed the ear and eye could neither hear the perverse words that were spoken (verse 4) nor see the evil deeds that were done (verse 6)? For, "He that chastiseth the heathen, shall not he correct? he that teacheth men knowledge, shall not he know? (verse 10).

There is here a fact that is not always recognised by us. We teach that knowledge brings responsibility and we think primarily of the individual's accountability to judgement. But, at a different level, the nations (and the world at large) have a moral responsibility. This too might vary according to the depth of their understanding, but

God holds people and nations responsible for the actions they take (see Amos 1,2). That God chastised the heathen (the nations) was a concept that most in Israel would have readily accepted. They would have rejoiced in the fact. But the implication of this truth for them was something that they blissfully ignored. For, "He that chastised the heathen, shall not he correct?" that is, correct those who committed such atrocities in the midst of Israel. Would He leave unpunished those who oppressed their own brethren? He who had given the knowledge to the heathen that established His right to judge amongst the nations – at this point the AV adds the words – "shall he not know?" to maintain the flow. It will be observed, however, that these words are not part of the original text and in the Hebrew there is a sudden and abrupt affirmation of the truth of the matter:

"The LORD knoweth the thoughts of man, that they are vanity." (verse 11)

In this positive way the writer answers the self-delusions of the wicked and the doubts of the faithless, for God who both hears and sees knows the very thoughts and devices of all men. It might be assumed that it is the "thoughts" that are "vanity", but the pronoun "they" is masculine and refers to men rather than to the feminine word "thoughts". Thus because man is vanity, like a breath, finite as compared with God who is infinite, all his thoughts and all his ways are laid bare before Him. It is for this reason that He is the judge of all the earth, and will ultimately be seen to be so. Paul quotes these words (verse 11) in the First Epistle to the Corinthians and his words confirm the meaning of the psalm: "Therefore let no man glory in men" (3:21).

God's Instruction (verses 12,13)

Once again David addresses God:

"Blessed is the man whom thou chastenest, O LORD, and teachest him out of thy law; that thou mayest give him rest from the days of adversity, until the pit be digged for the wicked." (verses 12,13)

What was true of the nations was, in a deeper, fuller sense, true of His covenant people. Truly happy were those who came to understand that God was instructing his servants through the circumstances of life and that these experiences, wrought together with the teaching of His word, would accomplish the will and purpose of God for them in their lives (see Proverbs 3:12; Deuteronomy 8:5 etc.). The wise man would recognise and welcome God's instruction but the fool would rebel against it.

The longing for God to take vengeance and the patient waiting for His works to be seen was part of their chastening. It was until God should give them rest from the days of evil and until the pit, prepared to swallow up the wicked, should envelop them. The metaphor is taken from the pit dug by the hunter to catch his prey. Although the wicked seemed secure, the pit was dug for them; God would establish His sovereignty in the sight of all Israel.

The reference to "giving rest" reiterates the sabbath theme and is perhaps an echo of the words of Joshua:

> "So Joshua took the whole land, according to all that the LORD said unto Moses; and Joshua gave it for an inheritance unto Israel according to their divisions by their tribes. And the land rested from war."
>
> (Joshua 11:23)

This was the rest into which the generation that perished did not enter (Psalm 95:10,11). When David brought the ark home to Zion (1 Chronicles 16:1), then God rested in His habitation (Psalm 132:8,14). The result was that God was recognised as king and David was confirmed in the kingdom and was delivered from the hand of all his enemies (see 2 Samuel 8).

The LORD is the Help of His People (verses 14-17)

The day of rest will come. The prayer of verse 3, "LORD how long?", will be answered:

> "For the LORD will not cast off his people, neither will he forsake his inheritance. But judgment shall return unto righteousness: and all the upright in heart shall follow it." (verses 14,15)

The words "his people" and "his inheritance" pick up the thought of verse 5 and echo again the words of Deuteronomy 32:

788

"For the LORD's portion is his people; Jacob is the lot of his inheritance."   (verse 9)

God will not cast off His people and the Apostle Paul quotes these words in the Epistle to the Romans to demonstrate the fact that His purpose with this people remains inviolate, for all Israel will be saved (11:1,2, 25,26).

Once again judgement shall be known in the land. It shall return unto righteousness, for it will be administered according to principles of equity, and all good-hearted men will embrace it. That this time will come the Psalmist is sure but until that day, "Who will rise up for me against the evildoers? or who will stand up for me against the workers of iniquity?" (Psalm 94:16).

It may seem inappropriate to think of these words as spoken by David the king, but there are suggestions that help. Literally the word "against" means 'with'. The word translated "stand up" carries the idea of 'setting up as in battle'. In effect David is asking, Who will stand with me to fight these workers of iniquity, these unrighteous judges that rule in the land?

We suggest that from the days of Saul, David always had enemies. They did not have the same vision of the kingdom; they did not share his aspirations. When David was threatened (e.g., Absalom and Ahithophel) then they revealed themselves openly, but throughout his reign David had to contend with these powerful and influential men who would have divided the kingdom if, like a true shepherd, he had not borne the reproach of them that reproached God (Psalm 69:9-13).

David's plea was not, Who shall stand *for* me? but, Who shall stand *with* me? for he knew that his help was in God:

"Unless the LORD had been my help, my soul had almost dwelt in silence."   (verse 17)

Unless God had sustained him through these troubles, then soon (RV) his lot would have been the coldness and stillness of the grave (see Psalm 115:17, etc.). God had delivered him out of the hands of evil men and finally David had triumphed. He had achieved his initial purpose and brought the ark to Zion.

The LORD Sustained Him (verses 18-21)

There had nevertheless been occasions when all had seemed lost, when from a human point of view there appeared to be no hope.

> "When I said, My foot slippeth; thy mercy, O LORD, held me up." (verse 18)

The *Cambridge Bible* has a pertinent comment: "The AV misses the picturesqueness of the tenses. 'When I said, My foot hath slipped, thy lovingkindness, LORD, was supporting me.'" Although David felt that his cause was lost, he discovered that in those darkest of times God still held his hand and supported him, for:

> "In the multitude of my thoughts within me thy comforts delight my soul." (verse 19)

The word "thoughts" means, as in the RV margin, 'doubts'. It carries the idea of anxious or distracting thoughts which divide the mind. It is natural to be beset with such cares when evil men appear to prevail. Faith, however, will not allow anxiety to dominate the mind. When perplexity threatens, then in the multitude of doubts the comfort and assurance of God's providential care will bring delight to the soul, for God will not allow injustice to prevail forever.

> "Shall the throne of iniquity have fellowship with thee, which frameth mischief by a law?" (verse 20)

The throne of iniquity is the judgement seat of evil men. The word translated "iniquity" is elsewhere rendered 'destruction' and the phrase conveys the idea of judges who were like 'a yawning gulf' ready to swallow up those who came to plead their cause before them. They did mischief and they did it 'by statute' (RV). They persecuted and oppressed the weak and they used a subterfuge of legality to give credence to their wickedness. For such tyranny there could be no escape from the righteous judgement of God. There could be no fellowship or association with the holiness that became His house (Psalm 93:5). This of course was the real wrong of the situation for, as judges, they represented God and in the unrighteousness of their judgement there remained the possibility that they could have claimed that God was on their side.

Final Reflections (verses 21-23)

Like a band of brigands they gathered themselves together against the righteous and condemned the innocent to death (verse 21). The word "righteous" is singular and the words had a most remarkable fulfilment when the Lord Jesus Christ appeared before Pilate and he, seeing that nothing could prevail "took water, and washed his hands before the multitude, saying, I am innocent of the blood of this just person" (Matthew 27:24).

In the face of all the wickedness and injustice of men David could affirm:

"But the LORD is my defence; and my God is the rock of my refuge. And he shall bring upon them their own iniquity, and shall cut them off in their own wickedness; yea, the LORD our God shall cut them off."

(verses 22,23)

The word rendered "defence" is elsewhere translated 'high tower' (Psalm 18:2) and once again David affirms his confidence in God because He is his rock. He is speaking of his own personal experience (i.e., "*my* God"), but because of this he can speak to faithful men of "*our* God" who will cause the way of the wrongdoing of the wicked to recoil upon their own heads. They will ultimately be swallowed up in the pit which they had dug for others.

PSALM 95

ALMOST all commentators who are not of the 'Critical School' agree in describing this psalm as a 'coronation anthem' relating to some event on which the God of Israel was perceived as enthroned in Zion. Strangely, they almost all agree again in their assertion that, contrary to the plain statement of Hebrews (4:7), David was not the author. This, of course, leads them to miss the obvious conclusion to which our considerations have led us, that David wrote this psalm to commemorate the bringing up of the ark to Zion. As already emphasised, the link with the sabbath is also established, for in this event the Lord entered into His rest (Psalm 132:8). That David did not see this event as an end in itself but a foreshadowing of the consummation of God's purpose in the earth, when all nations would acknowledge His sovereignty, is evident from the use made of the psalm by the writer to the Hebrews. The psalm is quoted three times in the context concerning the danger of falling away after the example of the generation that perished in the wilderness (3:1-11,15; 4:7). The link we have established between this group of psalms and the sabbath is confirmed by the apostle:

"For he spake in a certain place of the seventh day on this wise, And God did rest the seventh day from all his works."   (4:4, quoting Genesis 2:2; Exodus 20:11, etc.)

Space does not allow a detailed consideration of the argument in Hebrews 3 and 4 but this much is clearly apparent:

1. The rest into which Joshua led them was not the ultimate rest that God intended for His people, for He now spoke of another day.
2. The fact that David limited (i.e., fixed) a certain day (in Psalm 95) so long after the events of the

792

wilderness and the inheritance of the land, is proof
that "there remaineth therefore a rest to the people of
God" (Hebrews 4:9).

The words of David in Psalm 95 are clearly established as
being a prophecy of the age to come.

The psalm falls into two sections. The first (verses 1-7)
is a call to worship God enthroned in His rest; the second
(verses 8-11) is a solemn warning, first to David's
generation, lest through hardness of heart they should fail
to enjoy the blessings of that rest. Beyond the events of
that day, however, it speaks of "the rest that remaineth"
and the danger in which every generation stands of failing
to enter that rest because of unbelief.

A Call to Worship (verses 1-7)

"O come, let us sing unto the LORD, let us make a
joyful noise to the rock of our salvation. Let us come
before his presence with thanksgiving, and make a
joyful noise unto him with psalms."   (verses 1,2)

In another psalm God said, "Whoso offereth praise
glorifieth me" (50:23). It is in this spirit that David
encourages the people to join him in worship. God is
glorified because in praise and thanksgiving He is
recognised for everything He is; all that He has done and
will do to accomplish His purpose in the earth. All these
things met together in the bringing up of the ark to Zion.

The reference to praising him with psalms is
demonstrated by the number of psalms that David wrote
which are associated with this event, and in the actual
record (1 Chronicles 16) it is related that "on that day
David delivered first this psalm to thank the LORD into the
hand of Asaph and his brethren" (verse 7). What follows is
the substance of Psalm 105 (verses 1-15) and Psalm 96.
We comment further upon this in the consideration of
Psalm 96. The reason for praise and thanksgiving is:

"For the LORD is a great God, and a great King above
all gods. In his hand are the deep places of the earth:
the strength of the hills is his also. The sea is his, and
he made it: and his hands formed the dry land."
(Psalm 95:3-5)

793

The word *Elohim* translated "God" in the AV encompasses, we believe, the angels through whom God is manifest. It is used, however, of false gods, idols that were the work of men's hands (e.g., Psalm 96:5); human judges who were God's representatives (see Psalm 82:1; Exodus 21:6; 22:8) and on occasions in a precise way, of angels themselves (see Psalm 97:7, quoted in Hebrews 1:6). As a result there are a few occasions when it is difficult to know with certainty to whom the word is precisely applied.

The supremacy of the Lord described in verse 3, "a great King above all gods" is such an instance. We suggest that the reference here is to the angels. The emphasis noted in this group of psalms (beginning with Psalm 91:1), on "the Most High" lends itself to this conclusion. If we regard that title as encompassing the angels then, of course, it is expressing the truth that all who are included in that designation are exalted on high. The title, however, appears to us to exclude all others, including the angels, for He is *Most* High, unique in His exaltation. It refers we suggest exclusively to the great Uncreate. He is a great King above all *Elohim*, for even the angels acknowledge Him as such.

Not only has He created all things but He continues to sustain them, for the deepest recesses of the earth and the highest hills are all held in the hollow of His hand. The reference to creation in this psalm is characteristic of other psalms that relate to David bringing the ark to Zion:

> "The earth is the LORD's, and the fulness thereof; the world, and they that dwell therein. For he hath founded it upon the seas, and established it upon the floods."
>
> (Psalm 24:1,2)

It was, after all, "the ark of the covenant of the Lord of all the earth" (Joshua 3:11,13).

Once again David appeals to the congregation of Israel:

> "O come, let us worship and bow down: let us kneel before the LORD our maker. For he is our God; and we are the people of his pasture, and the sheep of his hand." (verses 6,7)

Literally, 'let us prostrate ourselves before Him'. This, no doubt, reflects the form of worship common among the people of Israel. It is not the manner in which we are accustomed to present ourselves before God. But there is a principle here, to which we have referred before; the danger of over-familiar thought and talk when referring to our Heavenly Father. The wonder of our relationship with Him arises out of the fact that He is so immeasurably great, so high and holy, beyond our feeble minds to comprehend, yet He condescends to call us His children. The closeness of our relationship must never be allowed to diminish the source of awe and reverence with which we must regard Him. We must always prostrate ourselves before Him, in spirit if not in posture. The reference to "the LORD our maker" is not to the original creation of man, but rather to the formation of the nation of Israel (see Isaiah 43:1). The allusion to Deuteronomy 32 in this group of psalms has been noted before and there appears to be another in these words (see Deuteronomy 32:6,15,18; note also the reference to the rock as in Psalm 95:1 and 94:22).

Not only was God their maker but He was also their shepherd. He led "(His) people like a flock by the hand of Moses and Aaron" (Psalm 77:20). He "made his own people to go forth like sheep, and guided them in the wilderness like a flock" (Psalm 78:52).

The last phrase of verse 7, although connected with the second section of the psalm (verses 8-11), opens up interesting connections with the Book of Exodus: "To day if ye will hear his voice". These are the words of David although the remaining verses of the psalm are spoken by God Himself. God, the shepherd of Israel, led His people through the wilderness but this Great King was represented and manifest in the midst of them by the angel of His presence:

"Behold, I send an angel before thee, to keep thee in the way, and to bring thee into the place which I have prepared. Beware of him, and obey his voice, provoke him not; for he will not pardon your transgressions: for my name is in him." (Exodus 23:20,21)

So with a reflection on these words David says, "To day if ye will hear (obey, Exodus 23:21) his voice". That angel with a special responsibility for Israel still dwelt among them and there was still a necessity to obey his voice. David is emphasising that the truths of the Exodus were continuing blessings for Israel. It was today, this day, in which they needed to hear his voice if they were to enjoy the blessings of God's rest. So it must ever be, for now is our time of opportunity and in the broadest sense every time we read the word of God it is "to day if (we) will hear his voice".

Harden Not Your Hearts (verses 8-11)

As the quotation from this psalm in Hebrews demonstrated (see above), David saw the ark resting in Zion as a type of the ultimate rest that remained for God's people when all the earth should say, "The LORD reigneth". So to those of David's generation and all subsequent generations God says:

"Harden not your heart, as in the provocation, and as in the day of temptation in the wilderness: when your fathers tempted me, proved me, and saw my work. Forty years long was I grieved with this generation, and said, It is a people that do err in their heart, and they have not known my ways: unto whom I sware in my wrath that they should not enter into my rest." (verses 8-11)

The RV translates the words rendered "provocation" and "temptation" as proper names. "Harden not your heart as at Meribah (strife), as in the day of Massah (temptation) in the wilderness". These were the names given to Rephidim, the place where they murmured at the beginning of the wandering (Exodus 17:1-7) and again in the fortieth year to Kadesh when they murmured there (Numbers 20:1-13).

They provoked God by putting Him to the proof. The question they asked was, "Is the LORD among us, or not?" (Exodus 17:7). Their lack of faith manifest itself in a demand that He should prove His fidelity by a display of His power. They had witnessed the work of God in the deliverance from Egypt and to that day they had known His providential care. However, they had not learned to trust God through these experiences but rather they had hardened their hearts.

In Hebrews 3 (verse 9) the words "forty years long was I grieved with this generation" are linked with the preceding sentence in a way that differs from the psalm. Verse 9 is not quoting either the Hebrew text or the Septuagint and, that the conjunction of the clauses is deliberate, is evident, as the psalm is referred to again in verse 17 in conformity with the text of the psalm. It is a divine commentary on the meaning of the psalm, demonstrating that what happened at Rephidim and Kadesh was typical of the attitude of that faithless generation throughout the wilderness journey.

Therefore God was grieved with them. It is a strong word expressing 'loathing or disgust' and it is a measure of the way their conduct separated them from their God. They erred in their hearts. Literally they 'went astray' in their hearts. More precisely, their hearts 'wandered'. It is the same word as that used in Psalm 107: "they wandered in the wilderness in a solitary way" (verse 4).

God sent an angel to keep them in the way and to bring them into the land (Exodus 23:20), but, because of their 'wandering hearts' they did not know His ways. They had not responded to the voice of the angel. So He sware unto them that they should not enter His rest. The reference is to the words of the Lord spoken to Moses (Numbers 14:26-32). When, at the borders of the land, Moses spoke to the people he said:

"For ye are not as yet come to the rest and to the inheritance, which the LORD your God giveth you. But when ye go over Jordan, and dwell in the land ... then there shall be a place which the LORD your God shall choose to cause his name to dwell there."

(Deuteronomy 12:9-11)

For David these words received their final fulfilment when he brought the ark to Zion. This event, however, he understood to be but a foreshadowing of the consummation of God's purpose when all the earth would acknowledge His sovereignty. We too believe that –

"there remaineth therefore a rest to the people of God ... Let us labour therefore to enter into that rest, lest any man fall after the same example of unbelief."

(Hebrews 4:9-11)

PSALM 96

THIS psalm carries forward the glorious theme that we have identified in this group of songs (Psalms 93-99). The sabbath association is maintained. God the Creator is honoured by all the works of His hands, animate and inanimate (verses 5,11,12). The psalm speaks especially of the manner in which God is recognised and acknowledged by all the nations of the earth (verses 1,9,10) because He judges amongst them righteously (verses 10,13).

We have previously identified this song, together with Psalm 95, as the key to our understanding of the group of psalms to which they belong, for they were both written by David (Psalm 95, see Hebrews 4:7; Psalm 96, see 1 Chronicles 16:7).

Psalm 96 is clearly associated with the occasion when David successfully brought up the ark of the covenant from the house of Obed-Edom to the tabernacle he had prepared for it in Zion. We read, "So they brought the ark of God, and set it in the midst of the tent that David had pitched for it" (1 Chronicles 16:1). Having appointed Levites to minister and to thank and praise the Lord God of Israel (see verses 4-6), then "on that day David delivered first this psalm ... into the hand of Asaph and his brethren" (verse 7).

What follows is a composite song containing verses 1-15 of Psalm 105 followed by Psalm 96, concluding with words that are repeated in Psalms 106 and 107. We defer consideration of the allusion in Psalms 106 and 107 to the chapters dealing with those psalms. We look more closely, however, at the manner in which Psalms 105 and 96 are linked together.

The section of Psalm 105 used by David in 1 Chronicles 16 and, presumably, elaborated upon to give the complete

798

song, dwells upon the wonderful covenant God made with Abraham. The second part of the psalm, that not included in the song recorded in 1 Chronicles, deals specifically with the manner in which God delivered Israel from the land of Egypt in fulfilment of those promises made to Abraham, Isaac and Jacob (verses 16-45).

In effect David sees a fulfilment of God's promises to Abraham in the manner in which the ark is now at rest in Zion and God rules in the midst of His people. He rejoices in God's purpose with Israel:

"Remember his marvellous works that he hath done, his wonders, and the judgments of his mouth; O ye seed of Israel his servant, ye children of Jacob, his chosen ones." (1 Chronicles 16:12,13)

But God's purpose with Israel was not confined to them alone. They were His chosen that they might be a light to the Gentiles, that ultimately they might be the vehicle for bringing salvation unto "all the ends of the earth" (Isaiah 45:22).

Thus it was that when Israel were brought into the bonds of the covenant at Sinai, God said:

"Now therefore, if ye will obey my voice indeed, and keep my covenant, then ye shall be a peculiar treasure unto me above all people: for all the earth is mine: and ye shall be unto me a kingdom of priests." (Exodus 19:5,6)

Israel's duty was to be a witness to the nations that ultimately all the earth should recognise and acknowledge her God.

Significantly, having emphasised the reality of the everlasting covenant that God made with the fathers of Israel, the section from Psalm 105 (verse 15) finishes, somewhat abruptly, with the words:

"Touch not mine anointed, and do my prophets no harm." (1 Chronicles 16:22)

We are then immediately introduced to Psalm 96 (verse 2): "Sing unto the LORD, all the earth; shew forth from day to day his salvation" (1 Chronicles 16:23).

What then did David mean when he described Abraham, and presumably Isaac and Jacob (and possibly

Sarah), as prophets? It should be noticed, first of all, that it is a reference (verses 21,22) to the words spoken to Abimelech (Genesis 20:7) when he took Sarah into his house. The truth of the matter is, however, that in the promises that God gave to Abraham, Isaac and Jacob, His whole purpose was encapsulated. As the custodians of those promises, in word and deed, they became forthtellers and fore-tellers of God's ultimate aim. Thus:

"The scripture, foreseeing that God would justify the heathen through faith, preached before the gospel unto Abraham, saying, In thee shall all nations be blessed."
(Galatians 3:8, with Genesis 12:3)

Again Abram "believed in the LORD and he counted it to him for righteousness" (Genesis 15:6). And:

"It was not written for his sake alone, that it was imputed to him; but for us also, to whom it shall be imputed, if we believe on him that raised up Jesus our Lord from the dead." (Romans 4:23,24)

It is with remarkable spiritual insight (not denying the power of inspiration) that David should link these two psalms in this way, concluding his use of Psalm 105 with the assertion that Abraham was a prophet and immediately, in his use of Psalm 96, carrying us forward to the fulfilment of those promises.

We have already noted verse 1 but the theme continues:

"Declare his glory among the heathen, his wonders among all people." (verse 3)

"Give unto the LORD, O ye kindreds of the people, give unto the LORD glory and strength." (verse 7)

"O worship the LORD in the beauty of holiness: fear before him, all the earth. Say among the heathen that the LORD reigneth: the world also shall be established that it shall not be moved: he shall judge the people righteously." (verses 9,10)

"The ark of the covenant of the Lord of all the earth" (Joshua 3:11,13) had come to Zion. In that fact David saw, in shadow, the ultimate fulfilment of the divine purpose. He appreciated also that, in that which he had done, he had contributed in no small way to the carrying forward of that purpose in the earth, "for he cometh to judge the earth: he shall judge the earth with righteousness, and the people with truth" (Psalm 96:13).

There are some minor variations between the text of Psalm 96 and the words recorded in 1 Chronicles 16. For information and accuracy we shall indicate these, as far as we are able to identify them, as we look at the substance of the psalm. In general terms we might say that the differences are due to the manner in which the psalm was used for liturgical purposes and in particular its use in the temple services.

There is a suggested structure:

1. God's glory proclaimed among all nations (verses 1-3).

2. A declaration of God's majesty (verses 4-6).

3. The nations acknowledge His greatness (verses 7-9).

4. The final proclamation of His sovereignty (verses 10-13).

As a point of interest, several writers point out that there is evidence that the psalm would be sung antiphonally (i.e., alternately by two groups). Two bands of Levites would sing alternately verses 1 and 2, 4 and 5, and 7 and 8; the whole choir then taking up the concluding verses of each stanza (i.e., verses 3,6,9). In the final stanza, verses 10-12 would be sung antiphonally and finally, with a chorus of voice and sound of instruments, the closing ascription of praise would sound forth (verse 13).

God's Glory Proclaimed (verses 1-3)

The psalm begins with a call to "sing unto the LORD a new song". There are seven 'new songs' in the Old Testament (Psalm 33:3; 40:3; 96:1; 98:1; 144:9; 149:1 and Isaiah 42:10). A 'new song' is invariably associated with God's work of redemption. The first of the 'new songs' (Psalm 33:3) was connected with the forgiveness of sins and the justification that comes by faith, for it is a meditation arising out of the circumstances of Psalm 32 which spoke of David's sin in the matter of Bathsheba and Uriah the Hittite. The new song is not necessarily Psalm 96. It is that psalm developing its theme of God's worldwide sovereignty that calls for the song to be sung. Some conjecture that the 'new song' is Psalm 97 and likewise that referred to in Psalm 98:1 is Psalm 99. We see no evidence to support that view and we suggest that, as it is always a song of the redeemed, all the Old Testament references must find their ultimate fulfilment in the words of Revelation 5:

> "And they sung a new song, saying ... for thou wast slain, and hast redeemed us to God by thy blood out of every kindred, and tongue, and people, and nation."
>
> (see verse 9)

The reference to a "new song" in Isaiah 42 is especially interesting, given the theme of Psalm 96, for the words are quoted verbatim from this psalm. Isaiah speaks prophetically of the Lord Jesus Christ: "Behold my servant, whom I uphold; mine elect, in whom my soul delighteth". His work is to "bring forth judgment to the Gentiles" (verse 1) and the Lord says He will "give thee for a covenant of the people, for a light of the Gentiles" (verse 6). The consequence of these "new things" that God has declared (verse 9) is that men "sing unto the LORD a new song, and his praise from the end of the earth" (verse 10). So the call in Psalm 96 is to –

> "sing unto the LORD ... all the earth. Sing unto the LORD, bless his name; shew forth his salvation from day to day."
>
> (verses 1,2)

In singing the "new song" the redeemed will bless His name, for it is the purpose embodied in that name that will have been consummated in them. In recognition of that truth and in their rejoicing in all the work of God fulfilled in their experience, they will bless His name in giving to Him the honour due. They will show forth His mercy perpetually for, from day to day, they will rejoice before Him with ceaseless praises.

David in his call to "show forth" once again anticipates Isaiah's prophecy. Literally the word means 'to proclaim' and it is the word so characteristic of the latter chapters of Isaiah's prophecy which speaks of the proclamation of the Gospel:

> "O thou that *tellest good tidings* to Zion ... O thou that *tellest good tidings* to Jerusalem."   (40:9,10, RV)

"How beautiful upon the mountains are the feet of him that *bringeth good tidings,* that publisheth peace; that *bringeth good tidings* of good."   (52:7)

"The LORD hath anointed me to preach good tidings unto the meek."   (61:1)

The word is connected by Isaiah with God's salvation, with the remission of sins, with the acceptable year of the Lord. It speaks of the deliverance of the poor and Zion's exaltation. It is the Hebrew word that encompasses in its meaning and associations everything for which the Greek word *evangelion,* rendered 'Gospel', stands. It is the proclamation of the good news of the kingdom of God.

Isaiah's more expansive use of David's words serves as a useful reminder to us that all the earth will rejoice in the kingdom age because of Zion's exaltation and because the Lord Jesus Christ is enthroned there on David's seat. This underlying truth is the foundation on which the theme of this psalm is based. God's glory is declared among the nations and His wonders among all people because the law goes forth from Zion "and the word of the LORD from Jerusalem" (Isaiah 2:2,3).

The word "wonders" (RV, "marvellous works") is characteristic of God's mighty acts in Egypt and the wilderness (e.g., Exodus 3:20; Psalm 78:4,11; 106:7). The things in which the earth now rejoices have been accomplished by God's marvellous works amongst the people of Israel.

Note that "sing unto the LORD, bless his name" (verse 2) is omitted from the song in 1 Chronicles 16, the reason for which we can offer no adequate explanation.

A Declaration of God's Majesty (verses 4-6)

"For the LORD is great, and greatly to be praised: he is to be feared above all gods. For all the gods of the nations are idols: but the LORD made the heavens."

(verses 4,5)

The greatness of Israel's God is asserted, for He alone is the living God, the Creator of the heavens. For this cause He is to be praised for all the gods of the nations, all those things in which they had put their trust, were but idols, the work of men's hands. They were "things of nought" (RV

803

margin), or literally 'nothings' – no power or strength; no existence at all. It was a truth that God had emphasised in the giving of the law:

> "Turn ye not unto idols, nor make to yourself molten gods: I am the LORD your God."   (Leviticus 19:4; 26:1)

It is a theme developed at some length by the prophet Isaiah and the 44th chapter of his prophecy is a classic illustration of the folly of those who put their trust in 'nothings', which were but the works of their own hands.

It appears that Hezekiah meditated upon this psalm when God delivered him out of the hand of Sennacherib and exalted him in the sight of the nations. Psalm 48 repeats verbatim the first phrase of verse 4: "Great is the LORD, and greatly to be praised" (verse 1).

Again Psalm 47 (verse 2) appears to allude to it, "For the LORD most high is terrible" (i.e., to be feared – same word as Psalm 96:4). Both are songs "for the sons of Korah" and are associated with Hezekiah. Psalm 47 in particular develops the same theme as Psalm 96; "For the LORD ... is a great King over all the earth" (verses 2,7,8).

But He who created the heavens and manifested His glory in the work of creation had now been pleased to dwell in the midst of His people, in the tabernacle that David had prepared.

> "Honour and majesty are before him: strength and beauty are in his sanctuary."   (Psalm 96:6)

It is to be noted that the words rendered "strength and beauty" are those applied to the ark of the covenant in Psalm 78 (verse 61) and their use here serves to confirm the background that has been outlined in this study. Also there is a difference between the psalm, which reads "sanctuary", and the record in 1 Chronicles 16, which reads "place". The difference might well be explained by the emphasis upon the word 'place' in earlier scripture (Exodus 15:17; Deuteronomy 11:5; 12:5,11,14,18,21,26; 14:23, etc.). All these scriptures were fulfilled when David brought the ark to Zion and God came to the place that "he (had) desired for his habitation" (Psalm 132:13). When the psalm was sung in the temple services, then the word 'sanctuary' would more appropriately be used, with no real change in the sense. There is, nevertheless, a most interesting play upon the language of both Psalm 69 and 1 Chronicles 16, when the prophet Isaiah brings both the words 'sanctuary' and 'place' together in a passage which speaks of the Gentiles bringing their gifts to the house of the Lord (Isaiah 60:10,11).

"For the nation and kingdom that will not serve thee shall perish." (verse 12)

That which they bring is "to beautify the place of my sanctuary" (verse 13). The verb "to beautify" is derived from the noun 'beauty' used in Psalm 96. Like the priest's garments that were "for glory and for beauty" (Exodus 28:40), the beauty of holiness adorned God's sanctuary, for He who dwelt there had revealed to His people all the loveliness of His character.

In the Hebrew text of Psalm 96 it is as though "honour and majesty" are personified, standing in attendance before Him. The words rendered "before him" mean more literally 'in his presence' (see 1 Chronicles 16:27). The Hebrew word is *pannim*. It is the plural of 'face' (see Genesis 4:14, "from thy face(s) shall I be hid"). It is appropriate to refer it to the faces of the cherubim between which God's glory dwelt.

The Nations Acknowledge God's Greatness (verses 7-9)

In the knowledge that He is enthroned in Zion, and reigns over all the earth, the nations are exhorted to join Israel in praise of her God:

"Give unto the LORD, O ye kindreds of the people, give unto the LORD glory and strength. Give unto the LORD the glory due unto his name: bring an offering and come into his courts. O worship the LORD in the beauty of holiness: fear before him, all the earth." (verses 7-9)

The word "kindreds" means literally 'families' and is so translated in Amos 3: "You only have I known of all the families of the earth" (verse 2). Most appropriately, however, it is the word used in God's promise to Abraham, "And in thee shall all families of the earth be blessed" (Genesis 12:3). It is in fulfilment of this promise that the call is made to all kindreds of the earth to join in this song of praise. The words are taken from an earlier psalm (29) and verses 1 and 2 of that song correspond generally to verses 7 and 9 of Psalm 96. Psalm 29 describes in a dramatic and poetic form the manner in which a storm of tremendous ferocity strikes terror into the hearts of men. The storm though is symbolic of the hand of God in human affairs and seven times the voice of God thunders (see verses 3-9). It reminds us of the seven thunders of Revelation 10 (verses 1-7) for when the thunders have sounded, "The LORD sitteth upon the flood; yea the LORD sitteth King for ever" (Psalm 29:10).

It is because they have been subdued before Him and compelled to recognise His greatness that the nations now "give unto the LORD the glory of his name" (verse 8, AV margin). That is, they recognise His character as revealed in His work among them and give honour to His name. They bring an offering into His courts. Again there is a variation between the psalm and 1 Chronicles 16. Here the word "courts" more aptly describing the temple is substituted for the words "before him". The offering (Hebrew, *minchah*) is normally associated with the meal offering (Leviticus 2:1) but here is used in its wider significance of bringing gifts or presents to the King in recognition of His greatness (see Isaiah 60:5,11, AV margin).

There is an important principle to be learned from these verses. The emphasis is upon giving. We cannot come into God's courts with empty hands and the principal purpose of coming before Him is to give rather than to get. We give Him the praise due for all that He has done for us, confident that He will continue to bless because of the offering of our thanks.

The call in verse 9 to worship him "in the beauty of holiness" has been variously translated: "In the glorious sanctuary", (AV margin); "In holy array", (RV margin and RSV); "In the honour of holiness", (*Young's Literal Translation*); "In the splendour of holiness" (NEB).

It has been pointed out (*Speaker's Commentary*) that the word rendered "majesty" in verse 6 is the masculine of that translated "beauty" here, and the word rendered "sanctuary" there is derived from the same root as that rendered "holiness" here. May it not be that the idea conveyed is of the beauty of holiness that pertains to God's sanctuary in all its parts? Consequently, as the priests of old were to present themselves in holy attire, even so now the nations that approach must be clothed in holiness, for all the earth must tremble and fear before Him – not in fright but in reverence and awe.

The Final Proclamation (verses 10-13)

The final call is to declare among the nations "that the LORD reigneth". In the Spirit David looks to the consummation of God's purpose in the earth when the Lord Jesus shall reign in righteousness and judge the people with equity. As a result, the world, i.e., that order of things that exists on the earth, is secure. It can no more be shaken (see Psalm 93:1; Hebrews 12:27,28). Note that the first and third lines of verse 10 are omitted from the record in Chronicles.

So all creation is called upon to rejoice in God's work of redemption:

"Let the heavens rejoice, and let the earth be glad; let the sea roar, and the fulness thereof. Let the field be joyful, and all that is therein: then shall all the trees of the wood rejoice." (verses 11,12)

The language speaks of all creation joining in the song of triumph for all that God's hands have made, both animate and inanimate, now rejoice in an earth restored. We can no doubt see in the language the symbology of the scripture, for the rulers, the common people, the nations generally all combine together in the chorus of praise.

In the *Companion Bible* attention is drawn to an apparent acrostic in the Hebrew text of verse 11. We do not reproduce the actual text but the first letters of each word form YHWH which, with the added vowels is Yahweh, the name of the God of Israel.

So the concluding verse of the psalm looks to the finality of God's work in the earth. All nature sings, "Before the LORD, for he cometh, for he cometh to judge the earth: he shall judge the world with righteousness, and the people with his truth (RV, in his faithfulness) (verse 13).

Once again there is a variation from the text of 1 Chronicles 16 as the last two lines of the psalm are omitted. However, the language directs our thoughts to the words of Paul spoken in Athens:

> "God ... now commandeth all men every where to repent: because he hath appointed a day, in the which he will judge the world in righteousness by that man whom he hath ordained; whereof he hath given assurance unto all men, in that he hath raised him from the dead."
>
> (Acts 17:30,31)

Paul's message is of the inclusiveness of the Gospel, for God who made the world giveth to all, life and breath and all things. He has made of one all nations of men and commands all men everywhere to repent, because ultimately He will judge (rule) the world in righteousness. Paul speaks in the spirit of Psalm 96. The assurance that we have, that the things of which the song speaks will become a reality in the earth, is the fact that God has raised His Son, the Lord Jesus Christ, from the dead.

PSALM 97

THERE is a similarity of language running right through the group of psalms we are considering (Psalm 93–99). They have a common theme, for they all arise out of that occasion when David brought the ark to Zion. This might lead us to conclude that there is little difference in emphasis between them but, if we did so, we would be mistaken. They are all concerned with God's sovereignty but the perspective from which this is viewed varies from song to song. There are clear links in word and thought between this psalm and that which precedes it (Psalm 96).

Psalm 96	Psalm 97
"Let the heavens rejoice, and let the earth be glad" (verse 11).	"Let the earth rejoice; let the … isles be glad (verse 1).
"Honour and majesty are before him" (verse 6).	"A fire goeth before him" (verse 3).
"Fear before him, all the earth" (verse 9).	"The earth saw, and trembled" (verse 4).

("fear" and "trembled" are the same Hebrew word)

"Declare his glory among the heathen" (verse 3).	"All the people see his glory" (verse 6).
"He is to be feared above all gods" (verse 4).	"Thou art exalted far above all gods" (verse 9).

Psalm 97 is, however, not a mere repetition of Psalm 96. In Psalm 96 the emphasis is upon the sovereignty of God, openly acknowledged and recognised throughout the earth, so that all creation joins in the glad chorus of praise (verses 9-12). The final verse of that psalm emphasises the inevitability of this state of blessedness; the consummation of all human history.

"For he cometh, for he cometh to judge the earth: he shall judge the world with righteousness, and the people with his truth."   (verse 13)

It is this advent, this coming of God in glory that is the substance of Psalm 97. Although arising out of the background of the events of David's days and drawing its imagery from the past manifestations of God in glory, it is essentially a prophecy. It speaks of the second coming of the Lord Jesus Christ, of the manifestation of God in judgement through His Son yet to be accomplished in the earth.

This truth is established by the manner in which the writer to the Hebrews quotes this psalm (verse 7) and applies it to the Lord Jesus Christ in developing his argument to demonstrate that the Son of God is superior to the angels (Hebrews 1). The AV margin, RV and NKJV rightly translate the text:

"And when he again bringeth in the firstborn into the world he saith, And let all the angels of God worship him."   (verse 6, RV)

"When he bringeth in again the first begotten into the world."   (AV margin)

"But when he again brings the firstborn into the world."   (NKJV)

The reference, we believe, is to the second coming of the Lord Jesus and the theme of the psalm is thereby established. Also the allusion to the angels, which we might not have detected in the psalm alone, is made clear and confirms the suggestion which we made in relation to Psalm 95 (verse 3).

It is interesting to compare the opening six verses of Psalm 97 and the first six verses of Psalm 50. In the language of God-manifestation, both psalms draw from the imagery of Mount Sinai. Psalm 50 is clearly in the future tense whereas Psalm 97 is descriptive of the events as they occur. Together, however, they confirm the conclusions we have reached. We look more closely at this language as we come to examine the text of the psalm.

It is generally agreed that the psalm falls into four stanzas, each comprising three verses, and we follow this construction in our general consideration of the subject matter.

The Earth Rejoices in His Coming (verses 1-3)

"The LORD reigneth; let the earth rejoice; let the multitude of isles be glad thereof." (verse 1)

Inasmuch as the Lord comes in judgement to overthrow this present world order and to establish God's kingdom founded on righteousness and justice, it is perhaps difficult sometimes to comprehend that the reaction of the people of the earth will be an overflowing spirit of joy and gladness. We ourselves, limited by our human nature and our daily association with the things of this present life, still see as through a veil. We too have our problems in trying to understand what the blessings of the future age will mean for us personally. In faith we believe that:

"Eye hath not seen, nor ear heard, neither have entered into the heart of man, the things which God hath prepared for them that love him."

(1 Corinthians 2:9)

By God's grace it is only in the experience itself that we shall come to appreciate all that is entailed in the transformation to spirit nature. But in similar fashion it will be true also for the mortal inhabitants of the earth. It is only when the transformation has been completed that men will truly understand what a dreadful and evil world they have lived in and appreciate how it took its toll of them, leaving them so often bitter and frustrated. So marked will be the change that men's hearts, recognising that "that LORD reigneth", will be overwhelmed with a sense of joy and true satisfaction.

The word "isles" is not to be understood simply in the manner that the English word suggests. Rather it means all those lands separated from the nation of Israel by the sea. It means the coastlines, the Gentile world at large – a fact that is established by comparing the words of Isaiah's prophecy with the words of the New Testament in quoting them.

"The isles shall wait for his law" (Isaiah 42:4) becomes in Matthew's interpretative comment, "In his name shall the Gentiles trust" (Matthew 12:21).

So his coming is described in language drawn from the Books of Exodus and Deuteronomy:

"Clouds and darkness are round about him: righteousness and judgment are the habitation of his throne. A fire goeth before him, and burneth up his enemies round about."   (verses 2,3)

The Hebrew words translated "clouds", "darkness", and "fire" are to be found in the Book of Deuteronomy in connection with the giving of the law at Sinai:

"And ye came near and stood under the mountain; and the mountain burned with fire unto the midst of heaven, with darkness, clouds, and thick darkness."

(Deuteronomy 4:11)

"These words the LORD spake unto all your assembly in the mount out of the midst of the fire, of the cloud, and of the thick darkness, with a great voice."

(Deuteronomy 5:22; see also Exodus 19:16-18)

Clouds and darkness do not belong to the nature of God for "God is light and in him is no darkness at all" (1 John 1:5). Why then are they associated in this way with the manifestation of His glory? They speak to mortal man of the uniqueness of God, separated from sinners who cannot approach to behold His glory. In this sense they are particularly relevant to the Mosaic dispensation, although the imagery and symbolism runs throughout scripture. It is our privilege to behold the glory of God in the Lord Jesus Christ (2 Corinthians 4:6), for we –

"are not come unto the mount that might be touched, and that burned with fire, nor unto blackness, and darkness, and tempest ... but unto mount Sion, and unto the city of the living God, the heavenly Jerusalem."   (Hebrews 12:18-22)

It is of this city that we hope to become constituent parts for in the grand consummation of the purpose of God "the city had no need of the sun, neither of the moon, to shine in it: for the glory of God did lighten it, and the Lamb is the light thereof" (Revelation 21:23).

The coming described in the psalm is, however, first in judgement, and it is mortal men, yet sinners, to whom He reveals Himself, convincing them that "righteousness and

812

judgement are the foundation of his throne" (verse 2, RV). None can withstand Him for "our God is a consuming fire" (Hebrews 12:29) and all that oppose Him are destroyed in the fire that "goeth before him".

God's Glory Manifest (verses 4-6)

The Psalmist continues his description of the coming of God in glory:

> "His lightnings enlightened the world: the earth saw, and trembled. The hills melted like wax at the presence of the LORD, at the presence of the Lord of the whole earth."   (verses 4,5)

We have previously drawn attention to the fact that Israel's deliverance from Pharaoh's army at the Red Sea was accompanied by lightning, thunders and an earthquake, factors that are not mentioned in the Exodus record (see Psalm 77:16-20). The earth beholding this awesome manifestation of power is depicted as trembling and the very hills become molten like wax; language that was to be appropriated later by Micah in a somewhat different context:

> "For, behold, the LORD cometh forth out of his place, and will come down, and tread upon the high places of the earth. And the mountains shall be molten under him, and the valleys shall be cleft, as wax before the fire, and as the waters that are poured down a steep place."   (1:3,4)

The context in Micah's prophecy is concerned with the outpouring of God's wrath against Israel (see verses 5-9) but in this psalm it describes the coming of the Lord in judgement upon the world at large. Clearly there is a kind of literality about the language, for the coming of the Lord will be accompanied by such physical manifestations of power when "the (LORD) ariseth to shake terribly the earth" (Isaiah 2:21).

Isaiah's prophecy, however, makes it clear that through such language a great truth is being emphasised:

> "The lofty looks of men shall be humbled, and the haughtiness of men shall be bowed down, and the LORD alone shall be exalted in that day. For the day of the LORD of hosts shall be upon everyone that is proud and

lofty, and upon every one that is lifted up; and he shall
be brought low."   (verses 11,12)

The theme is developed by describing how the Lord will be
upon "the cedars of Lebanon ... the oaks of Bashan ... the
high mountains ... all the hills ... every high tower ...
every fenced wall" (verses 13-15). In other words, all these
features are descriptions of the pride and arrogance of
man. Similarly in Psalm 97, through the literal nature of
the language, the song is describing the manner in which
all the stubbornness and loftiness of men will dissolve
before the awful and dreadful manifestation of God's
power. Thus the Psalmist declares:

"The heavens declare his righteousness, and all the
peoples have seen his glory."   (verse 6, RV)

The whole earth, all peoples and nations are brought into
subjection because of the "presence of the LORD, the
presence of the Lord of the whole earth" (verse 5).

The double emphasis upon "the presence of the LORD"
serves to emphasize the reality of God's presence, in the
person of His Son, in the midst of these physical
convulsions of the earth. The phrase "Lord of the whole
earth" was of course associated with the ark of the
covenant and serves as a reminder of the background to
this group of psalms that we have consistently noted.

Thus the ark of the covenant of "the Lord of all the
earth" (Joshua 3:11,13) and the use of the phrase in the
context of Psalm 97 is an indication of all that is involved
in the teaching of scripture on the ark of the covenant. As
in past ages God reigned from between the cherubim, so
now in the Lord Jesus Christ all the earth recognises and
acknowledges His sovereignty.

False Worship Put to Shame (verses 7-9)

Faced by the irresistible power of God's might and the
establishment of His kingdom, all those who have put
their trust in false gods are confounded and ashamed. The
idols, of course, are "nothing" or "things of nought" (see
Psalm 96:5). This was true of the gods of wood and stone
that were built by men in the days of the Psalmist. It is,
however, equally true of the gods of this world, the
material things that men seek after and long for in our

days. These too will be found to be vanity with no power to save or sustain in the day of the Lord's coming. All false worshippers (and, of course, covetousness is idolatry) will be compelled to recognise and acknowledge that God is sovereign and in shame and confusion they will be brought to appreciate the emptiness of those things in which they had trusted previously (verse 7).

Even the angels in heaven will acknowledge the greatness of the Lord Jesus Christ (see previous comments and quotation in Hebrews 1:6). The victory won has a remarkable effect upon Zion, for:

"Zion heard, and was glad; and the daughters of Judah rejoiced because of thy judgments, O LORD. For thou, LORD, art high above all the earth: thou art exalted far above all gods." (verses 8,9)

The joy and gladness resulting from the Lord's coming that is to be felt by all the people of the earth (verse 1) is particularly associated with Zion, for this is "the city of the great King". Here he will make his throne and David's experiences in bringing the ark to Jerusalem were a fitting reminder and type of the manner in which God's purpose would ultimately be fulfilled.

At a later date, in psalms written to commemorate Judah's deliverance from Sennacherib in the days of Hezekiah, these words of Psalm 97 (verses 8,9) were recalled and quoted as the king and the faithful remnant in Judah rejoiced in the victory won:

"Let mount Zion rejoice, let the daughters of Judah be glad, because of thy judgments." (Psalm 48:11)

"For the LORD most high is terrible; he is a great King over all the earth ... for the shields of the earth belong unto God: he is greatly exalted." (Psalm 47:2,9)

Another psalm (83) which describes the alliance of surrounding nations, confederate together in common purpose to destroy the people of Israel (verse 4), also quotes from verse 9 of Psalm 97 the words, "For thou, LORD, art high above all the earth" (RV).

"That they may know that thou alone, whose name is JEHOVAH, art the Most High over all the earth."
(verse 18, RV)

So will men come to appreciate the reality and supremacy of the God of Israel.

Israel's Response (verses 10-12)

The final section of the psalm contains words of exhortation that are meaningful for every generation. Those who first read the psalm when David brought the ark to Zion who, in faith, understood that one day all the earth would acknowledge the sovereignty of their God, would take the words to their hearts and treasure them there. We who await the coming of the Lord and understand the judgement of the world at large associated with his advent, will be equally exercised by them.

Finally, those in Israel who witness the fulfilment of the events described in the psalm will, in like manner, be constrained to live by the standards and principles emphasised:

> "Ye that love the LORD, hate evil: he preserveth the souls of his saints; he delivereth them out of the hand of the wicked." (verse 10)

There is an appropriateness about the exhortation that we do well to heed. It is because of the evil that fills the world that God will bring upon it the judgements declared in this psalm. If we love the Lord and look expectantly for the coming kingdom, it follows that we too must hate the evil that surrounds us. There is no better yardstick by which to measure ourselves; Do we hate evil? Psalm 119 has a series of verses that make the issue clear:

> "Horror hath taken hold upon me because of the wicked that forsake thy law". (verse 53)

> "Rivers of waters run down mine eyes, because they keep not thy law." (verse 136)

> "I beheld the transgressors, and was grieved; because they kept not thy word." (verse 158)

Is that how we feel about the world in which we live? Do we feel a sense of horror? Are we grieved because of the way men break God's law and commandments? Or do we rather acquiesce in the wickedness, perhaps even, on occasions, delighting in it. Like righteous Lot we must be "vexed with the filthy conversation of the wicked" (2 Peter 2:7).

816

To love the Lord is to hate evil and they who do so are assured of His blessing for He preserveth their souls. The word rendered "preserveth" means literally 'to hedge about, to guard or protect' (*Strong*). It is an assurance that if we strive to be holy (i.e., saints) as He is holy, then the angel of the Lord will encamp round about us (see Psalm 34:7).

We shall live in the confidence that "the eyes of the LORD are upon the righteous, and his ears are open unto their cry ... (for) the LORD heareth, and delivereth them out of all their troubles" (Psalm 34:15,17). We know that ultimate deliverance is in the kingdom, in the gift of eternal life; yet surely there is comfort and consolation now too in the conflict with sin.

For David, and others like him, the words about being "(delivered) out of the hands of the wicked" had a very real and literal meaning and we might find it difficult to find a parallel in our experiences. Nevertheless we do well to remember that on occasions men might still seek to do us harm because of our faith and, if such circumstances should arise, our God is powerful to deliver. However, in a more general sense, the wicked who surround us are by their influence a constant threat to our spiritual health. We must never minimise the danger and we do well to pray, "Lead us not into temptation, but deliver us from evil" (Matthew 6:13), knowing that our Heavenly Father who guards and protects us "is able to keep (us) from falling and to present (us) faultless before the presence of his glory" (Jude verse 24). In this manner, by His providential hand, God continues to deliver us out of the hand of the wicked, lest we become like them and perish in their transgressions.

In the appreciation of all these things we can but cry with the Psalmist: "Light is sown for the righteous, and gladness for the upright in heart" (verse 11). There is here a beautiful and expressive figure illustrated by other scripture:

"The wicked worketh a deceitful work: but to him that soweth righteousness shall be a sure reward."

(Proverbs 11:18)

817

> "For they have sown the wind, and they shall reap
> the whirlwind." (Hosea 8:7)

So now the light sown through the word of God in the lives
of the righteous will finally bear fruit in the coming of the
Lord Jesus, for: "Unto you that fear my name shall the sun
of righteousness arise with healing in his wings" (Malachi
4:2). Because they live now in the light of God's
countenance, gladness also is sown in their hearts that
will finally blossom in everlasting joy. So the final
exhortation of the psalm encapsulates the joy that has
been characteristic of the recipients of God's mercy (verses
1,8,11). "Rejoice in the LORD, ye righteous; and give thanks
at the remembrance of his holiness" (verse 12).

To rejoice in the Lord is to know a happiness that the
world cannot give. Earthly joys are subject to the
vicissitudes of life – they can be so easily snatched away.
But joy which is in God no man can take from us, for He
changeth not and His promises are sure. It is for that
reason that the righteous "give thanks to His holy name"
(RV); literally 'the memorial of his holiness' (*Cambridge
Bible*). His name is His memorial, that by which He is
remembered throughout all generations (Exodus 3:15). It
is that which is expressive of all that He is and does. By it
He has made Himself known to men in all His wonderful
works.

In that day, when the Lord shall come, that name will
finally be made known through the many sons that God is
bringing unto glory. It is the hope of all who are upright in
heart to be numbered amongst them.

PSALM 98

THIS is the only psalm in the group we are considering (Psalm 93–99) that bears an inscription. In the AV it says simply "a Psalm"; in the Hebrew *Mizmor*, according to *Strong*, 'a poem or song accompanied by music'. It is in fact the only psalm in the Psalter that bears this single inscription (in contrast, for example, to "a Psalm of David", etc.).

The *Speaker's Commentary* points out that the verb from which the Hebrew noun *Mizmor* is derived means 'to cut or prune'. This can be confirmed by the use of the usual aids for those without a knowledge of Hebrew (*Strong's Concordance and Lexicon* and *Gesenius' Lexicon*). See, for example, Leviticus 25:3,4 where the verb is translated "prune" and also Genesis 43:11 where another derivative of the verb is translated "best fruits". The question is, have these associated meanings any significance in relation to the context of the psalm?

Well, we know that if pruning is done properly then it will produce the very best fruit. With this thought in mind we suggest that Psalm 98 be read carefully for the picture is of a world reconciled to God. It is a song of victory (verse 2). His righteousness has been openly manifest in the sight of the nations. He has fulfilled His promises to Israel and all the ends of the earth have seen the salvation of God (verses 2,3).

There is no suggestion of false worship, no stubborn and rebellious hearts, but all the earth sings God's praise because of the marvellous things He has done (verses 4-8). In effect God has pruned the earth. He has cut away all that would hinder and inhibit growth; the wickedness of man no longer prevails and in consequence the peoples of the earth bring forth their best fruits, for it is a wonderful picture of the kingdom age.

Psalms 96 and 98

There is a striking similarity between Psalm 96 and Psalm 98 as the comparison in the following table indicates.

Psalm 96	Psalm 98
"O sing unto the LORD a new song" (verse 1).	"O sing unto the LORD a new song" (verse 1).
"His wonders among all people" (verse 3). "Declare his glory among the nations" (verse 3, RV).	"For he hath done marvellous (same Heb. word as "wonders") things ... in the sight of the nations" (verses 1,2, RV).
Righteousness and truth (verse 13).	Righteousness and truth (verses 2,3).
"The LORD reigneth" (verse 10).	"The LORD, the King" (verse 6).
"Let the sea roar, and the fulness thereof" (verse 11).	"Let the sea roar, and the fulness thereof" (verse 7).
"Before the LORD ... for he cometh to judge the earth" (verse 13).	"For he cometh to judge the earth" (verse 9).

It will be recalled that Psalm 96 with some minor variations is recorded in 1 Chronicles 16 (verses 23-33), and has an undoubted association with the occasion when David brought the ark of God from the house of Obed-Edom to Zion. We demonstrated the way in which, linked in the record with Psalm 105 (verses 1-15; see 1 Chronicles 16:8-22), it spoke of the manner in which God would ultimately, through the fulfilment of His promises to Israel, bring His salvation to all nations.

If there is any significant difference between the two psalms it is to be found in the fact that Psalm 98 includes Israel in the worldwide knowledge of God's salvation in which all the earth rejoices. "He hath remembered his mercy and his truth toward the house of Israel", and the result is that "all the ends of the earth have seen the salvation of our God" (verse 3).

So alike are the psalms that there seems little to be said by way of exposition of Psalm 98 than that we have already written regarding Psalm 96. There is however, a very obvious question that needs to be asked: Why then are both psalms included in the inspired record?

We believe that if the psalms are read carefully a subtle difference will be observed. Psalm 96 is addressed to the people of Israel. For example:

"Shew forth his salvation from day to day. Declare his glory among the heathen."   (verses 2,3)

Psalm 98, however, is a declaration of the accomplishment of that work:

"The LORD hath made known his salvation: his righteousness hath he openly shewed in the sight of the heathen."   (verse 2)

This difference in emphasis can be traced throughout both psalms. The one then speaks of Israel's responsibility to declare God's righteousness and salvation amongst the nations, whereas the other speaks of the accomplishment of that purpose, often using the identical language of the other song.

Exodus 15

An appreciation of these facts leads to a deeper insight into both Psalms 96 and 98 for there are clear allusions in both, although not as apparent in Psalm 96, to the Song of Moses in Exodus 15. Then Moses and the children sang their song to celebrate God's deliverance from the Egyptians (verse 1) whom God swallowed up in the sea (verses 4-10). Now as the psalms celebrate a greater deliverance and an earth redeemed, they sing "a new song".

God "hath done marvellous things: his right hand, and his holy arm, hath gotten him the victory. The LORD hath made known his salvation" (Psalm 98:1,2). So Moses sang, "he hath triumphed gloriously" (Exodus 15:1). "He is become my salvation" (verse 2).

"Thy right hand, O LORD, is become glorious in power: thy right hand, O LORD, hath dashed in pieces the enemy."   (verse 6; see also verse 11)

As God had triumphed over Pharaoh and his host so now He had gained the victory, through the Lord Jesus Christ, over the power of sin (Psalms 96,98).

821

We have demonstrated that the background to this group of psalms (93–99) is the sabbath rest and David bringing the ark to Zion. How significant it is therefore, that in the song that Moses sang, to which the psalm alludes, he should have looked forward to the day when God would dwell in Zion:

"Thou shalt bring them in, and plant them in the mountain of thine inheritance, in the place, O LORD, which thou hast made for thee to dwell in, in the Sanctuary, O LORD, which thy hands have established."

(verse 17; see also verse 2)

Upon such passages David meditated. From these grew his desire to bring the ark to Zion and to build a house for God to dwell in.

Concluding Observations

Psalm 98 is shorter than Psalm 96 and falls into three sections:

1. God victorious through His wonderful works (verses 1-3).
2. All the earth recognises His sovereignty (verses 4-6).
3. Nature joins in the chorus of praise (verses 7-9).

Additional points to note in conjunction with the previous exposition of Psalm 96 are set out below:

Firstly, the prophet Isaiah uses the language of this psalm on several occasions. Compare for instance, "The LORD hath made bare his holy arm in the eyes of all nations; and all the ends of the earth shall see the salvation of our God" (52:10, with Psalm 98:1,3).

"And I looked, and there was none to help; and I wondered that there was none to uphold: therefore mine own arm brought salvation unto me; and my fury, it upheld me."   (Isaiah 63:5, with Psalm 98:1,2)

Note also the connection between salvation and righteousness (Psalm 98:2) which is emphasised in the later chapters of Isaiah's prophecy (45:8,17-19; 46:13; 51:5,6,8; 56:1; 59:16,17; 61:10; 62:1).

Secondly, "He hath remembered his mercy and his truth towards the house of Israel" (verse 3). God, of course, cannot forget. Thus when God remembers it is not a calling to mind of something that, in human terms, had been forgotten. The Hebrew word means 'to mark or to recognise' (*Strong*). Thus when God remembers, it speaks of God marking the occasion and recognising individuals who fall within the purview of His purposes. Thus when the scripture speaks of God remembering, then it is always associated with action (See Genesis 8:1; 19:29; 30:22; Exodus 2:24; 6:5; etc.).

We might notice particularly that these words were recalled by Mary after the Holy Spirit had come upon her and she waited for the birth of the Lord Jesus Christ:

"He hath holpen his servant Israel, in remembrance of his mercy; as he spake to our fathers, to Abraham, and to his seed forever."　　　　　(Luke 1:54,55)

Thirdly, the reference to the trumpets and sound of cornets (verse 6) is perhaps an indication of the priestly function of the people of Israel (or the saints). For "ye shall be unto me a kingdom of priests" (Exodus 19:6). The trumpets were initially for the use of the priests alone, although it appears that in later times they were used more generally.

The word translated "trumpets" is the Hebrew *chatzotzeroth* and it is that used in Numbers 10 to describe "the silver trumpets" that the priests used to assemble the people or to break camp (Numbers 10:1-8). It is an onomatopoeic word, that is, it is formed from the sound associated with it (e.g., 'cuckoo'). Its name apparently was formed from the quavering sound it made. It was distinctive and easily recognisable and its use in the psalm (the only time it is used in the Psalter) is perhaps an indication that it was calling the people to praise the God of Israel and that, consequently, it points to a time when the ideal of the people of Israel as a nation of priests has finally been realised.

Fourthly, in recognition of the King (verse 6), "the floods clap their hands" (verse 8). It is a striking figure, for the clapping of the hands was a characteristic way to acknowledge royalty. See for instance the coronation of Joash:

"And he brought forth the king's son, and put the crown upon him, and gave him the testimony; and they made him king, and anointed him; and they clapped their hands, and said, God save the king."

(2 Kings 11:12)

Perhaps also, given the references to Exodus 15, there is an allusion to God's victory over the Egyptians when the waters of the Red Sea overwhelmed them. In token of that typical victory, the waters now clap their hands at the fulfilment of that which was foreshadowed.

Finally, we note that the words of verse 7, "Let the sea roar, and the fulness thereof; the world, and they that dwell therein", are an obvious echo of the words of Psalm 24 (verses 1,2). This is a psalm almost universally recognised as relating to David bringing the ark to Zion. The allusion serves to establish the fact that this psalm also, with the others in this group of songs, is connected with that event.

PSALM 99

IN our introduction to Psalm 92 which bears the superscription, "A Psalm or Song for the sabbath day", we gave reasons why we believed that Psalm 92 was written by Joshua and the seven following psalms (93–99) by David who associated this series of songs with Psalm 92 – seven being a most appropriate number of psalms to connect in this way with the sabbath.

We have endeavoured to show that the theme of these psalms is the sovereignty of God manifested openly in the earth and acknowledged first by Israel and then by all the nations of the earth – a theme that is consistent with the sabbath rest that remains for the people of God. We have traced also a historical background for the psalms, seeing in David's bringing the ark of God to Zion the event which provided the platform for the theme of sovereignty as God entered into His rest (Psalm 132:14). Prophetically the psalms speak of the kingdom age when the Lord Jesus Christ will be enthroned in Zion, when the glory of God will be manifest in him and the multitude of the redeemed; when all the earth shall recognise his authority and render to him the praise and honour that is his due.

Characteristically, Psalm 99, the last of the series, opens with the words, "The LORD reigneth" as did the first psalm (93) (also Psalm 97). This psalm appears to be addressed to Israel or, to be more precise (in its prophetical implications), to the covenant people of God. He is "great in Zion" (verse 2) and has executed judgement in Jacob (verse 4). He is the "LORD our God" (verses 5,8,9) and the latter part of the psalm emphasises the holiness of those who draw near to worship Him, for He, "the LORD our God is holy" (verse 9).

The psalm falls easily into three sections, each closing (as verse 9 above) with an affirmation of the holiness of

825

God. "Holy is he" (verses 3,5, RV). Thus the three sections might be identified as follows:

1. "The LORD reigneth" (verses 1-3).
2. The Righteousness and Justice of His reign (verses 4,5).
3. Kings and Priests unto God (verses 6-9).

"The LORD reigneth" (verses 1-3)

The striking similarity of the language between the psalms in this series of songs continues. This is the third that opens with the majestic declaration that "the LORD reigneth" (Psalm 93:1; 97:1). The consequence of this open manifestation of God's presence in the earth is reflected throughout the songs: "let the people tremble" (verse 1) (see also Psalm 96:9; 97:4; etc.). The word rendered "tremble" means 'to quiver with violent emotion, either with anger or rage' (*Strong*). Clearly the sense in these psalms is primarily that of fear and awe, although perhaps we should not discount completely the idea of anger.

The initial reaction of the nations when God sets His king upon His holy hill of Zion is anger for, "Why do the heathen rage?" (Psalm 2:1), and it is only when they have been humbled before His might and have come to recognise the utter futility of opposition to His will, that the anger moves through frustration to fear and the acknowledgement that they can do nothing but bow the knee in worship before the King of all the earth.

It hardly needs to be said that arising out of the circumstances of David's experiences, he is moved by the Spirit to prophesy of the advent of the Lord Jesus Christ in glory and his exaltation in the earth. It is of this wondrous day that the psalm speaks. It is particularly appropriate given the historical background that David should, in the parallel phrases of the first verse, exclaim: "He sitteth between the cherubims; let the earth be moved."

Yahweh's reign is parallel with, "He sitteth between the cherubims" and the people trembling with the earth being moved. The verb rendered "moved" appears to occur only in this one instance and means 'to quake' (*Strong*). One

826

could well imagine that it would speak of some physical phenomenon like an earthquake. However, the fact that it appears as an extension of the previous expression of the fear and awe experienced by the people is an indication that the language is purely figurative and describes the response of all the earth to the fact that the Lord is King.

The reference to sitting (literally, 'dwelling', see 2 Samuel 6:2; 2 Kings 19:15; 1 Chronicles 13:6, etc.) is a clear indication that God is manifest as King not just from heaven but in the earth. The language establishes that God reigns from His temple in Zion (verse 2), where, in times past, He dwelt in the midst of His people.

The cherubim in the tabernacle are not described in the detail that we are given by Ezekiel, and those carved figures in the most holy place must to some extent remain a matter of conjecture as to their form and faces. It is not our intention to consider the cherubim in any detail, but the most complete description we have is in Ezekiel chapter 1. Amongst the characteristics described, the following might be noted particularly:

1. They were associated with whirlwind, cloud and flashing fire (verses 4,5, RV).
2. They had the appearance of four living creatures, yet their likeness was that of a man.
3. They had four faces (i.e., man, lion, ox and eagle).
4. They had wheels full of eyes.

Clearly the picture is of chariots which carry the cherubim where they were intended to go (verses 19,20), and the picture that emerges is of a vehicle that bears and carries forth the glory of God.

We appreciate that this is a very superficial insight into everything that the cherubim represent, but we suggest the idea that they are the vehicles whereby God's power and glory are manifest is a simple fact that holds the key to further investigation (see Genesis 3:24; Psalm18:10; Ezekiel 10; Daniel 7; Revelation 4:5, etc.).

The four faces correspond to the standards of the camp of Israel which, although not delineated in scripture, are well established by universal ancient tradition in Israel. Thus the lion was for Judah on the east; the eagle for Dan on the north; the ox for Ephraim on the west, and the man for Reuben on the south.

We know also of the extent to which the cherubic figures were represented in the tabernacle and the temple and thereby the Israelitish character of the cherubim is confirmed. In stating this, however, we must be careful not to forget that the four cherubim represent the universality of God's power – His sovereignty over all the earth. Israel is but the means whereby God brings all people of the earth to recognise and acknowledge this fact.

The meaning of the word "cherubim" is obscure. In *Kitto's Cyclopaedia of Bible Literature*, F. W. Farrar lists nine possible derivations of the word that he considers to be worthy of consideration. We mention just three.

1. It is derived from a word that means 'the plougher', hence an ox. This was apparently the most commonly held view by leading Hebrew authorities at the time of the publication of the work (late 19th Century) and Ezekiel 10:14 is quoted to substantiate this view.

2. By transposition of the vowels it is argued that it is derived from the word for 'chariot'. This is the view we have heard expressed by brethren most often. The association of the cherubim with the concept of a chariot is beyond dispute (see Psalm 18:10 etc., and comments above). These connections are, of course, in no way diminished even if the actual meaning of the word is different.

3. In ancient times (i.e., 1st Century AD) it appears to have been almost universally believed that it was derived from a combination of two words meaning abundance and knowledge. We believe that it was from this derivation that the late Brother Elwyn Humphreys suggested that the meaning of the word was 'a host or a multitude'. More precisely 'a host of knowing ones'.

This last suggestion has an aptness as we consider the consummation of God's purpose, when His glory will be revealed in a multitude, the many sons whom God is bringing unto glory. Doubt about the meaning of the word, however, in no way prevents us from coming to the conclusion from the things revealed in scripture, that the cherubim represent the power and glory of God manifest in a variety of ways throughout human history, but ultimately to be seen in the manifestation of God in the Lord Jesus Christ and the glorified saints. Throughout Ezekiel's vision of the cherubim (chapter 1) there is this repeated emphasis upon man.

Apart from the fact that one of the faces was the face of a man, Ezekiel says of the four living creatures that their appearance was the likeness of a man (verse 5) and they had the hands of a man under their wings (verse 8). The four faces recall God's work of creation. The eagle represents the fowl of the air; the ox, the cattle of the field, and the lion, the beasts of the earth. Yet over them all man was given dominion (Genesis 1:26-28) and the cherubim perpetuate and illustrate the truth that ultimately God's purpose in creation will be fulfilled when, through the Lord Jesus Christ, man will be given dominion over all the works of His hands.

In that day it will be said, "The LORD is great in Zion; and he is high above all the people" (Psalm 99:2). He is a great God and a terrible (Deuteronomy 7:21, RV; 10:17) and through the understanding of His name, His moral perfection is appreciated and all peoples of the earth are moved to give praise and thanks unto Him in the knowledge that "Holy is He" (verse 3, RV).

The Righteousness and Justice of His Reign (verses 4,5)

"The king's strength also loveth judgment". The construction appears awkward but the sense is clear. The God who reigns in Zion does not exercise His power and might as men would. There is nothing arbitrary about His actions but His strength is characterised by judgement. "The strength (or might) of a king who loveth judgment ... Thou (even Thou) hast established; equity, judgment, and righteousness, Thou (even Thou) hast executed" (verse 4, *Speaker's Commentary*). There is great emphasis upon the pronoun which can best be demonstrated in English by the repetition of the word "Thou".

These qualities are of course characteristics of David's throne when the Lord Jesus shall sit upon it forever. So men are exhorted to "exalt the LORD our God, and worship at his footstool" (verse 5).

We might imagine that the familiar words of Isaiah's prophecy, "Thus saith the LORD, The heaven is my throne, and the earth is my footstool" (66:1) are no more than poetic imagery to describe the unimaginable greatness of the Creator. The context, however, is illuminating for the passage continues, "Where is the house that ye build unto me? and where is the place of my rest? For all those things hath mine hand made". If we might so put it, the language has now taken on a distinctly 'cherubic' character and the ultimate dwelling place of the Lord is not a literal building but a house composed of faithful men and women:

"But to this man will I look, even to him that is poor and of a contrite spirit, and trembleth at my word."
(Isaiah 66:2)

This sovereignty that the God of Israel exercised over all the earth was represented by the cherubim of glory over the ark and the mercy seat in the most holy place. Thus the reference to God's footstool in the Old Testament scriptures is found to have particular reference to those representations of God's power and glory. The following passages demonstrate the point:

"As for me (David), I had in mine heart to build an house of rest for the ark of the covenant of the LORD, and for the footstool of our God." (1 Chronicles 28:2)

"We will go into his tabernacles: we will worship at his footstool. Arise, O LORD, into thy rest; thou, and the ark of thy strength." (Psalm 132:7,8)

'The glory of Lebanon shall come unto thee, the fir tree, the pine tree, and the box together, to beautify the place of my sanctuary; and I will make the place of my feet glorious." (Isaiah 60:13)

"(He) hath ... cast down from heaven unto the earth the beauty of Israel, and remembered not his footstool in the day of his anger!" (Lamentations 2:1)

"And he said unto me, Son of man, this is the place of my throne, and the place of the soles of my feet, where I will dwell in the midst of the children of Israel for ever." (Ezekiel 43:7)

If we might reverently put it so, He sat upon the mercy seat between the cherubim and the soles of His feet symbolically touched the ground and hallowed it. It was to this place that men were to come and worship Him and to prostrate themselves before His footstool for "Holy is He" (verse 5, RV).

Kings and Priests unto God (verses 6-9)

This final section of the psalm is based upon Israel's past history. The names recorded and the imagery used are prophetic of the kingdom age, but to understand their significance we have to consider their original scriptural associations:

> "Moses and Aaron among his priests, and Samuel among them that call upon his name; they called upon the LORD, and he answered them." (verse 6)

Strictly speaking Moses was not a priest although he performed the functions of the priesthood until Aaron's consecration for the office (Exodus 24:8; Leviticus 8:6-13 etc.). Samuel is not described as a priest in this passage but he also appears to have undertaken priestly tasks in addition to his prophetic office (1 Samuel 9:12,13; 11:14,15).

The emphasis, however, is not upon the offering of sacrifices but upon the prayers that these men offered on behalf of the people of Israel. It is their work as intercessors that is being recalled. We might remember particularly Moses' prayer when Israel sinned in the matter of the golden calf (Exodus 32:3,32); Aaron at the rebellion of Korah, Dathan and Abiram when "he stood between the dead and the living" (Numbers 16:48); Samuel who cried unto the Lord on behalf of the children of Israel to deliver them out of the hand of the Philistines (1 Samuel 7:8; see also 12:18-20).

At a later date to emphasize the sins of the people of Israel, God said, "Though Moses and Samuel stood before me, yet my mind could not be towards this people" (Jeremiah 15:1). The naming of these great characters, however, is not to highlight their personal responsibilities in the kingdom age, although beyond doubt they will be there. Rather they are selected as representatives of all those in the kingdom of God who will be "kings and priests" unto God (Revelation 5:10) and who will perform for Israel and for all the nations of the earth the functions that Moses, Aaron and Samuel fulfilled in the past.

What we have in the psalm is "a predictive representation of the combined worship of the risen saints, and of those who shall be Christ's at his coming, in that great day of his appearing which the Psalm describes" (*Speaker's Commentary* – Psalms, page 398).

> "He spake unto them in the cloudy pillar: they kept his testimonies, and the ordinance that he gave them."
> (verse 7)

Again, if we apply these words strictly to the three men named in verse 6, as with the priesthood, there is an inconsistency. Only Moses is specifically spoken of as entering into the cloud and speaking with God although it is also recorded of Samuel:

> "And the LORD appeared again in Shiloh: for the LORD revealed himself to Samuel in Shiloh by the word of the LORD." (1 Samuel 3:21)

The question is, Who is referred to as "them"? (verse 7). We suggest that in the past history of the people of Israel, God spoke to the nation through the mediation of these men. The pillar of cloud was the token of the presence of God in the midst of His people. The reference in this verse is in keeping with the earlier declaration that "He dwelleth between the cherubim" (verse 1). As in days of old when God spoke through priest and prophet, so now the message is that once again, in the visible manifestation of His presence in the earth, God has drawn nigh to those that are His and through them (the saints) He speaks to His people Israel and indeed to all the peoples of the earth. God does not change. He is the same God, true to Himself, who now deals with the mortal nations of the earth by the same principles that He showed in times past.

Then under the guidance of Moses, Aaron and Samuel, the people received and kept His testimonies and ordinances. He answered the prayers of His servants and showed His compassion in forgiving the sins of the people. Even so, His justice demanded that although He was prepared to pardon their sin they sometimes could not escape the consequences of their actions and they were punished for their doings (verse 8, RV). Thus, we believe, the context establishes that those spoken of in verses 7 and 8 are not the three men of God, but the people on whose behalf they interceded.

"Thou answeredst them, O LORD our God: thou wast a God that forgavest them, though thou tookest vengeance of their doings." (verse 8, RV)

It is a remarkable insight into the priestly functions of the saints in the kingdom age. The principles by which God operated in the midst of His people Israel will not be changed, but by the same means He will administer righteousness and judgement among the peoples of the earth. In this work the saints, represented here by Moses, Aaron and Samuel, will have an important part to play.

It is in the realisation of the wondrous things that God has brought to pass in the earth that the people of God can only exclaim:

"Exalt the LORD our God, and worship at his holy hill (i.e., His footstool, verse 5, RV); for the LORD our God is holy." (verse 9)

Addendum

Readers will discover that there is a body of opinion that would place some, at least, of this group of psalms in the days of Hezekiah – see the *Speaker's Commentary,* for example. One suggestion is that three of the psalms (93,97,99) were actually written by the prophet Isaiah.

There can be no doubt that some of the language could appropriately be applied to Isaiah's day, but this need not be surprising if both circumstances are looking forward to the same event (i.e., the kingdom age). We know on the authority of scripture that two of the psalms, at least, were written by David (Psalms 95,96) and by long tradition the Jews regarded this group of psalms (93–99) as one song. We believe that on balance, with the background of the ark and the sabbath, the evidence points to the view we have presented. In any event the essential message of the psalms (i.e., "The LORD reigneth") is not affected which ever point of view is adopted.

A final interesting suggestion to be found in the *Speaker's Commentary* that this group of psalms (Psalm 99 in particular) forms the basis of the words to be found in the Book of Revelation chapter 11:

"And the seventh angel sounded; and there were great voices in heaven, saying, The kingdoms of this world are become the kingdoms of our Lord, and of his Christ; and he shall reign for ever and ever. And the four and twenty elders, which sat before God on their seats, fell upon their faces, and worshipped God, saying, We give thee thanks, O Lord God Almighty, which art, and wast, and art to come; because thou hast taken to thee thy great power, and hast reigned. And the nations were angry, and thy wrath is come, and the time of the dead, that they should be judged, and that thou shouldest give reward unto thy servants the prophets, and to the saints, and them that fear thy name, small and great; and shouldest destroy them which destroy the earth. And the temple of God was opened in heaven, and there was seen in his temple the ark of his testament: and there were lightnings, and voices, and thunderings, and an earthquake, and great hail."

(verses 15-19)

PSALM 100

W^E have suggested that Psalms 90, 91 and 92
were psalms of Moses. In Psalm 90, a psalm
of the wilderness, the emphasis was upon the
generation that perished in the wilderness. Psalm 91
is addressed to Joshua who lived through all the
privations of the wilderness to enter the land
because God had promised that no evil should befall
him, and He had given His angels charge concerning
him.

Psalm 92 bears the inscription "a Psalm for the
sabbath day" and is appropriately linked with Joshua
(Psalm 91) who led the children of Israel into their
promised rest.

There follow seven psalms (93–99) which have a
common theme – "The LORD reigneth", and speak of the
time when God will enter into His rest and be
acknowledged by all the people of the earth as their
sovereign Lord. They are all reflections upon this
common theme seen from different perspectives and
inevitably they contain many repetitions of thought.

We concluded that all seven psalms were written by
David against the background of the ark of the covenant
being brought into the tabernacle that he had prepared
for it in Jerusalem – this event foreshadowing the
eventual consummation of God's purpose when the Lord
Jesus shall reign on David's throne in the kingdom.

It is not possible to read Psalm 100 without realising
that it reflects beautifully and precisely the spirit of the
previous seven psalms. Its language is an echo of all that
has been expressed in them. Indeed the language of
Psalm 95 in particular seems to be reproduced as
demonstrated in the comparisons that are tabulated
overleaf:

Psalm 95

"Let us come before his presence with thanksgiving, and make a joyful noise unto him with psalms" (verse 2).

"For he is our God; and we are the people of his pasture, and the sheep of his hand" (verse 7).

Psalm 100

"Make a joyful noise unto the LORD, all ye lands. Serve the LORD with gladness: come before his presence with singing" (verses 1,2).

"We are his people, and the sheep of his pasture" (verse 3).

Psalm 100 stands as a doxology to the previous group of psalms. It is the grand finale to their wondrous message of God's sovereignty. It bears no indication of authorship. It is probable that this psalm also was composed by David. Equally it could have been written at a later date by an unknown author (Hezekiah?), who was moved by the Spirit to gather together the thoughts and expressions of the previous series of psalms at the time the Psalter was compiled.

There is nevertheless an inscription at the head of the psalm. It says, "A Psalm of praise". The AV margin has, "A Psalm of thanksgiving" and with this agrees the RV, although the RV margin reads, "A Psalm for the thank offering". This latter rendering would link the psalm with the record in Leviticus (7:11-15) and may have arisen because of the liturgical use of the psalm in the temple. The recognition that it is a psalm of thanksgiving links naturally with the ideas expressed in verse 4:

"Enter into his courts with thanksgiving, and into his courts with praise: be thankful unto him, and bless his name."

Interestingly in the Syriac Version, the psalm bears the title, "A psalm for the conversion of the heathen to the true faith", and although we do not believe that this is authentic (i.e., part of the inspired record) it nevertheless expresses a true understanding of what the psalm is about.

The song is sung on behalf of Israel. It is a call to all the world to come and recognise that, in His final mercy to Israel, is to be seen blessing for all the earth. The nations are invited to come and to join in Israel's worship that there might be a common recognition that there is one God who is enthroned as King of all the earth. This is a picture of Israel fulfilling their destiny to be "a kingdom of priests and an holy nation" (Exodus 19:5,6), recognising that they are truly God's witnesses (Isaiah 43:10).

In this respect the psalm anticipates the prediction of the prophet Isaiah:

"Also the strangers, that join themselves to the LORD ... even them will I bring to my holy mountain, and make them joyful in my house of prayer ... for mine house shall be called an house of prayer for all peoples."
(Isaiah 56:6,7, RV)

These words were written against the background of King Hezekiah's exaltation in the sight of the nations (see 2 Chronicles 32:22,23).

The Text

This short psalm of thanksgiving needs no subdividing. It is one. Of the word "joyful" in verse 1, *Strong* says that it means 'to shout (usually with joy)' and the words, "Make a joyful noise unto the LORD, all ye lands" (verse 1) are again an echo of Psalm 98 (verses 4-6). There all the earth salutes its king and it is evident that 'a shout' was the traditional method of recognising and welcoming a king, who entering the city sits on the throne of his glory. Now at last, the blessing of Abraham is enjoyed by all the families of the earth. Note the progression:

"(They) serve the LORD with gladness: (and) come before his presence with singing." (verse 2)

In Psalm 2 where "the heathen rage, and the people imagine a vain thing" (verse 1) they are compelled to submit to the divine authority and they "serve the LORD with fear" (verse 11). Now, in the understanding of all that He had accomplished in His people Israel, they come with gladness and singing. No longer do they merely submit, but now they come in worship. They come before His presence (literally, His face), and the reference to the presence of God and the faces of the cherubim in the most holy place seems to be an appropriate conclusion to make.

Israel's appeal to the nations who come to worship is, "Know ye that the LORD he is God" (verse 3). Yahweh, alone is recognised as God and consequently, because He is one, there is now universal recognition of His sovereignty: there is one religion and the dire effect of the tower of Babel which resulted in confusion is now reversed:

"For then will I turn to the people a pure language, that they may all call upon the name of the LORD, to serve him with one consent." (Zephaniah 3:9)

The implication of the verb 'to know' is that it is a knowledge gained by experience. How have the nations come to this understanding? It is because they have witnessed and meditated upon the wonder of all that He has accomplished in and through Israel. So in support of their plea to come and worship with them, Israel proclaim:

"It is he that hath made us, and not we ourselves; we are his people, and the sheep of his pasture."
(Psalm 100:3)

So it has ever been. He did not just create them but He made them what they are – His people – from the call of Abraham, Isaac's miraculous birth, the sojourn in Egypt, the Exodus, the inheritance of the land, the establishment of the kingdom. It was all of God and though they might be carried away captive, their restoration was through the good hand of their God. Thus it will be when they are finally reconciled to Him, established in their land and all His promises brought to fulfilment. In that day it will be said again, "It is he that hath made us and we are his" (RV) (see Deuteronomy 32:6,15; Psalm 95:7).

The translation given in the RV is, perhaps, confirmed by the prophet Isaiah's allusion to the psalm:

"But now thus saith the LORD that created thee, O Jacob, and he that formed thee, O Israel, Fear not: for I have redeemed thee, I have called thee by thy name; thou art mine." (43:1)

Not only was He their Maker but He was also their Shepherd, and His pasture into which He led them was surely the land of promise and the blessings that He bestowed upon them there (see Psalm 77:20; 78:52).

In the knowledge of all that God had done for Israel and the blessings that flowed through them to the Gentiles, all peoples of the earth could "enter into his gates with thanksgiving, and into his courts with praise".

The Hebrew word translated "thanksgiving" also carries the idea of 'confession' (see *Strong*). It is on a few occasions rendered thus and the verb from which it is derived is commonly translated 'confess'. Thus it would be that the man who brought his peace and thank offerings would first bring a sin offering, before these offerings which spoke of fellowship with God could be accepted.

So those who come to offer thanksgiving and praise can do so only because they have acknowledged their sin and God has graciously forgiven them. Consequently, "be thankful unto him, and bless his name" (verse 4). God's name will be blessed when men, in appreciation of all that the name conveys, recognise that God has fulfilled that purpose enshrined in it:

"For the LORD is good; his mercy endureth for ever; and his faithfulness unto all generations." (verse 5, RV)

Thus the grand anthem of praise is brought to a conclusion. As the psalm began by calling all people of the earth to shout with joy at the coronation of the 'King Eternal', so now all people rejoice in the goodness of God for they have experienced His grace and mercy. His faithfulness stands forever; the purpose enshrined in His promises can never be frustrated. It stands unto all generations reminding those who in every age seek the salvation that He offers, that God will be true to His name for that is His memorial unto all generations (Exodus 3:15). Could this series of psalms together with their doxology end on a more sublime note than this?

Excursus Upon Psalms 93–100

It is a strange thing but we have not discovered a single orthodox writer who is prepared to accept that these psalms were written by David. We have of course the evidence of scripture (1 Chronicles 16:23-33 for Psalm 96 and Hebrews 4:7 for Psalm 95) that two of them at least were, beyond question, from his pen.

What is interesting, however, is that although denying the Davidic authorship, there is a consensus of opinion that, given the common theme that runs throughout, all these songs have a common author. Notable in developing this point are Kay (*Psalms with Notes*) and the *Speaker's Commentary*. In the latter case there is a seven-page excursus upon Psalms 91-100 (pages 506-512), where the writer presents evidence for this view and draws attention to the close affinity between the language of the psalms and the Book of Isaiah. In connection with the question of authorship he writes:

"The indications of mutual connection and common authorship ... are traced mainly in the identity of similarity of the subject matter ... in the general resemblance of style ... and in the facts that Psalm 93 is a part of Psalm 92 in twelve Codices, that Psalm 95 is joined to Psalm 94 in nine Codices, that Psalm 96 is a part of Psalm 95 in four Codices, that Psalm 97 is a part of Psalm 96 in fourteen Codices, and that Psalm 99 is connected with Psalm 98 in eight Codices."

Commenting further on the links with Isaiah's prophecy he writes:

"The following table of coincidences will suffice to show that if the Psalms and the prophecies were not the compositions of the same writer, the Psalmist must have borrowed from the Prophet or the Prophet from the Psalmist." (page 506)

We do not believe that they were coincidences or that they were borrowed in the sense the above quotation seems to mean, for we are speaking of the inspired word of God. Neither do we believe that the psalms are quoting Isaiah but rather given the Davidic authorship established by scripture, it is the prophet who quotes the Psalms. As a point of interest we have extracted from the *Speaker's Commentary* some of the points of contact established between the two scriptures.

The following table is a selection from a much greater list of points of contact, many depending on an appreciation of the Hebrew text. It will be noted that Psalm 98 in particular seems to be referred to frequently.

PSALMS

"The LORD reigneth" (93:1). *These words form the keynote of this series of psalms and are repeated in 96:10; 97:1; 99:1, coupled in the last instance with the declaration* "the LORD is great in Zion" (99:2).

"He is clothed with majesty; the LORD is clothed with strength" (93:1).

"O sing unto the LORD a new song (96:1; 98:1).

"Let the sea roar, and the fulness thereof; the world, and they that dwell therein" (98:7; see also 96:11).

"Let the heavens rejoice, and let the earth be glad" (96:11).

"His holy arm, hath gotten him the victory" (98:1).

"All the ends of the earth have seen the salvation of our God" (98:3).

"The voice of a psalm (or song)" (98:5).

"Clap their hands" (98:8).

ISAIAH

"When the LORD of hosts shall reign in mount Zion" (24:23). "That saith unto Zion, Thy God reigneth" (52:7).

"Awake, awake, put on strength, O arm of the LORD" (51:9). "Awake, awake; put on thy strength, O Zion; put on thy beautiful garments, O Jerusalem, the Holy City" (52:1).

"Sing unto the LORD a new song" (42:10).

"The sea and the fulness thereof, the isle and the inhabitants thereof" (42:10, AV with margin).

"Sing, O heavens; and be joyful, O earth" (49:13).

"The LORD hath made bare his holy arm" (52:10).

"All the ends of the earth shall see the salvation of our God" (52:10).

"The voice of melody (or psalm or song)" (51:3).

"Clap their hands" (55:12)

This phrase occurs in no other psalm

"He hath remembered his mercy (lovingkindness) and his truth toward the house of Israel" (98:3).

"I will mention the lovingkindness of the LORD ... and the great goodness toward the house of Israel ... according to the multitude of his lovingkindnesses" (63:7).

841

"He shall judge the world with righteousness, and the peoples with equity" (98:9, RV).

"But with righteousness shall he judge the poor, and reprove with equity for the meek of the earth" (11:4).

"Holy is he ... holy is he ... for the LORD our God is holy" (99:3,5,9, RV).

"Holy, holy, holy, is the LORD of hosts" (6:3).

There can be no doubt that Isaiah meditated upon this group of psalms. He understood their significance and saw in the events of his own times both the need for the purpose indicated to be fulfilled and the manner in which the events surrounding the life of Hezekiah pointed forward to the same grand climax in the affairs of men.

PSALM 101

THE song bears the inscription "A Psalm of David" and even the more critical commentators seem prepared to accept that this psalm is truly his. The substance of the psalm is concerned with the practical way in which David desired to rule the kingdom in righteousness and equity. It has been called "David's mirror for rulers", "the prince's Psalm", "a mirror for magistrates" and it is recorded of some rulers that they sent a copy of this psalm to unfaithful counsellors. (*Cambridge Bible,* page 590).

There are only two occasions in David's life to which this psalm might appropriately apply. The first is when he assumed his sovereignty over all twelve tribes of Israel (2 Samuel 5:7-9). The second is when he endeavoured to bring the ark to Zion. We believe that the evidence points to the second of these suggestions. The psalm was clearly written when David was enthroned in Jerusalem – the city of the Lord (see verse 8). The general tone of the psalm suggests that the conduct of would-be ministers in that kingdom should be appropriate to those who served in the presence of a divine guest. It will be remembered that when David first attempted to bring the ark to Zion the venture ended in disaster, for Uzzah, seeking to steady the cart, touched the ark and was struck dead for his presumption. It was against this background that it is recorded:

"And David was afraid of the LORD that day, and said, How shall the ark of the LORD come to me?"

(2 Samuel 6:9)

Two psalms written at that time reflect how David's meditations led him to appreciate the qualities of life necessary in those who would approach the Eternal God and have Him dwell in the midst of His people. Psalm 15 asks:

> "LORD, who shall abide in thy tabernacle? who shall dwell in thy holy hill?" (verse 1)

The answer which, perhaps, sums up the details of the remainder of the Psalm is:

> "He that walketh uprightly, and worketh righteousness, and speaketh the truth in his heart." (verse 2)

Psalm 24 has a similar message:

> "Who shall ascend into the hill of the LORD? or who shall stand in his holy place? He that hath clean hands, and a pure heart; who hath not lifted up his soul unto vanity, nor sworn deceitfully." (verse 3,4)

The words of 2 Samuel 6 spring from the heart of David once more in the words of Psalm 101:2: "O when wilt thou come unto me?" for this is David's desire; this is the hope of his aching, longing heart. As Psalms 15 and 24 emphasise the principles that God looks for in those who seek to approach Him, so David gives them practical expression in the qualities he will look for in those who assume positions of authority in the city where God has chosen to dwell.

We can divide the psalm into two parts:

1. David's resolution as to his own conduct (verses 1-4).
2. His intention to eradicate wickedness and to banish evil men (verses 5-8).

Verses 1-4

> "I will sing of mercy and judgment: unto thee, O LORD, will I sing." (verse 1)

Mercy (Hebrew, *chesed*) and judgement are qualities associated with God's rule. They are the bond that establishes any relationship between man and God. If a man would truly know God, then not only must he recognise and meditate upon them as manifest by God but he must reproduce them, as much as he is able, in his own life. These principles are emphasised throughout the Old Testament, but the prophet Hosea's message seems particularly relevant:

"And I will betroth thee unto me for ever; yea, I will betroth thee unto me in righteousness, and in judgment, and in lovingkindness, and in mercies. I will even betroth thee unto me in faithfulness: and thou shalt know the LORD."   (2:19,20)

The practical expression of these qualities in God's activity amongst men, when truly appreciated, will always result in a knowledge of God.

This was Israel's failure. God had manifested His grace in His dealings with them, but:

"My people are destroyed for lack of knowledge: because thou hast rejected knowledge, I will also reject thee."   (4:6)

Israel's failure is highlighted in chapter 6:

"O Ephraim, what shall I do unto thee? O Judah, what shall I do unto thee? for your goodness (AV margin, Hebrew, *chesed*) is as a morning cloud, and as the early dew it goeth away."   (verse 4)

"For I desired mercy, and not sacrifice; and the knowledge of God more than burnt offerings. But they like men have transgressed the covenant: there have they dealt treacherously against me."   (verses 6,7)

So the exhortation came again:

"Therefore turn thou to thy God: keep (RSV, 'hold fast') mercy and judgment, and wait on thy God continually."   (12:6)

In celebration of these divine virtues David says that he will sing psalms (verse 1) and endeavour to reproduce them in his own life:

"I will behave myself wisely in a perfect way. O when wilt thou come unto me? I will walk within my house with a perfect heart."   (verse 2)

The RV margin says, "I will give heed unto the perfect way" and this seems to have the support of most translators. In effect David is expressing his sense of responsibility, his understanding of the need for personal integrity. It is so easy for men in positions of power to be dazzled and blinded by the opportunity to indulge themselves in their whims and passions. This was, no doubt, particularly true of eastern potentates in those times, and no less true of men today if they are given opportunity. But David had resolved "to walk within his house in the integrity of his heart" (RV margin). Even in the privacy of his own palace, hidden from prying eyes, he would not indulge himself and mercy and judgement would prevail in all his ways.

The cry, "O when wilt thou come unto me?" echoes the words of 2 Samuel (6:9) but given the background, could also be a reflection of David's meditations on the Book of Exodus:

"In all places where I record my name I will come unto thee, and I will bless thee."   (20:24)

So David expresses the manner in which he would behave himself in exercising his royal authority:

"I will set no wicked thing before mine eyes: I hate the work of them that turn aside; it shall not cleave to me. A froward heart shall depart from me: I will not know a wicked person."   (Psalm 101:3,4)

If verse 2 describes the manner in which David will behave privately, then verse 3 tells of the way in which he will conduct himself publicly. He would set no wicked thing before his eyes. That is, he would not make it his aim or ambition in life. The RV renders it, "no base thing" but it is literally, 'no matter of Belial'. Although superstition has led men to regard 'Belial' as a proper name and even to render it thus on occasions in the historical books, it is in fact a compound noun meaning 'that which profiteth not', i.e., worthless (compare Deuteronomy 15, 'a heart of belial', verse 9, AV margin). If in fact David was thinking of men of belial – vain or worthless individuals – then he was asserting that such should not be allowed to abide in his presence as a pattern for imitation or object of regard.

David had no sympathy with evil men; he hated "the doing of unfaithfulness" (RV margin, verse 3) and men who lacked moral integrity would be banished from his court. David of course, would know from practical experience in the court of Saul how such men behaved. He had experienced their slander, talebearing and false praise as they endeavoured to bring about his downfall. He would take particular care not to be contaminated by their wickedness. It should not "cleave" to him. Literally, the word rendered "cleave" means 'to adhere or to stick', or as we would say, 'to be glued to'. It is the word used of the marriage bond in Genesis (2:24) and it is used in Deuteronomy where Israel are exhorted to cleave unto the Lord (4:14; 10:20; 11:22; 13:4). David would allow "no cursed thing" to cleave to him (see Deuteronomy 13:17). So a "froward heart", that is a crooked character, a man that was not upright in his way, should not abide in his presence. He would repudiate wickedness in all its forms, for:

"They that are of a froward heart are abomination to the LORD: but such as are upright in their way are his delight."   (Proverbs 11:20)

Verses 5-8
David's description of those whom he will not suffer to abide in his royal court gives us a vivid insight into the way in which men so often behave when personal ambition drives them to achieve precedence over their fellows:

"Whoso privily slandereth his neighbour, him will I cut off: him that hath an high look and a proud heart will not I suffer."   (verse 5)

The desire to ingratiate oneself with those in authority is something that is a characteristic of human nature in almost every sphere of human activity. Sadly it often resorts at the lowest level to tittle-tattle and gossip, but more seriously to slanderous assertions made privately when those accused not only have no opportunity to defend themselves but are also totally unaware that the allegations have been made. Those who behave in such a way, says David, he will cut off. He will not suffer them to continue in his service.

Likewise the man with a high look (literally, 'lofty of eyes'); the man who, as it were, looks down upon his fellows, considering himself superior to them and better qualified in every respect to serve. The high look is the token of a proud heart. His arrogance is indicative of a heart that is blown up with pride (literally, 'a wide heart'). Such a man is motivated, not by a desire to serve, but to promote his own interests. For such there would be no place in David's court. Instead he would look for men of integrity to be his confidential ministers:

> "Mine eyes shall be upon the faithful of the land, that they may dwell with me: he that walketh in a perfect way, he shall serve me."
>
> (verse 6; RV, "minister unto me")

David's closest advisors would be chosen not because of accident of birth or because of their wealth. He would not be influenced by flattery or what we would describe today as 'Yes-men'. The quality he would look for was faithfulness, and surely the sense is faithful to God, for such men could be relied upon to be faithful to him. They should be those who walked "in a perfect way"; those who lived by the same standards that David had set for himself (see verse 2). Thus:

> "He that worketh deceit shall not dwell within my house: he that telleth lies shall not tarry in my sight."
>
> (verse 7)

The basis of all human relationships is trust. If deceit is practised and lies told, then there can be no confidence in such a man. David would not allow such to dwell with him; he would expel them from his presence. It was his resolve, not only to cut off such men from his court but to drive them from the land. It was his spiritual ambition to make Jerusalem a city that was truly worthy to be described as "the city of the LORD":

> "Morning by morning will I destroy all the wicked of the land; to cut off all the workers of iniquity from the city of the LORD." (verse 8, RV)

It was a daily task as he sought to purge the city from wickedness. He recognised it was not something that could be accomplished in a short period of time. That David was not more successful in his purpose was in some measure due to his own weakness. His sin in the matter of Bathsheba and Uriah the Hittite diminished his authority amongst those who were closest to him, not least his own family.

The psalm, however, is not merely a description of David's earnest desire to establish mercy and judgement as the foundation of his kingdom. It is also a prophecy of the day when the Lord Jesus Christ shall sit on David's throne and establish his righteous judgement over all the earth. The qualities of those who will be his ministers in that day are clearly portrayed. If we would be with him we must show those characteristics in our daily lives, in our relationship with our brethren and sisters in our ecclesial life, and indeed in our dealings with all men.

For all his longing to purge his kingdom from wickedness David did not succeed. We can be assured that when the Lord Jesus comes again nothing will frustrate him from accomplishing that end and Jerusalem will be universally recognised as "the city of the LORD".

PSALM 102

A CAREFUL reading of Psalm 102 and its title establishes the following facts about the author and his circumstances:

1. That he is in great adversity (title).
2. Through sickness and disease he appears to be close to death (verses 23,24).
3. Because of the circumstances in which he finds himself he feels an overwhelming sense of loneliness (verses 6,7).
4. He expects God to act to deliver Zion and to exalt her in the sight of the nations (verses 13-18).

A majority of writers place this psalm at a time when the captivity in Babylon was coming to its close. This means that we cannot identify the author and although some have suggested Daniel, we know nothing in his life that is comparable to the facts revealed in the psalm. Nevertheless the reference to "the time to favour (Zion), yea, the set time, is come" (verse 13), would certainly be appropriate in terms of the seventy years captivity.

As an alternative to this view we suggest that the detail outlined above is true, as far as information revealed in scripture is concerned, of one man only and that is King Hezekiah. (Prophetically it is true also of the Lord Jesus Christ, but we are thinking now particularly of authorship.)

Of course, essentially, the question of who wrote the psalm is not vital to our understanding of it, or God would have given us irrefutable evidence. However, as we have written before, a historical setting does give a framework in which the words and exhortations of the psalm become more readily appreciated.

The psalm is unique in respect of its title. All other psalms which bear titles, give either musical or historical information. This is purely devotional and seems designed to reflect the feelings of all who were in similar circumstances to the writer: "A Prayer of the afflicted, when he is overwhelmed, and poureth out his complaint before the LORD."

The structure of the psalm can be identified as:

1. The Prologue (a general cry for God's help) (verses 1,2).

2 A description of the Psalmist's distress (verses 3-11).

3. His comfort and consolation in God (verses 12-22).

4. An Epilogue (a contrast between the transience of the writer and the unchanging nature of God) (verses 23-28).

The Prologue (verses 1,2)

"Hear my prayer, O LORD, and let my cry come unto thee. Hide not thy face from me in the day when I am in trouble; incline thine ear unto me: in the day when I call answer me speedily." (verses 1,2)

Simple words, such as these, often repeated in the psalms, can sometimes lose their impact. It has been pointed out (*Cambridge Bible*) that each of these phrases reflects the words and thoughts of earlier psalms. For instance; "Hear my prayer" (18:6); "Hide not thy face from me" (27:9); "in the day when I am in trouble" (59:16); "incline thine ear unto me" (31:2); "in the day when I call" (56:9); "answer me speedily" (69:17). All the examples given are from psalms of David and they indicate that the writer was a man who constantly meditated upon the psalms. Their language became his also, and when he was in distress he poured out his heart in those words and expressions that had been characteristic of David in his times of affliction centuries before.

In all his ways, the man of God will meditate upon the word of God and draw from its language the words appropriate to the particular circumstances in which he finds himself.

The Psalmist's Distress (verses 3-11)

The reason why he cries to God to hear him and answer him speedily is because –

"my days consume away like smoke, and my bones are burned as a firebrand. My heart is smitten like grass, and withered. For I forget to eat my bread."

(verses 3,4, RV)

Both the AV and the RV margin give "hearth" instead of "firebrand". These are the words of a man made acutely aware of his mortality by the sickness that would consume him. The grass withering is used in scripture to describe the transience of human life:

"As for man, his days are as grass: as a flower of the field, so he flourisheth. For the wind passeth over it, and it is gone; and the place thereof shall know it no more." (Psalm 103:15,16; see also Isaiah 40:6-8)

The words of the Lord Jesus are also relevant, illustrating as they do the reference to the hearth or the firebrand:

"Wherefore, if God so clothe the grass of the field, which today is, and to morrow is cast into the oven, shall he not much more clothe you, O ye of little faith?"

(Matthew 6:30)

In this instance dried grass, as hay, would be used in the oven to provide heat for baking. He is a man distressed by sickness which has taken the form of a burning fever. Like grass which withers in the heat of the sun, his energy and natural vigour have dried up, so that he is like a plant without sap. So weakening has his illness been that he has lost all appetite for food, and this in its turn has added to his general state of debility, for:

"By reason of the voice of my groaning my bones cleave to my skin." (Psalm 102:5)

As a result of his distress he has become, as we would say, 'nothing but skin and bones' – such was the state of emaciation to which he had been reduced. The distress, however, was not just physical but seems also to embrace the worry and anxiety with which it was associated. It was also by reason of his groaning and sighing that he had been reduced to this condition.

This kind of affliction can lead to a sense of isolation, a tendency to become introspective, to turn in on oneself as it were, and to show no desire for the company or fellowship of family and friends. So the Psalmist says:

"I am like a pelican of the wilderness: I am like an owl of the desert. I watch, and am as a sparrow alone upon the house top." (verses 6,7)

He likens himself to solitary birds that inhabit waste places, or like the sparrow, deprived of her mate, perched forlornly upon the housetop. Authorities differ in their identification of the birds referred to. Some say these are the vulture and the night-raven and point out that the Hebrew word indicates any small bird that 'twitters', not necessarily a sparrow. The precise identification does not affect the sense of the words in any way, and the picture is of a man enveloped in lonely, sleepless misery; the word translated "watch" conveying the idea of wakefulness.

To add to his sufferings there were the 'taunts' of his enemies who derided him with bitter insults:

"Mine enemies reproach me all the day; they that are mad against me do curse by me." (verse 8, RV)

It would appear that as they beheld his sorry plight they used his predicament as a means of cursing others. In effect they would say, 'Let that which has befallen him, befall you'. Well might they do so, says the Psalmist:

"For I have eaten ashes like bread, and mingled my drink with weeping." (verse 9)

Mourning and tears had been his food and drink. And all this:

"Because of thine indignation and thy wrath: for thou hast lifted me up, and cast me down. My days are like a shadow that declineth; and I am withered like grass." (verses 10,11)

Life is like a shadow that disappears as the sun sets below the horizon. The shadows grow longer as sunset approaches, only to disappear quickly as night falls – a process that is particularly rapid in southerly latitudes. Figures of his mortality and transience are uppermost in his mind. He attributes his mortal condition to God's indignation and wrath, but note that there is no confession of sin on his part.

We feel that this is particularly appropriate to the circumstances of Hezekiah. It was the sin of the people that brought calamity upon Judah. The keenness of Hezekiah's worry and anxiety because of the threat of the Assyrian is reflected in his prayers (Isaiah 36–38). It was at this time that he was stricken with the disease that, if allowed to take its course, would have seen him cut off in the midst of his days. As king, he was representative of the nation as a whole and it seems that Hezekiah saw his affliction as a just retribution for the collective guilt of the people. If we accept that the latter half of Isaiah's prophecy springs out of the background of Hezekiah's sickness and recovery and the destruction of the Assyrian host, with the resultant exaltation of Zion in the sight of the nations, then the words of this psalm are particularly apposite. Isaiah 53 speaks of the suffering of the Lord Jesus with a remarkable precision. But it also reflects the experience of Hezekiah, for not only did he feel a connection between his sickness and the sin of the people, but they themselves, particularly his enemies, showed an inclination to regard it in this way:

"He is despised and rejected of men; a man of sorrows, and acquainted with grief: and we hid as it were our faces from him; he was despised, and we esteemed him not. Surely he hath borne our griefs, and carried our sorrows: yet we did esteem him stricken, smitten of God, and afflicted." (Isaiah 53:3,4)

So God had lifted him up and cast him down. It was true of Judah's present humiliation, but in Hezekiah's personal experience it was as if a great wind had gusted into his life, carrying him up and casting him down, bringing apparent disaster both for him personally and for the people over whom he reigned.

His Consolation (verses 12-22)

What comfort then can Hezekiah find in this situation? It is only in the God of Israel: in His faithfulness; in the abiding nature of His character; in the certainty that in the midst of all life's vicissitudes and differing circumstances He changes not:

"But thou, O LORD, shalt endure forever; and thy remembrance unto all generations." (verse 12)

He turns from his own frailty and finds consolation in the words by which he contrasts his own transience with the permanence of God: "But thou, O LORD, sittest enthroned for ever." This is the true sense of the Hebrew text. The RV says "abide" and the margin "sittest as king". The same phrase occurs in Psalms 9:7 and 29:10, and the words of the psalm are quoted by Jeremiah in the Book of Lamentations (5:19), where the word "throne" is substituted for that rendered "remembrance". The word is rightly translated by the RV as "memorial", and the phrase "thy memorial unto all generations" is an unmistakable reference to the name of God by which He made Himself known to Moses (Exodus 3:14,15).

The Psalmist rests his confidence not simply on the fact that God is King but upon the knowledge that His sovereignty is eternal. The name by which He revealed Himself at the Exodus is His memorial to all generations. It is an assurance that "I will be that I will be" is the living God who will manifest Himself in judgement and salvation for the outworking of His purpose in the earth. That which He revealed Himself to be at the time of the Exodus, He will continue to be for all subsequent generations. It is therefore in the confidence that he has a place in that purpose and that God will remain true to the things He has promised concerning Zion that the Psalmist cries:

"Thou shalt arise, and have mercy upon Zion: for the time to favour her, yea, the set time is come."

(verse 13)

The Hebrew word translated "set time" means 'fixed time, appointed time'. Its meaning is well expressed by the words of the Lord Jesus:

"The time is fulfilled, and the kingdom of God is at hand." (Mark 1:15)

It is this phrase that appears to convince commentators that the psalm belongs to the captivity, but we know that in its ultimate fulfilment it refers to the time of the end and in the context of the sovereignty of God perhaps we can best understand it in the sense that all times are in His hand, for He "hath determined the times before appointed" (Acts 17:26). He rules in the kingdom of men and all things are done according to His hand and counsel (Acts 4:18). So now the Psalmist says, the distress of Zion has lasted long enough, for the time to favour Zion has surely come. Just as "the LORD loveth the gates of Zion more than all the dwellings of Jacob" (Psalm 87:2), so also "thy servants take pleasure in her stones, and have pity upon her dust" (Psalm 102:14, RV).

If they are concerned about this city, how much more so the God who has chosen this place to put His name there. He will arise and favour Zion:

"So the heathen shall fear the name of the LORD, and all the kings of the earth thy glory."

(verse 15, see 2 Chronicles 32:23)

They would do this when the Lord builds up Zion and appears in His glory. The words have a recurring fulfilment: true of the deliverance in Hezekiah's day; true also of the appearing of the Lord Jesus Christ in his glory.

It is not only Hezekiah the king who prayed, for there remained a faithful remnant in Judah and their prayer too would be heard. It was for this reason that:

"This shall be written for the generation to come: and the people which shall be created shall praise the LORD." (verse 18)

In his condemnation of the Assyrian, God said:

"For out of Jerusalem shall go forth a remnant, and they that escape out of mount Zion." (Isaiah 37:32)

It is to this faithful remnant, "a seed (that) shall serve him (and) shall be accounted to the LORD for a generation" (Psalm 22:30), that the latter chapters of Isaiah's prophecy are addressed initially. It is of this seed (Isaiah 53:10) that chapters 54–66 speak. They are indeed a new creation. Nevertheless they are but the backcloth against which the work of the Lord Jesus is described; his saving work on behalf of all those who fear the Lord. The tense of the verb (verse 19) indicates that which will have come to pass when the words of verse 18 have been fulfilled.

The groaning of the prisoner will be no more; those appointed to death (literally, 'the sons of death') will be set free (verse 20). This was fulfilled in the experience of Hezekiah by those who were delivered out of the hand of the Assyrian, and their return to Jerusalem was accompanied by a gathering of the nations to worship the God of Israel (see again 2 Chronicles 32:23).

"That men may declare the name of the LORD in Zion, and his praise in Jerusalem; when the peoples are gathered together, and the kingdoms, to serve the LORD." (verses 21,22, RV)

Epilogue (verses 23-28)

From the contemplation of this glorious deliverance the Psalmist turns again to his own sad plight, yet surely now convinced that whatever might befall him, God would prove Himself faithful to the things that He had promised. Once more he is moved to compare the brevity of his own life with the enduring and unchanging nature of God:

"He weakened my strength in the way; he shortened my days. I said, O my God, take me not away in the midst of my days." (verses 23,24)

He had come to the end of his days. His pathway through life had brought him to this weak and emaciated state and, it would appear, a premature death. Yet with great pathos he turns again to the one who abides, who changes not, in whose eternal sovereignty the future of His people and His land were assured:

"Thy years are throughout all generations."

(verse 24)

It is an echo of the words of verse 12. In the purpose embodied in His name the confidence of His people must rest:

"Of old hast thou laid the foundation of the earth: and the heavens are the work of thy hands. They shall perish, but thou shalt endure: yea, all of them shall wax old like a garment; as a vesture shalt thou change them, and they shall be changed: but thou art the same, and thy years shall have no end." (verses 25-27)

857

There are two ideas expressed in these verses concerning the heavens and the earth. The first is that, compared with God, they are transient. He has created them and consequently He can destroy them. Although to man in his frailty they may appear as an emblem of permanence, God is the only ultimate reality. This is not a statement of intent. There is no contradiction of other scripture. "The earth abideth for ever" (Ecclesiastes 1:4). This is because God has decreed that it should be so.

Secondly, there is the idea of change. In a bold and dramatic figure, the manner in which God changes the face of the heavens and the earth is likened to a man changing his clothes: "As a vesture shalt thou change them." Here there is a subtle difference in emphasis, for the God who in the beginning created the heaven and the earth is the Sovereign Lord who determines the order of things that shall prevail on the earth. The language has moved from the literal to embrace also the symbolic. Thus we read in Isaiah's prophecy:

"For, behold, I create new heavens and a new earth: and the former shall not be remembered, nor come into mind. But be ye glad and rejoice forever in that which I create: for, behold, I create Jerusalem a rejoicing, and her people a joy."   (65:17,18; see also 66:22)

One generation comes and another passes away, but God remains eternal in the heavens. We know that even the Millennium is a transitional period that will eventually give way to the order of things when God shall be "all in all".

The words of the psalm are a wonderful declaration of the immutable, omnipotent God who alone is eternal in the heavens. "Thou art the same" says the AV. Literally, 'Thou art he' (as Deuteronomy 32:39) – an emphatic assertion of the unique personality of Israel's God in whose unchanging character the future of His people was assured.

These verses (25-27) are quoted in the Epistle to the Hebrews as part of the apostle's argument in chapter 1 (verses 10-12) to demonstrate that the Lord Jesus, as Son of God, was superior to the angels. The first question to be asked is, Who is addressed as "Lord" in this passage in

Hebrews? Is it God, the Father, or is it His Son, the Lord Jesus Christ? How we answer this question will determine our interpretation of the phrase in Hebrews.

The view that the person addressed is the Lord Jesus Christ, we suggest, does not satisfy the emphatic language of the psalm, or indeed the context which demands a literal meaning as well as a symbolic interpretation as set out above.

Note that the words, "Thou Lord", are not in verses 25 to 27 which form the main part of the quotation from Psalm 102. They are, however, in the earlier recognition of the unchanging nature of the Eternal God:

"But thou, O LORD, shalt endure for ever." (verse 12)

We suggest that these two passages have been merged and the words of verse 12 attached as an introduction to verse 25, confirming that the person addressed is God Himself. This leads to the question as to why the apostle should have quoted this particular passage in the context of his argument about the superiority of the Lord Jesus over the angels?

We do not believe that there is an easy answer to this question. It is interesting to read the opinions of orthodox writers who, naturally, have no difficulty in ascribing the words to the 'deity' of the Lord Jesus in conformity with their Trinitarian convictions. The reason why it should be quoted, however, is something that either perplexes them or they quietly fail to address. It is important that our anxiety to refute their false views does not lead us also to overlook the questions of context and purpose. We give below a tentative answer to the questions raised that we hope will at best point the way to a proper understanding.

An examination of the passages quoted to prove the Lord's superiority indicates that they are all related to the covenant that God made with David and to this point have all laid emphasis upon his personal status as Son of God:

"Thou art my Son; this day have I begotten thee."
(Hebrews 1:5; quoting Psalm 2:7)

"I will be to him a Father, and he shall be to me a Son." (verse 5; quoting 2 Samuel 7:14)

859

"Again, when he bringeth in the firstbegotten into the world." (verse 6; quoting Psalm 89:27)

In his next quotation the apostle introduces not just the status of the Lord Jesus but also the authority that, as a consequence, has been committed to him:

"But unto the Son he saith, Thy throne, O God, is for ever and ever: a sceptre of righteousness is the sceptre of thy kingdom. Thou hast loved righteousness, and hated iniquity; therefore God, even thy God, hath anointed thee with the oil of gladness above thy fellows." (verses 8,9; quoting Psalm 45:6,7)

It is important to appreciate that Psalm 102 is not a Messianic psalm simply because its words are quoted in Hebrews. Rather, the quotation in Hebrews is made because it is in itself a psalm concerning Messiah. It speaks of the time when the Lord shall arise and have mercy upon Zion, when the set time is come, when the nations shall fear the Lord; Zion shall be built up and God will be manifest in His glory. It is a time when God shall hear the groaning of the prisoner and deliver those appointed to death; when the name of the Lord shall be declared in Zion and His praise in Jerusalem (verses 13-22). It speaks of a people that shall be created (verse 18) and of children who shall be established for ever (verse 28). The psalm also speaks of the suffering of Messiah. It is the spirit of Christ in the psalm that is foreshadowed in the experience of the psalmist.

Note that the picture of Zion's exaltation (verses 13-22) is sandwiched between the two verses that are merged together in Hebrews 1 (i.e., verses 12 and 25). Observe also that the experiences of Hezekiah reflect those of the Lord Jesus:

"I said, O my God, take me not away in the midst of my days." (verse 24; see also Isaiah 53:8-11)

We return to Hebrews 1. The quotation from Psalm 45 had emphasised that Messiah's throne would be established "for ever". What then of defecting Jews who had put their trust in a crucified Messiah raised from the dead? Where was this kingdom of which the psalm spoke? They had lost their faith; they were returning to the weak and beggarly elements of the law. Psalm 102 with its entire Messianic context was relevant. A suffering and crucified Christ was now anointed with the oil of gladness above his fellows. The kingdom age described in Psalm 102 would be established when the set, or appointed, time came, and as the song emphasised it was certain because of the eternal nature of God who had promised. In the midst of all that was transient and ephemeral, He remained faithful and, moving from the literal to the figurative, at the appointed time He would create a new heavens and a new earth. They would be changed. Indeed the Mosaic constitution itself was shortly to pass away for in an echo of the words of the psalm the apostle wrote:

"In that he saith, A new covenant, he hath made the first old. Now that which decayeth and waxeth old is ready to vanish away."   (Hebrews 8:13)

The quotation from Psalm 102 should, we suggest, be regarded as a parenthesis inserted to emphasise the immutability of those things that God had promised. In effect the apostle says to the faithless Jewish believers – it must be so that the kingdom is not yet established for –

"to which of the angels said he at any time, Sit on my right hand, until I make thine enemies thy footstool?"
                    (Hebrews 1:13; quoting Psalm 110:1)

The concluding thought of the psalm, in keeping with the observations above is, "The children of thy servants shall continue, and their seed shall be established before thee" (verse 28). The "Godly seed" have the assurance of an eternal future because of the unchanging and abiding nature of the God whom they serve. The eternal inheritance will be theirs and they will be admitted into the very presence (literally meaning, 'before thee') of God Himself.

PSALM 103

IN the study of the psalms there are occasions when words cannot be found to describe adequately the beauty and pathos of the thoughts expressed. Psalm 103 is such a psalm. It has been described as "a song of the redeemed" and it anticipates the love of God manifest in the Lord Jesus Christ in a way that few other psalms can rival. In words that touch the heart and give hope to the downcast, the Psalmist expresses the infinite pity and compassion that God shows towards them that fear Him, seen particularly in the manner in which He extends forgiveness and shows forbearance towards human weakness.

The psalm bears the inscription, "A Psalm of David" and the Syriac Version adds the comment that it was written by him in his old age. This seems particularly apt given the substance of the song. Reflecting on all the varied experiences of his life, David, more appropriately than most, could utter this paean of praise to the God who had so wonderfully cared for him, pitied and forgiven him through all the changing circumstances of life.

We have commented previously on the differing nature of Messianic psalms and this, although as far as we are aware, is not quoted directly in the New Testament, reflects in a wonderful way the work of God as portrayed in the ministry of the Lord Jesus. How better could the expressions of the psalm be illustrated than by the words of the Gospel records?

"A leper ... beseeching him ... If thou wilt, thou canst make me clean. And Jesus, moved with compassion, put forth his hand, and touched him, and saith unto him, I will; be thou clean." (Mark 1:40,41)

"He went into a city called Nain; and ... behold, there was a dead man carried out, the only son of his mother,

862

and she was a widow ... and when the Lord saw her, he
had compassion on her, and said unto her, Weep not.
And he came and touched the bier ... And he said, Young
man, I say unto thee, Arise. And he that was dead sat
up, and began to speak. And he delivered him to his
mother." (Luke 7:11-15)

"And Jesus, when he came out, saw much people, and
was moved with compassion toward them, because they
were as sheep not having a shepherd: and he began to
teach them many things." (Mark 6:34)

These few passages, from the many that might be quoted,
illustrate how the Lord Jesus was touched with the feeling
of our infirmities; how his compassion overflowed as he
associated himself with the needs of men and how
particularly he was moved by bereavement in the case of
the widow who had lost her only son.

It is difficult to detect an overall pattern to the psalm.
The first five verses are in the form of a soliloquy as David
consults, as it were, with his own heart. The main body of
the psalm (verses 6-18) is a declaration of the goodness of
God in all its varied forms, and the last few verses (19-22)
are a call to recognise the greatness and majesty of God.

Verses 1-5

"Bless the LORD, O my soul: and all that is within me,
bless his holy name. Bless the LORD, O my soul, and
forget not all his benefits." (verses 1,2)

The Psalmist summons his whole being, all the seats of
thought and emotion to unite in praise to the Lord. With
all his faculties he will praise His holy name, that is, what
He has revealed Himself to be, and which the Psalmist
describes in the subsequent verses of the song.

Forgetfulness is something to which human nature is
particularly prone. In purely human terms, time and
chance, the concentration upon our own lives and present
circumstances, so often causes us to forget those who have
helped and supported us in the past. Conversely, those
who have given such help are sometimes hurt and
bewildered by the manner in which, in later life, they are
ignored.

Human nature forgets God just as readily as it does its brethren and sisters. It is a recurring theme of the Book of Deuteronomy:

"Then beware lest thou forget the LORD."

(6:12; see also 8:11; 8:14; 8:19, etc.)

Forget not all His benefits. The sum total of God's goodness towards us is something that only meditation and constant reflection upon the circumstances of life will help us to appreciate. David, looking back over his life, could think of nothing that for him so adequately summed up that goodness than the way that God had covered his sin:

"Who forgiveth all thine iniquities; who healeth all thy diseases; who redeemeth thy life from destruction; who crowneth thee with lovingkindness and tender mercies." (verses 3,4)

There is no greater benefit that God offers than the forgiveness of sins. It is, however, only appreciated by those who, convicted by God's word, feel the burden of shame and guilt that separation from God brings. For those who seek it there is no greater happiness (Psalm 32:1) than sin forgiven. It needs, nevertheless, an act of faith on our part. God has assured us of His forgiveness if sin is confessed, yet there is no outward token of the reality of His mercy. This is why at Capernaum the Lord Jesus needed to demonstrate his authority to forgive sin by means of a miracle:

"But that ye may know that the Son of man hath power on earth to forgive sins, (he saith to the sick of the palsy,) I say unto thee, Arise, and take up thy bed." (Mark 2:10,11)

We must believe that God is faithful to do that which He has promised.

"If we confess our sins, he is just, and may be trusted to forgive our sins and cleanse us from every kind of wrong." (1 John 1:9, NEB)

Forgiveness is linked in the psalm with the healing of disease. No doubt this was true of the experience of David. Certainly at the time of Absalom's rebellion he was a sick man (see Psalm 41), and David linked his sickness with his sin. "Heal my soul; for I have sinned against thee (Psalm 41:4). Sometimes a life of excess in some way or other can lead to bodily sickness, but it would be wrong to equate sickness and disease generally with specific acts of sin. Nevertheless, we do well to recognise that sickness of the soul, guilt and shame, can affect the whole body and sometimes this can be manifest both in infirmity of mind and body. This is not a matter for us to identify in the experience of others. David knew it to be true in his life and in a similar fashion those who have trodden the same path can testify to their own experiences.

This surely is why David linked forgiveness and disease together in this way. In this mortal life God does not heal from every kind of disease, but ultimately He will deliver us from this "body of our humiliation (RV), that it may be fashioned like unto his glorious body" (Philippians 3:21), for it is He "who redeemeth thy life from destruction" (literally, 'the pit').

We could have no clearer indication that it is salvation at the heart of these wonderful words. No doubt the words of Exodus were in David's mind, "I am the LORD that healeth thee" (15:26), and we do well to remember that "with his stripes we are healed" (Isaiah 53:5). In scripture, physical sickness and disease become the symbols of spiritual infirmity, and ultimately our deliverance will be from both when "mortality is swallowed up of life". Truly, He crowneth us with lovingkindness and tender mercies. Like a royal crown, He has and will anoint us with His love and faithfulness to the covenant.

The final thought of this personal meditation is: "Who satisfieth thy mouth with good things; so that thy youth is renewed like the eagle's" (Psalm 103:5). If indeed David wrote the psalm in his old age, then these words are most appropriate. At face value they seem to refer to our daily bread, and if that is so we know it to be true. The word translated "mouth", however, is the subject of much debate. The Targum says, "the days of thine old age". This commends itself in that the two parts of the verse will then correspond:

"Who satisfies thine age with good: so that thy youth is renewed as the eagle."   (*Speaker's Commentary*)

God's goodness continued even to length of days. The eagle with its strength and speed was a fitting symbol of perpetual youth, and although in a sense David is rejoicing that even in old age God gave him renewed strength, surely he is thinking of eternal youth:

> "But they that wait upon the LORD shall renew their strength; they shall mount up with wings as eagles; they shall run, and not be weary; and they shall walk, and not faint."   (Isaiah 40:31)

The God who showers us with His goodness through every stage of life will finally reward us with the blessing of everlasting youth.

Verses 6-8

The Psalmist turns now from his own experience to apply the principles, for which he has praised the Lord with his whole being, to all God's people who have been redeemed by Him. The passage about which this whole section of the psalm revolves, and from which its thoughts seem derived, is Exodus 34 when God proclaimed His name to Moses. Thus :

> "The LORD executeth righteousness and judgment for all that are oppressed. He made known his ways unto Moses, his acts unto the children of Israel."
>   (verses 6,7; see Exodus 34:6,7)

The words translated "righteousness" and "judgment" are both in the plural, indicating that it was not in a single decisive act that God manifested Himself on behalf of His people, but through a whole series of interventions in the affairs of men by which He delivered them from the oppression of Egypt and revealed His character. Verse 7 is an obvious allusion to the prayer of Moses:

> "Now therefore, I pray thee, if I have found grace in thy sight, shew me now thy way, that I may know thee."   (Exodus 33:13)

So God revealed His way and His doings to Moses when He revealed His glory and declared His name:

> "And the LORD passed by before him, and proclaimed, The LORD, The LORD God, merciful and gracious, longsuffering, and abundant in goodness and truth, keeping mercy for thousands, forgiving iniquity and

transgression and sin, and that will by no means clear the guilty; visiting the iniquity of the fathers upon the children, and upon the children's children, unto the third and to the fourth generation." (Exodus 34:6,7)

So David reflects upon these words :

"The LORD is merciful and gracious, slow to anger, and plenteous in mercy. He will not always chide: neither will he keep his anger for ever. He hath not dealt with us after our sins; nor rewarded us according to our iniquities." (Psalm 103:8-10)

David, of course, had good cause to rejoice in these words. As far as the Law of Moses was concerned there was no forgiveness for David's sin in the matter of Bathsheba and Uriah the Hittite. There was no sacrifice permitted. The three words translated, "sin", "iniquity" and "transgression" cover every kind of sin, and in the declaration of His name, God indicated His willingness to forgive all three. Thus in Psalm 103 all three are mentioned as being covered by the kindness and forbearance of God:

"He hath not dealt with us after our sins; nor rewarded us according to our iniquities ... as far as the east is from the west, so far hath he removed our transgressions from us." (verses 10,12)

In both his great penitential psalms (32 and 51) David places particular emphasis on those three words (32:1,2; 51:1-3) and recognises that although the law made no sacrificial provision, there was a sacrifice that God would accept:

"The sacrifices of God are a broken spirit: a broken and a contrite heart, O God, thou wilt not despise." (Psalm 51:17)

That occasions arise when God in His anger will punish His people is a fact that has to be recognised, but "He will not always chide (literally, 'contend'): neither will he keep his anger for ever".

This was a lesson that Moses himself had learned and faced by the wrath of God when the children of Israel refused to go up and inherit the land. It was the words of Exodus 34:6 that he quoted, adding:

"Pardon, I beseech thee, the iniquity of this people according to the greatness of thy mercy, and as thou hast forgiven this people, from Egypt even until now."
(Numbers 14:19)

In all His dealings the forbearance of God had been seen, for:

"If thou, LORD, shouldest mark iniquities, O Lord, who shall stand? But there is forgiveness with thee, that thou mayest be feared." (Psalm 130:3,4)

He had not treated them as their sins deserved (verse 10) for His mercy was infinite. It could not be measured:

"For as the heaven is high above the earth, so great is his mercy toward them (literally, 'over them') that fear him." (verse 11)

As the heavens are stretched out through the boundless realms of space, so the lovingkindness of God cannot be limited. East is east and west is west – they never meet and so far has His measureless mercy removed our sins from us. It is as though we had never committed them. There is another possible allusion in these words. In the tabernacle, the gate where men approached the altar of burnt offering was on the east, the most holy place with the mercy seat was on the west. Could it be that as far as the east, where men brought their sin offerings, was from the west, where the presence of God dwelt in the midst of His people, so far had God removed their sin. His forgiveness was absolute; they could, as it were, come into His very presence – presented "faultless before the presence of His glory" (Jude verse 24). God's pity can only be compared to the love and tenderness of a human father (Psalm 102:13). The reason He has such compassion is that "He knoweth our frame; he remembereth that we are dust" (verse 14).

Our human frailty is known to God. It is a reference to the familiar words of Genesis 2:7 when, "The LORD God formed man of the dust of the ground". The Hebrew word translated "frame" is directly related to that rendered "formed". He who made us understands our weakness:

"As for man, his days are as grass: as a flower of the field, so he flourisheth. For the wind passeth over it,

868

and it is gone; and the place thereof shall know it no more." (verses 15,16)

"As for man (*enosh*) ..." The word means literally 'mortal man' – man in all his frailty and weakness. As the scorching wind from the desert withereth the flower of the field, so is man in 'his flourishing': transient and ephemeral, so soon gone with no more a place "under the sun".

But although men may fade away, for "one generation passeth away, and another generation cometh" (Ecclesiastes 1:4), God's lovingkindness, His faithfulness to the covenant endures. The eternity of God is the foundation upon which our faith is built. It is the assurance of our everlasting future:

"But the mercy of the LORD is from everlasting to everlasting upon them that fear him, and his righteousness unto children's children." (verse 17)

God makes His sun to rise on the just and the unjust. He extends His mercy to all men in the provision He makes for their daily needs. The covenant love of God, however, is for those only "that fear him". Three times this phrase occurs (see also verses 11,13), emphasising that forgiveness and redemption depend upon a man's response to God. It is not for all men; but the blessings described are "to such as keep his covenant, and to those that remember his commandments to do them" (verse 18).

Verses 19-22

The psalm closes with a declaration of God's universal sovereignty:

"The LORD hath prepared his throne in the heavens; and his kingdom ruleth over all." (verse 19)

God's eternal reign encompasses the past, the present and the future. He is the "King Eternal" and our prayer, "Thy kingdom come, Thy will be done in earth, as it is in heaven", is a recognition of that fact and a plea that God will manifest Himself visibly in the earth; that all men might recognise His universal sovereignty, that as His throne is established in the heavens, so also it might be seen and acknowledged in the earth.

Not only is man called to praise Him, but the angelic host itself, which performs His will:

> "Bless the LORD, ye his angels, that excel in strength, that do his commandments, hearkening unto the voice of his word. Bless ye the LORD, all ye his hosts; ye ministers of his, that do his pleasure." (verses 20,21)

It is a remarkable insight into the work of angels. They are "mighty in strength" (AV margin), or more literally 'strong warriors' and we remember the archangel who appeared to Joshua with drawn sword in his hand, and identified himself as "captain (literally, Prince) of the host of the LORD" (Joshua 5:14). The myriad of the heavenly host are but His servants, His ministers who do His pleasure (Hebrews 1:14). Who, more appropriately, can sing His praises until the multitude of the redeemed join their voices in strong immortal song?

So the Psalmist calls upon all creation to join in this anthem of praise:

> "Bless the LORD, all ye his works in all places of his dominion." (verse 22)

And as this universal hymn of praise sounds forth, David would humbly lift up his voice to join in song. In the realisation of all that our Heavenly Father has done for us, we too can but say:

> "Bless the LORD, O my soul."

PSALM 104

IT is generally acknowledged that this psalm is from the same pen as Psalm 103. They both begin and end with the same benediction, "Bless the LORD, O my soul"; the final "Praise ye the LORD" (verse 35) being connected with the psalm following (105). Whereas Psalm 103 extols the mercy of God towards His spiritual creation, those who have made a covenant with Him by sacrifice (Psalm 50:5), this song praises God for His work in creating the heavens and the earth. It is clearly based upon the Genesis record (chapter 1) but the emphasis of the psalm is different, for it shows God not just as Creator but also as Sustainer:

"God who made the world and all things therein ... he giveth to all life, and breath, and all things ... for in him we live, and move, and have our being." (Acts 17:24-28)

The psalm has been extolled for its poetic beauty by both sacred and profane writers and, giving all due consideration to the Spirit that inspired him, the psalm remains as a wonderful testimony to the spiritual insight of the man David. From his own experience he could speak of the magnitude of God's love, seen in His pity and compassion towards them that fear Him. But also from his meditation upon scripture and his observation of the marvels of creation, he could give this wonderful insight into the might and power of the God who upholds all things by His own power:

"O LORD, how manifold are thy works! in wisdom thou hast made them all: the earth is full of thy riches."
(verse 24)

It is a recognition that in creation all things were made for His pleasure (Revelation 4:11) and that consequently God's purpose will be fulfilled. It is for this reason that the psalm closes with the prayer:

871

> "Let the sinners be consumed out of the earth, and let the wicked be no more."   (verse 35)

Finally, all things that offend and that disturb the harmony of God's creation will be eradicated:

> "But as truly as I live, all the earth shall be filled with the glory of the LORD."   (Numbers 14:21)

Genesis 1

Strictly there is no poetic structure to the psalm, but it is possible to relate the words recorded to the account in Genesis 1. There is a general, but not a precise correlation with the order of the days of creation. But, in a remarkable way, the Genesis record is not so much quoted as alluded to in the Psalmist's meditation. He reflects not on the simple fact that God did these things, but on the reason why He performed them and the manner in which each of these acts of creation, in its own way, contributes to the overall unity of the work. It is seen, for example, in the harmony and interdependence that exists between vegetation and trees, and the birds and beasts of the field. The Psalmist does not speak just of the creation of sea and land and vegetation on the third day (Genesis 1:9-13), but proceeds to describe how these works provide sustenance for every beast of the field, fowl of the air and even for man himself (Psalm 104:10-18), although they were not created until the fifth and sixth days of creation.

This feature will best be seen in our examination of the psalm. As intimated above, there is no identifiable structure to the psalm but we have divided it in an arbitrary fashion to facilitate consideration of the thoughts and ideas conveyed.

Verses 1-4

> "In the beginning God ... Let there be light: and there was light."   (Genesis 1:1,3)

As Genesis emphasises that God is the ultimate reality and that all creation is a reflection of His glory, so David begins his psalm with a contemplation of the greatness and majesty of God:

> "O LORD my God, thou art very great; thou art clothed with honour and majesty. Who coverest thyself with

872

light as with a garment: who stretchest out the heavens like a curtain." (verses 1,2)

Light, the creation of the first day, is described as the garment with which God covers Himself. "God is light, and in him is no darkness at all" (1 John 1:5). Thus the light of that first day shone forth from the very presence of God. That light continues to shroud Him as a garment and in the physical sense makes it impossible for man to approach Him:

"Who only hath immortality, dwelling in the light which no man can approach unto; whom no man hath seen, nor can see." (1 Timothy 6:16)

The light both reveals and hides. It would be folly to imagine that we in our mortal weakness could penetrate that light with which He is arrayed, to behold His majesty and glory. Yet that light has shone forth to give life in all its varied forms, so that in His works of creation God is seen:

"For the invisible things of him from the creation of the world are clearly seen, being understood by the things that are made, even his eternal power and Godhead." (Romans 1:20)

He stretches out the heavens like a curtain. It is the figure of a man pitching a tent. Just as easily God has stretched out the canopy of the heavens and by them also His glory is veiled. It is interesting to reflect that the word rendered "curtain" is used in this one instance only in the psalms, but it is the common word used in the construction of the tabernacle. Might it be that as the curtain of the tabernacle veiled the glory of God so also God who dwells in "the heaven of heavens" is hidden, as it were, by heaven's expanse? It is pointed out that the verbs for "coverest thyself" and "stretchest out" are present participles and indicate that they are not just complete acts but continuing operations. By them is all creation sustained.

The reference that follows would appear to be to the second day of creation when God divided the waters which were under the firmament from the waters which were above the firmament (see Genesis 1:6-8) for, "(He) layeth the beams of his chambers in the waters: who maketh the

873

clouds his chariot: who walketh upon the wings of the wind" (verse 3).

In a bold figure, David describes God as constructing His secret chamber, that which a man would build for privacy, upon the very beams of the firmament; hidden from man in His majesty yet manifesting Himself amongst men in a manner symbolically described as storm and tempest.

We note Brother John Thomas' use of this passage in his exposition of the cherubim, and would draw attention to the record of Ezekiel's vision of the cherubim which is introduced by a whirlwind out of the north, a great cloud and a fire unfolding itself (1:4). Whereas men might see only storm, cloud and wind, so often behind these forces of nature the hand of God is at work through His angelic ministers: "Who maketh his angels spirits (or winds); his ministers a flaming fire" (Psalm 104:4). Truly, as another psalm declares, it is a case of "stormy wind fulfilling his word" (148:8).

Verses 5-9

This section of the psalm appears to relate directly to the work of the third day of creation. The work of that day is divided into two parts: first the separation of land from water and secondly the creation of grass, herbs and trees (Genesis 1:9-12). It is the first part of the work of day three that is the subject of these verses and the second part is considered in the verses following (10-18):

"... who laid the foundations of the earth, that it should not be removed for ever. Thou coveredst it with the deep as with a garment: the waters stood above the mountains. At thy rebuke they fled; at the voice of thy thunder they hasted away. They go up by the mountains, they go down by the valleys unto the place which thou hast founded for them. Thou hast set a bound that they may not pass over; that they turn not again to cover the earth." (verses 5-9)

It is a poetic meditation upon the language of Genesis 1. It uses imagery and symbolism to convey the grandeur of the work of God. Behind it lies the solid fact of what God did

874

– it is not the language of science and we should not be disturbed by the lack of precise scientific data.

The earth is likened to a building erected upon solid foundations (see Job 38:4-8 for a similar imagery). Yet mountain, hill and valley alike were covered by the waters of the great deep. The tense of the original is a graphic imperfect – "the waters were standing above the mountains" (*Cambridge Bible*).

At God's rebuke the waters flee, "the mountains ascend, the valleys descend" (AV margin). God's rebuke is the thunder of His voice; He spoke and it was done. They went "unto the place which thou hast founded for them" (Psalm 104:8), a reference surely to Genesis 1:9: "Let the waters under the heavens be gathered together unto one place".

The words of Psalm 104:9 recall the language of the covenant that God made with Noah after the flood (Genesis 9:8-17). Then God confirmed His purpose in the original separation of land from water and indicates that the effect of the flood was to produce a new creation.

Verses 10-18
The separation of land from water made possible the next stage in God's creative work – the creation of vegetation in all its various forms. David's vision is not just of the initial provision but of the manner in which God continues to sustain it that it might provide necessary sustenance for the beasts of the field, the birds of the air and for man also, the crowning work of God's creation. In this way the dependence of the creatures created on the fifth and six days upon the work of the third day becomes apparent. The land is fertilised by springs and rain whereby bountiful provision is made for the need of men and animals.

It is interesting, but natural, that David's description in verses 10,11,13 should be a reflection of the language used to describe the land of promise:

> "But the land, whither ye go to possess it, is a land of hills and valleys, and drinketh water of the rain of heaven." (Deuteronomy 11:11)

Wine, oil and bread were also among the chief products of the land (Deuteronomy 12:17). So the Lord gives:

> "Wine that maketh glad the heart of man, and oil to
> make his face to shine, and bread which strengtheneth
> man's heart."   (Psalm 104:15)

These products were the basis of an oriental feast and the
references teach us that God does not simply provide for
our sustenance but also for our enjoyment.

So the beasts of the wilderness, the wild goats and the
conies (verse 18), are sustained as well as the cattle for
whom he causes the grass to grow and man who is
provided with the means of cultivating the ground (verses
13,14).

The emphasis is all upon the work of God:

> "The trees of the LORD are full of sap; the cedars of
> Lebanon, which he hath planted."   (verse 16)

They are not simply stately and majestic trees but they
are His planting. That is, the reference is to the great wild
forests sustained by the rain from heaven and not to the
trees planted by men. In these the great birds (the stork)
find a place to make their nests (verse 17).

Verses 19-24

The Psalmist reverts to day four when "God made two
great lights; the greater light to rule the day, and the
lesser light to rule the night" (Genesis 1:16).

The Hebrew word translated "made" is the same as that
rendered "appointed" in Psalm 104:19: "He appointed the
moon for seasons: the sun knoweth his going down". The
set times, the feasts of the Lord, were all determined by
the moon. Their year was lunar not solar. Yet there was a
wonderful harmony, for sun and moon together played
their part: "The sun knoweth his going down. Thou
makest darkness, and it is night" (verses 19,20).

Just as "evening and morning" measured the length of
the day, so the moon is mentioned first and the sunset
brings the night with all its creatures that live their busy
lives under the cloud of darkness (verses 20,21). The sun
rises and the beasts return to their dens, and man goes
forth to his daily toil until the evening comes again (verses
22,23).

The Psalmist has come to the sixth day – to man the
crowning work of God's creative activity. In contemplation

of all the wonders that God's hand has wrought David can only stand in awe:

"O LORD, how manifold are thy works! in wisdom hast thou made them all: the earth is full of thy riches."

(verse 24)

The idea of the word translated "riches" is that of prosperity or possessions. It is illustrated by the words of Abraham concerning the Most High God, "possessor of heaven and earth" (Genesis 14:19).

Verses 25-30

The Psalmist's vision is broadened:

"The earth is full of thy riches. So is this great and wide sea, wherein are things creeping innumerable, both small and great beasts." (verses 24,25)

It is as though the writer was beholding from a hilltop the vast expanse of the ocean stretching into the distance. There too is life in all its varied forms to be found. There go the stately ships, there leviathan, the sea monster (probably the whale) disports himself (verse 26). It is as though these greatest and strongest of beasts are seen enjoying life in the sea to emphasise the might and power of the One who created them and takes pleasure in the fulness of their life.

All creatures, whether on land or in the sea, depend upon Him. God opens His hand to satisfy them. He hides His face and they are troubled. Their very life comes from Him for:

"Thou takest away their breath, they die, and return to their dust. Thou sendest forth thy spirit, they are created: and thou renewest the face of the earth."

(verses 29,30)

"One generation passeth away, and another generation cometh." (Ecclesiastes 1:4)

Creation continues; life is renewed as God, through the Spirit by which He created all things in the beginning, renews the face of the earth.

Verses 31-35

It is the Psalmist's prayer that God may rejoice in His works:

877

"The glory of the LORD shall endure for ever: the LORD shall rejoice in his works."   (verse 31)

It is a staggering thought that there are creatures both on land and in the sea, that the eye of man could not behold until our days. It is only the wonder of modern science and photography that has made it possible for us to marvel at life in the depths of the ocean particularly. Why then are they there? That God may rejoice in all His works. He takes pleasure in them, and the human mind staggers to contemplate the wonders that may yet be revealed when through the Lord Jesus Christ all things will be put under the dominion of man. It is for this reason that God allows creation to continue. If He were to look at or touch the earth then it would tremble or consume away like smoke (verse 32).

So the song draws to its conclusion:

"I will sing unto the LORD as long as I live: I will sing praise to my God while I have my being. My meditation of him shall be sweet: I will be glad in the LORD."
                                    (verses 33,34)

The sense of the word translated "sweet" is 'acceptable'. It is particularly associated with sacrifice. As God rejoices in that which His hands have made, so David would rejoice in God. If the days of creation have been the background against which the Psalmist has developed his thoughts then surely the seventh day, the sabbath of rest, is in his mind as he concludes his meditations. The rest that remains for the people of God:

"Let the sinners be consumed out of the earth, and let the wicked be no more."   (verse 35)

Let all things that offend, that mar God's work and that give Him no joy, be finally destroyed. The harmony of His creation will only eventually be restored when sinners are no more. For this day the Psalmist prays and with those who will sing God's praise in that day, he would gladly join his voice:

"Bless thou the LORD, O my soul. Hallelujah"*

---

* The Hallelujah at the conclusion of the psalm is considered to be part of the psalm following. Both psalms 105 and 106 would then begin and end with the words, "Praise ye the LORD".

PSALM 105

PSALMS 105 and 106 are clearly connected. As Psalm 105 (verses 1-15) is joined with Psalm 96 in the song that David sang when he brought the ark to Zion (1 Chronicles 16), we may safely assume that he is the author of both psalms. On this question of authorship, orthodox commentators are almost unanimous in attributing both psalms to the time of the captivity. They, of course, do not believe in the inerrancy of scripture and have no difficulty in suggesting that the song of David in 1 Chronicles is a late addition to the text by another hand, or by the writer of Chronicles who invented the Davidic authorship and borrowed from these late psalms. We place our trust in the word of God and see little profit in pursuing or seeking to combat their contrary opinions. We might nevertheless offer an observation. There is no mention of any historical incident in either of these psalms that occurred after the time of David (this is true of other Davidic psalms where authorship is questioned). Is not this strange given the covenant God made with David and the glories of Solomon's kingdom, not to mention the deliverance in Hezekiah's days, if they were written during Israel's captivity? There is no hint of the covenant that God made with David and this of course, is what we would expect, given that the covenant was made after the ark was brought to Zion.

The two psalms (105,106) stand in contrast to each other. Psalm 105 describes the faithfulness of God towards His people from the beginning of their national history in the call of Abraham to their inheritance of the land. Psalm 106 is a song of penitence and contrition describing how the people failed to respond to God's grace. They have been well summed up as songs, firstly of God's faithfulness (105), and secondly of Israel's faithlessness (106).

879

As regards the use of the first fifteen verses of Psalm 105 in David's song (1 Chronicles 16), we have already written of this in our consideration of Psalm 96.

The psalm appears to fall into four sections, that in historical terms might be described as follows:

1. God's covenant with Abraham (verses 1-15).
2. Israel goes down into Egypt (verses 16-26).
3. God's wonders in the land of Egypt (verses 27-38).
4. Israel brought through the wilderness to the land of promise (verses 39-45).

God's Covenant with Abraham

It was Israel's calling to be "a kingdom of priests, and an holy nation" (Exodus 19:6). They were to be God's witnesses in the midst of the earth. So they are exhorted now to proclaim the wonderful works of God to all the people of the earth:

"O give thanks unto the LORD; call upon (literally, 'proclaim') his name: make known his deeds among the people."   (verse 1)

These words are quoted by the prophet Isaiah (12:4) in a context that makes clear that they have their truest expression when Israel finally fulfil their destiny in the kingdom age.

It has been pointed out that the first five verses of this psalm present us with ten features of true worship:

1.   Give thanks unto the Lord (verse 1).
2.   Call upon His name (verse 1).
3.   Proclaim His deeds among the people (verse 1).
4.   Sing psalms unto Him (verse 2).
5.   Talk of His wondrous deeds (verse 2).
6.   Glory in His name (verse 3).
7.   Let your heart rejoice (verse 3).
8.   Seek the Lord (verse 4).
9.   Seek His face (i.e., His presence) (verse 4).
10.   Remember His marvellous works (verse 5).

The RV margin renders the word "talk" (verse 2) as "meditate". The reference to seeking the Lord (verse 4) would appear to suggest presenting oneself at His tabernacle where the face (presence) of the Lord and the ark of the covenant (His strength – see Psalm 78:61; 132:8) dwelt in the midst of His people. They were called to remember the wonderful works He had performed and the judgements that He had spoken in and against the land of Egypt (verse 5), for they were the seed of Abraham, His servant and the children of Jacob, His chosen (verse 6). Grammatically, "His servant" could refer either to Abraham or to his seed, but given the parallelism with "the children of Jacob his chosen" it would appear that the reference is to Israel and not to the patriarchs themselves. In these things Israel were to rejoice, for:

"He is the LORD our God: his judgments are in all the earth. He hath remembered his covenant for ever, the word which he commanded to a thousand generations. Which covenant he made with Abraham, and his oath unto Isaac; and confirmed the same unto Jacob for a law, and to Israel for an everlasting covenant."

(verses 7-10)

Notice that the covenant was renewed and confirmed to Isaac and Jacob because it was through this line of Abraham's family that God's purpose was to be carried forward, i.e., "in Isaac shall thy seed be called" (Genesis 21:12; Romans 9:7).

Covenants between men are usually negotiated between equal parties. They are often arrived at by compromise. God's covenants are different, as the Hebrew word *berith* indicates. It is imposed by a greater upon a lesser. It is the word which He commanded and confirmed for a law. God lays down the conditions and to enjoy the benefits men must accept them. So God promised:

"Unto thee will I give the land of Canaan, the lot (literally, 'line') of your inheritance."   (Psalm 105:11)

These promises God had made when they were few in number (see Genesis 34:30) and when they wandered in the land they should afterwards inherit, as pilgrims and strangers (verses 12,13).

During all this period they dwelt among the inhabitants of the land as foreigners without any rights of citizenship and they depended on the providential hand of God to protect them. For their sakes (verses 13,14) God had

881

reproved kings (Pharaoh, Genesis 12; Abimelech, Genesis 20 and 26). God said:

> "Touch not mine anointed, and do my prophets no harm."   (verse 15)

The words echo the Genesis record:

> "Therefore suffered I thee not to touch her ... Restore the man his wife; for he is a prophet." (Genesis 20:6,7)

> "He that toucheth this man or his wife shall surely be put to death."   (Genesis 26:11)

For comment upon the Patriarchs as prophets please refer to the study of Psalm 96.

Down into Egypt (verses 16-23)

We could have no finer example of providence at work than that presented in the history of Joseph:

> "(God) called for a famine upon the land: he brake the whole staff of bread."   (verse 16)

It was the direct result of divine agency, and God had sent a man before them in preparation for this day. All that befell Joseph, the hatred of his brothers, the evil designs of Potiphar's wife, the dreams of the baker and the butler were all part of the outworking of God's hand. Not that He was responsible for the actions of any of those involved. What they did was of their own volition, but God had the right man (and woman) in the right place at the right time, and had taken their reactions to the circumstances of life into account in the grand design that He was working out. Joseph recognised the hand of God at work and it was with marvellous insight that he could tell his brothers:

> "God did send me before you to preserve life."
> (Genesis 45:5)

There is additional information in the psalm to that given in Genesis. The record in Genesis 39 does not suggest that Joseph was treated cruelly during his imprisonment, but the psalm says:

> "Whose feet they hurt with fetters: he was laid in iron."
> (verse 18)

It may well be that initially, when he was first thrust into prison, his treatment was harsher than his later experience. The phrase, "he was laid in iron" could be parallel to that preceding it, but some suggest that the true reading is, 'into iron entered his soul'. If this be true, then it is giving us an insight into the mental and emotional anguish that Joseph experienced as a result of the false accusation made against him and his subsequent imprisonment. In any event this may still have been true, for we do well to remember that these men of God were men of "like passions" and we do them a disservice if we imagine that they sailed placidly through all the storms that overtook them, unmoved by the buffeting of life.

So it was that:

"Until the time that his word came: the word of the LORD tried him." (verse 19)

That which was revealed to Joseph in dreams was eventually fulfilled by the command of the word of God. Until that time Joseph was tried, his faith was put to the test, and perhaps it helps us to appreciate his resilience when we remember that he was in Egypt for thirteen years before he was exalted by Pharaoh.

"He made him lord of his house, and ruler of all his substance: to bind his princes at his pleasure; and teach his senators wisdom." (verses 21,22)

His power was such that his authority extended over all the princes and rulers of the people.

So it was that Israel came down into Egypt. "Jacob sojourned in the land of Ham" (verse 23) and there the people increased greatly until they were perceived to be a threat by the Egyptians. Notice that it is God who "turned their heart to hate his people" (verse 25). Throughout this psalm it is the hand of God at work. His blessings upon Israel provoked the antagonism of the Egyptians "to deal subtilly with his servants" (verse 25). They devised schemes and crafty plans to destroy Israel.

God's Wonders in the Land of Egypt (verses 24-38)

The God of Israel, however, remained in control and "He sent Moses his servant; and Aaron whom he had chosen" (verse 26). By them He showed His signs and wonders in the land of Ham. The AV margin rightly interprets the Hebrew text when it renders the phrase, "the words of his signs" (verse 27). That is, they came in fulfilment of His word, or perhaps that the signs bare witness to the command that God had given to let His people go.

In the verses that follow, only eight of the ten plagues are mentioned, the fifth and sixth being omitted, and those that are mentioned are not presented in the order in which they occur in Exodus. It is the ninth plague that is mentioned first:

"He sent darkness, and made it dark; and they rebelled not against his word."　　　　　　(verse 28)

Why this plague is mentioned first it is difficult to say. Certainly it had the effect of producing some kind of conviction amongst the Egyptians that they must let Israel go (see Exodus 10:24; 11:2,3). Nevertheless it still needed the death of the firstborn finally to convince them. It may be also that in a country where the sun was reverenced as a god, the plague of darkness established the superiority of Israel's God over those who were no gods at all.

It is difficult to know to whom the words, "they rebelled not against his word" refer. Some apply it to the partial acceptance of Moses' words by the Egyptians referred to above; others to Moses and Aaron who, in for them what must have been a more stressful situation than we sometimes appreciate, refused to compromise with Pharaoh's limited offer of obedience (Exodus 10:24-26) and held steadfastly to the word of God. After this mention of the plague of darkness, the Psalmist refers briefly to most of the other plagues. He turned the water into blood (verse 29; Exodus 7:17) and brought frogs upon their land (verse 30; Exodus 8:2). These were followed by the flies and the lice, the third and fourth plagues being inverted (verse 31; Exodus 8:21; 8:16). Omitting the fifth and sixth, the psalm speaks next of the seventh – the plague of hail (verse 32; Exodus 9:22-25) and then adds the plague of locusts (verses 34,35; Exodus 10:4), and finally the death of the firstborn (verse 36; Exodus 11:5).

The God of Israel was triumphant. Israel came forth like a victorious army. The Egyptians gave them their jewels of silver and jewels of gold and raiment as they required (verse 37; Exodus 12:35,36). We might say that this was a debt the Egyptians had incurred for the long involuntary service that they imposed upon Israel. The record in Exodus says:

"The children of Israel went up harnessed (AV margin, "by five in a rank") out of the land of Egypt."
(13:18)

It is a reflection of these words when David says:

"There was not one feeble person among their tribes. Egypt was glad when they departed: for the fear of them fell upon them." (verses 37,38)

The gladness is seen in the urgency with which they prevailed upon them to depart (Exodus 12:31-33), and the fear in their reaction to the destruction of Pharaoh's host in the Red Sea (Exodus 15:14-16).

The Wilderness and the Land of Promise (verses 39-45)

Three miracles are mentioned to illustrate the care and protection of God in the wilderness. The pillar of cloud and of fire, the manna and the water out of the rock (verses 39-41). It might be wondered why it is that these three are mentioned particularly? It would seem they are intended to emphasise that it was God's protection and provision that brought them to the promised land. Concerning the manner in which God led them, the Book of Exodus records:

"The LORD went before them by day in a pillar of cloud, to lead them in the way; and by night in a pillar of fire, to give them light; to go by day and night."
(Exodus 13:21)

In Exodus 14 (verses 19,20) the cloud separated the people of Israel from the Egyptians, so that it was light to Israel and darkness to the Egyptians. Here in the psalm, however, the emphasis is upon the act of covering and the words of Isaiah help us to reconcile the two aspects:

"And the LORD will create upon every dwelling place of mount Zion, and upon her assemblies, a cloud and smoke by day and the shining of a flaming fire by night: for upon all the glory shall be a defence." (4:5)

("for above all the glory shall be a covering",
AV margin)

885

Does it not mean that the pillar of cloud and of fire were but the token of God's presence? For above them was a covering – the overshadowing protection that God afforded to this people to ensure that ultimately they should enter the land.

The people asked and God responded with the manna, the bread of heaven (verse 40). There is no mention here of the murmuring of the people for it is the mercy and faithfulness of God that is being emphasised. So also the rock was opened and the waters gushed forth like a river (verse 41). The Hebrew word for "rock" (*tsur*) is the same as that used to describe the provision of water at Rephidim (Exodus 17). The word used in Numbers 20 for the similar provision in Kadesh is different: it means a cliff.

All these things God has done because He remembered His promise and Abraham, His servant (verse 42). He brought them forth from Egypt with joy and gladness (verse 43). The allusion is to the rejoicing on the shores of the Red Sea when Moses and the Children of Israel sang their song of triumph (Exodus 15).

So God "gave them the lands of the heathen: and they inherited the labour of the people" (verse 44). It was not their kingdom, it was God's. That which others had laboured to provide, God gave them that the glory might be His alone. Moses had testified:

"And it shall be, when the LORD thy God shall have brought thee into the land which he sware unto thy fathers, to Abraham, to Isaac, and to Jacob, to give thee great and goodly cities, which thou buildest not, and houses full of all good things, which thou filledst not, and wells digged, which thou diggedst not, vineyards and olive trees, which thou plantedst not; when thou shalt have eaten and be full; then beware lest thou forget the LORD, which brought thee forth out of the land of Egypt." (Deuteronomy 6:10-12)

All this God had done for them "that they might observe his statutes, and keep his laws" (verse 45).

The blessings were conditional upon their reaction to God's mercy, and the response of Israel to all that God had done for them is the subject of the next psalm (106) to which this song is closely related. Hallelujah!

886

PSALM 106

AS previously indicated, this is a companion song to
Psalm 105 and stands in contrast to it. Here too the
history of Israel, from the Exodus to the inheritance
of the land is recapitulated. The emphasis, however, is
different. In Psalm 105 the people rejoice in the goodness
of God shown to them throughout this period of their
history. In this psalm, Israel is indicted for her sin; for her
failure to respond to the lovingkindness of God. It is a song
of penitence leading to a final prayer for God once again to
show mercy to His people in their adversity (verse 48).

As was the case with Psalm 96 and 105, a section of this
psalm also appears in David's song at the bringing up of
the ark. It will be found that the conclusion of that song (1
Chronicles 16:34) includes verse 1 of Psalm 106 followed
by a prayer and doxology (verses 35,36).

We suggest that these psalms were written in earlier
periods of David's life (Psalms 105,106 possibly before he
became king). At that time the effects of the anarchy that
prevailed as the time of the Judges came to a close was
still felt. David brought the various sections of these
earlier psalms together because they were appropriate to
that occasion. The use of Psalm 106, its first and final two
verses, suggests that in the ark at last resting in
Jerusalem, David saw a token of the fact that God had
forgiven Israel the sins described in the body of the psalm
and that God had finally answered the prayer contained in
verse 47.

The introductory section of the psalm (verses 1-5) is a
call to Israel to recognise the goodness and mercy of God
in which David himself joins. There follows the long
description of Israel's sins (verses 6-46) before the final
prayer and doxology (verses 47,48). The doxology serves as
an appropriate conclusion to the Fourth Book of the

Psalms. Nevertheless, it appears to have been part of the original song that David composed.

Verses 1-5

The psalm is prefaced by a call to praise God for His goodness in the knowledge that His mercy endures for ever. Israel's sin cannot exhaust His kindness towards them (verse 1). His mighty acts and the praise which they call forth are beyond the ability of man to celebrate adequately (verse 2). Nevertheless:

> "Blessed are they that keep judgment, and he that doeth righteousness at all times." (verse 3)

These are the qualities that God looks for in those who will participate in His deliverance and David would share in that salvation when God manifested it:

> "Remember me, O LORD, with the favour that thou bearest unto thy people: O visit me with thy salvation; that I may see the good of thy chosen, that I may rejoice in the gladness of thy nation, that I may glory with thine inheritance." (verses 4,5)

Although it is an expression of David's desire to be involved in the blessing of God towards His people, it also gives us a wonderful insight into the privilege that is theirs: "Thy chosen ... thy nation ... thine inheritance".

> "Blessed is the *nation* whose God is the LORD; and the people whom he hath *chosen* for his *inheritance*."
> (Psalm 33:12)

The Purpose of the Psalm (verse 6)

> "We have sinned with our fathers, we have committed iniquity, we have done wickedly."

In these words David and his generation are linked inseparably with the generations past. There is a national solidarity, in which they are all involved. Israel as a nation had been unworthy of the mercy for which David and his contemporaries now pleaded. They could not shrug it off but they needed to remember the collective responsibility of the nation. (Compare Daniel's prayer (9:5) and read Leviticus 26:40-42.) We also come from sinful stock and the attitude of men like David and Daniel is something that we need to give careful thought to in our prayers.

A careful reading of the psalm reveals that there are seven sins committed in the wilderness that David recalls as illustrating the transgressions of the nation:

1. "They understood not ... remembered not ... but provoked him" (verses 7-12).

2. The lusting for food (verses 13-15).

3. Challenging the authority of Moses and Aaron (verses 16-18).

4. The golden calf (verses 19-23).

5. They despised the promised land (verses 24-27).

6. Baal-peor (verses 28-31).

7. The murmuring at Meribah (verses 32,33).

"They understood not ... remembered not ... but provoked him" (verses 7-12)

At the Red Sea they rebelled against the God who so recently had delivered them out of the hand of Pharaoh (Exodus 14:11,12). That sin is attributed to the fact that they "understood not ... remembered not ... but provoked him" (verse 7). They lacked insight into the character of their God and the purpose of His deliverance:

"For they are a nation void of counsel, neither is there any understanding in them. O that they were wise, that they understood this, that they would consider their latter end!" (Deuteronomy 32:28,29)

"They remembered not." To remember was the repeated exhortation of the Book of Deuteronomy and how needful it was is illustrated by this psalm, for forgetfulness is emphasised as the source of so much of their sin (see verses 13,21).

They "provoked him". This is the root from which the proper noun *Marah* is derived. It means 'to be bitter or unpleasant, to be rebellious' (*Strong*). So it was that the bitterness of their souls caused them to rebel and thereby provoke the One who had delivered them from bondage.

What they forgot was "the multitude of his mercies" (verse 7), and consequently in purely human terms He would have been justified in granting their request and letting them return to Egypt.

"Nevertheless he saved them for his name's sake, that he might make his mighty power to be known."

(verse 8)

It was for His name's sake. He cannot deny Himself. He will always be true to the character and purpose that He has revealed to men and those that oppose Him (the Egyptians) will come to know His might and power.

So He dried up the waters of the sea and led them through the midst on dry land. He destroyed their enemies in the midst of the sea, so that there was not one of them left. The result was this: "Then believed they his words; they sang his praise" (verse 12). For a short while there was a show of faith and they rejoiced in their deliverance (see Exodus 14:31; 15:1). How transitory was their repentance is seen in the second sin to be related.

The Lusting for Food (verses 13-15)

"They soon forgat (Hebrew, 'they made haste to forget') his works; they waited not for his counsel: but lusted exceedingly in the wilderness, and tempted God in the desert."   (verses 13,14)

They had only travelled three days from the Red Sea when they murmured for water (Exodus 15:22-27). A few weeks later (Exodus 16:1) and they were complaining about the lack of food. At Rephidim (Exodus 17:1,2) they were resentful again because of lack of water. God was putting them to the proof but they lacked the staying power to wait for God to reveal His counsel on these matters.

"They lusted a lust" (AV margin). The phrase is taken from the record in Numbers 11 (verse 4) when they tempted God, that is, endeavoured to put Him to the proof. God granted their request by sending the quails but with them came the plague, with which God afflicted them. The place was called Kibroth-hattaavah (the graves of lust). The comment of the psalm is that God sent leanness into their soul. Israel said, "our soul is dried away" (Numbers 11:6) and in context it clearly means their body or their life. Leanness is a word which describes the effect the plague had upon their bodies. It was a wasting disease, a withering sickness, and the idea conveyed may be that it was the fattest of them, or the strongest of them, who were struck down first (see Psalm 78:30,31).

On a spiritual level, we can all draw lessons from this episode. If in our hearts we lust for something, if it becomes a consuming passion, then sometimes God will give it to us. But with it He will send leanness into our souls; what we might describe as spiritual malnutrition. Our life in Christ will wither and die and we shall be found to have dug for ourselves "the graves of lust".

Challenging the Authority of Moses and Aaron (verses 16-18)

The third sin emphasised is the rebellion of Korah, Dathan and Abiram (Numbers 16,17) when they envied Moses and Aaron. Aaron is described as "the saint of the LORD" because he was set apart and consecrated to perform the duties of priest. Their complaint was "all the congregation are holy, every one" (Numbers 16:3). Moses' response was, "the LORD will shew who are his, and who is holy" (verse 5).

The Psalmist mentions only Dathan and Abiram because the family of Korah were not swallowed up (Numbers 26:11; Deuteronomy 11:6). The reference to the fire that burnt up the wicked is, of course, to the two hundred and fifty men that offered incense (Numbers 16:35) who are described by Moses as "wicked men" (verse 26).

The Golden Calf (verses 19-23)

The record of this incident is in Exodus 32, but the Psalmist appears to be following the record in Deuteronomy (9:8-29) where Moses recapitulates this event. Horeb (the Mount of God) rather than Sinai is the distinctive mark of Deuteronomy. At the very time that the Lord their God was revealing Himself to them, while Moses was yet in the mount, they expressed their defiance of the explicit command that He had given them. They made a golden calf and by doing so "they changed their glory into the similitude of an ox that eateth grass" (Psalm 106:20). Their God was their glory, for:

891

"What nation is there so great, who hath God so nigh unto them, as the LORD our God is in all things that we call upon him for?"   (Deuteronomy 4:7)

It was in that very context that God had said to them:

"Only take heed to thyself, and keep thy soul diligently, lest thou forget the things which thine eyes have seen."   (Deuteronomy 4:9)

So David recalls these words:

"They forgat God their saviour, which had done great things in Egypt; wondrous works in the land of Ham, and terrible things by the Red sea." (Psalm 106:21,22)

God would have destroyed them had not Moses "stood before him in the breach" (verse 23). It is a bold figure – a military metaphor. Moses interceded on their behalf and put his own life at risk, like a soldier defending the breach of a city wall. (For the same figure see Ezekiel 22:30 where the word is translated 'gap'.)

They despised the Promised Land
(verses 24-27)

When the spies returned (Numbers 14), instead of going up to inherit the land:

"They despised the pleasant land, they believed not his word: but murmured in their tents, and hearkened not unto the voice of the LORD."   (verses 24,25)

The picture is of a cowardly, unbelieving multitude, sulking in their tents, rather than boldly setting forth to conquer this pleasant (literally, 'desirable'; see also Jeremiah 3:19) land as God had commanded them.

Again, but for the intervention of Moses, He would have destroyed them in the wilderness. It is interesting to notice how the psalm draws on the language of the Books of Moses to describe this event. "They despised" (verse 24; Numbers 14:31); "they murmured in their tents" (verse 25; Deuteronomy 1:27); "he lifted up his hand" (verse 26; see Numbers 14:30, AV margin – as He "lifted up his hand" to bless now He would do so to curse); "make them fall" (verse 26 RV margin; Numbers 14:29,32). David was "a man of the word". He had meditated upon the Books of Moses so that their language became the natural way for him to express himself about the events recorded.

892

There is one interesting piece of additional information in the psalm that is not given in Numbers. God "lifted up his hand against them ... to overthrow their seed also among the nations, and to scatter them in the lands" (verses 26,27).

A similar reference occurs in Ezekiel 20 (verse 23) where the prophet appears to be quoting the psalm. It seems to have been at this stage that God first warned them that He would scatter them for disobedience; words that were repeated later in different contexts (Leviticus 26:33; Deuteronomy 28:64).

Baal-peor (verses 28-31)

"They joined themselves also to Baal-peor, and ate the sacrifices of the dead."   (verse 28)

Literally, this means 'they yoked themselves', the same word being used in the record in Numbers 25 (verses 3,5). See also the words of the Apostle Paul in 2 Corinthians 6: "Be ye not unequally yoked" (verse 14); and also in 1 Corinthians 6, "he which is joined to an harlot" (verse 16).

Baal was the god whom the Moabites worshipped on Mount Peor. There they ate the sacrifices of the dead, the reference being to the lifeless idols of the nations as compared with "the living God" of Israel.

Thus they provoked God "with their doings" (RV), so that "the plague brake in upon them" (verse 29). The word "plague" means literally 'smiting' and usually conveys the idea of a divinely inflicted pestilence. There is no record of such an event in Numbers, but God used human agency to destroy with the sword those that sinned against Him. Nevertheless it might be that we have yet another significant detail originally omitted, but now added to the record.

God made a breach upon them, for the verb is from the same root as the noun in verse 23. (For similar usage of this figure see Exodus 19:24; 2 Samuel 6:8.)

The anger of the Lord was turned away and the plague was stayed because, "Then stood up Phinehas, and executed judgment" (verse 30; Numbers 25:7,8). Because of his zeal in taking this action, the wrath of God was turned away from the Children of Israel (Numbers 25:11).

Note that the Israelite who was slain was a prince of the tribe of Simeon, whereas the woman was the daughter of a prince of Midian (Numbers 25:14-18). We might say that it was at the highest levels that this yoking together took place and the behaviour of those who had authority would have encouraged many in Israel to follow their example.

Phinehas performed an act of faith and for that reason it "was counted unto him for righteousness" (verse 31); just as Abram centuries before believed in the Lord and it was counted to him for righteousness (Genesis 15:6). Faith is the quality that, above all else, commends a man to God, and faith is shown to be real by the works it produces – not always what the world would regard as 'good works', but actions that demonstrate that God's word has been believed (read Hebrews 11).

The Murmuring at Meribah (verses 32,33)

It was in the fortieth year of their wanderings that the Children of Israel came to Kadesh and chided with Moses and Aaron because there was no water for them to drink (Numbers 20:1-13). They angered God at the waters of Strife or Meribah. (Because of that which happened there, it became a proper name.) "It went ill with Moses for their sakes" (verse 32). Faced with their provocation Moses showed an uncharacteristic lack of patience. He allowed himself to be influenced by the general turmoil and instead of speaking to the rock, he struck it with his rod twice. He spoke "unadvisedly with his lips" (verse 33) (*Strong*, to babble, to vociferate angrily). Moses was caught in a paroxysm of rage and the result was that he did not sanctify God in the eyes of the people, but rather sought to justify himself: "Hear now ye rebels; must we fetch you water out of this rock?" (Numbers 20:10). There is some discussion as to whose spirit was provoked. Was it God's or was it Moses'? The words of the prophet would seem to suggest that it was the spirit of God; "But they rebelled, and vexed his holy Spirit" (Isaiah 63:10). In any event the general sense of the verse is not affected.

Disobedience in the Land (verses 34-46)

They had received explicit instructions as to how they were to deal with the nations in the land (Exodus 23:31-33).

Nevertheless they did not destroy the nations, as God had commanded them (verse 34), but they mingled themselves with the nations (verse 35, RV). The result was that through intermarriage, trade and social intercourse they "learned their works, and ... served their idols which were a snare unto them" (verses 35,36). They plumbed the depths of wickedness, "sacrificing their sons and daughters unto devils" (verse 37; RV, 'demons'). Who the devils / demons were is indicated in the verse that follows:

"(They) shed innocent blood, even the blood of their sons and of their daughters, whom they sacrificed unto the idols of Canaan." (verse 38)

The devils / demons were the idols and in the only other passage where the Hebrew word is used in the Old Testament this meaning is emphasised:

"They sacrificed unto demons, which were no God, to gods whom they knew not." (Deuteronomy 32:17, RV)

The demons were 'dumb idols'. This meaning is carried over into the New Testament and is the basis of our understanding there. As a result of their actions the land was polluted with blood. The word is taken from the Book of Numbers (35:33).

It was for this kind of behaviour that the Canaanites had defiled the land and the land had vomited them out (Leviticus 18:24,25). The Canaanites were condemned to be wiped out for their iniquity, but now Israel had followed their ways. So Israel went "a whoring" after their own inventions (verse 39). Israel's relationship to their God is likened to the marriage bond and like an unfaithful wife they had gone "a whoring" (see Exodus 34:14-17).

Because of these things the anger of the Lord was kindled against them. He abhorred His inheritance and gave them into the hand of the nations, so that those who hated them ruled over them and oppressed them:

"Many times did he deliver them; but they provoked him with their counsel, and were brought low for their iniquity." (verse 43)

As they had not waited for God's counsel (verse 13), so now in their self-will they pursued their own counsel which was not in accord with God's:

895

> "For they are a nation void of counsel, neither is there any understanding in them." (Deuteronomy 32:28)

They were brought low (AV margin, 'impoverished or weakened') for their iniquity (verse 43). The verb is very similar to that in the Book of Leviticus:

> "And they that are left of you shall pine away in their iniquity." (26:39)

In the foregoing verses we have a vivid description of the days of the Judges when God delivered them into the hands of their enemies to oppress them that they might cry unto Him for deliverance. The God of Israel heard them:

> "He regarded their affliction, when he heard their cry: and he remembered for them his covenant, and repented according to the multitude of his mercies."
> (verses 44,45)

Though they forgot, He remembered and in His lovingkindness He pitied them, for He softened the hearts of their oppressors so that they treated them with kindness (verse 46).

The Final Prayer (verse 47)

The long catalogue of Israel's sins now finds its object in this final prayer. Their intermingling among the nations meant that many still dwelt in their lands. David would have them all united once more, that together they might fulfil that purpose for which God had created them:

> "Save us, O LORD our God, and gather us from among the heathen, to give thanks unto thy holy name, and to triumph in thy praise." (verse 47)

As stated earlier, it is a prayer that David saw finally fulfilled when he brought the ark to Zion. In a final paean of praise he acknowledges the Holy One of Israel, who has done such wondrous things for His people:

> "Blessed be the LORD God of Israel from everlasting to everlasting: and let all the people say, Amen. Praise ye the LORD." (verse 48)